Sociology of Leisure

Occupational

Therapy

Occupational Therapy

# Sociology of Leisure

A reader

Edited by

## C. Critcher

Communications
Sheffield Hallam University
UK

## P. Bramham

Leisure and Consumer Studies
Leeds Metropolitan University
UK

and

## A. Tomlinson

Chelsea School
University of Brighton
UK

**E & FN SPON**
An Imprint of Chapman & Hall

London · Glasgow · Weinheim · New York · Tokyo · Melbourne · Madras

**Published by E & FN Spon, an imprint of Chapman & Hall,
2–6 Boundary Row, London SE1 8HN, UK**

Chapman & Hall, 2–6 Boundary Row, London SE1 8HN, UK

Blackie Academic & Professional, Wester Cleddens Road, Bishopbriggs,
Glasgow G64 2NZ, UK

Chapman & Hall GmbH, Pappelallee 3, 69469 Weinheim, Germany

Chapman & Hall USA, One Penn Plaza, 41st Floor, New York,
NY 10119, USA

Chapman & Hall Japan, ITP-Japan, Kyowa Building, 3F, 2-2-1 Hirakawa-
cho, Chiyoda-ku, Tokyo 102, Japan

Chapman & Hall Australia, Thomas Nelson Australia, 102 Dodds Street,
South Melbourne, Victoria 3205, Australia

Chapman & Hall India, R. Seshadri, 32 Second Main Road, CIT East,
Madras 600 035, India

First edition 1995

© 1995 E & FN Spon

Phototypeset in 10/12pt Times by Intype, London
Printed in Great Britain by T.J. Press (Padstow) Ltd, Padstow, Cornwall

ISBN 0 419 19420 7

A catalogue record for this book is available from the British Library

Library of Congress Catalog Card Number: 94-68793

While every effort has been made to trace copyright holders and obtain
permission, this has not been possible in all cases. Any omissions
brought to our attention will be remedied in future editions.

∞ Printed on permanent acid-free text paper, manufactured in accordance with
ANSI/NISO Z39.48 - 1992 and ANSI/NISO Z39.48-1984
(Permanence of Paper)

# Contents

# Preface

The idea for a reader in the sociology of leisure came out of discussions amongst the editors and with others about the kinds of books needed to cope with the ever-increasing numbers of students in higher education following introductory courses in the subject. Many of the texts we regarded as central were out of print. Even when in print, college libraries cannot be expected to stock enough copies to cater for groups of around a hundred students at a time. Often at this level, only a particular chapter or extract is needed for the purposes of background reading, assignment completion or examination preparation.

Though there are some textbooks which review the essential arguments, notably Haywood *et al.* (1990), the original arguments and studies frequently remain inaccessible. There thus seemed a strong case for putting together a collection of readings which would remedy this deficiency. It would complement existing course material from textbooks and lectures. The objective would be to provide a basic introductory overview of the central arguments in the British sociology of leisure. It would aim less to incorporate the most recent empirical studies or theoretical disputes than to cover the key conceptual debates.

This reader has been designed to meet these aims. Part One (wholly given over to a recent article by Kenneth Roberts) reviews leisure trends in recessionary Britain. The rest of the reader is divided into four inter-related but distinct sections. Part Two, Leisure and Common Experiences, examines how leisure is affected by social experiences we virtually all share and encounter: paid work, family relationships and the life cycle. Most of us go through these in one form or another and each has been argued to have particular effects on how we spend our leisure time. Thus this part considers whether or to what extent paid work structures leisure expectations, why the family has come to be so central to leisure and how the meaning of leisure changes as we move through different phases of our lives.

Part Three, Leisure and Social Relations, looks less at experiences common to us all than those which vary our leisure opportunities and expectations. Three topics are examined for the extent to which they can identify and explain differences in the quantity and quality of leisure between social groups. The arguments centre on what differences in leisure, if any, can be attributed to membership of class, gender and ethnic groups.

In Part Four, Types of Leisure Provision, we encounter a range of examples from the commercial, voluntary and public sectors. The objectives, organization and ethos of each sector are analysed for the assumptions made in each case about the varieties and categories of leisure aspirations.

Finally in Part Five, Theories and Prognostications, we tackle two more topics, more difficult because more abstract. Theories of leisure we present by juxtaposing three distinctive perspectives, those of pluralism, Marxism and feminism. To make some of these arguments more specific, we conclude with an extract which looks at the difficulties of forecasting leisure demand and behaviour.

Any selection of key readings is bound to be arbitrary. Other actual or potential editors would be likely to come up with a slightly or significantly different selection. In making our decisions, we were guided by the principle that readings should provide essential material in a form which is accessible to students who may not have encountered leisure studies or sociology before. This did cut down the field considerably and there were few disputes amongst the editors about what should be included. Much less easy was the task of editing down lengthy arguments into the few thousand words available for each extract. We are grateful to all the authors for their forbearance in tolerating such violence as we may have done to the integrity of their original arguments.

Our sources are all British. There is a need for international comparisons but we felt that, at this introductory level, students would find it easier to understand arguments based on one society and the one they know best.

We hope the student will find the readings logically ordered and accessible. Teachers and lecturers will no doubt adapt the book to their own needs and interests. We have offered some brief exercises and essay titles at the end of each part to indicate how we would use the texts ourselves. But, as in leisure itself, what is intended by the providers is no guarantee of the uses to which it will be put.

## REFERENCE

Haywood, L., Kew, F., Bramham, P. *et al.* (1990) *Understanding Leisure*, Stanley Thornes.

# PART ONE

# Contemporary Trends

# Introduction

Any sociologically adequate understanding of leisure needs to situate it historically, politically and economically. Contemporary trends cannot be grasped in terms only of activity rates or participation figures. Leisure cultures are developed over time, and under the influence of political and economic as well as social forces. It is vital, therefore, to appreciate the wider context in which leisure takes place, and to consider how trends in leisure are interconnected with political and economic factors.

In political terms, for instance, leisure has often been put on the political agenda and claimed by governments as a source of social discipline, as a means of moral transformation – particularly so during times of social unrest or instability. For at such times governments have seen in leisure a means of diverting disruptive elements, and channelling what are seen as antisocial or undesirable energies towards less threatening outcomes.

Rational recreation in the mid- and late nineteenth century was an attempt to render respectable that of which the dominant culture and authorities disapproved, and this has had its equivalents in the Depression years of the 1930s, when widespread concerns were expressed about the use of free time; and in the 1970s and 1980s, when rising unemployment was euphemized as 'enforced leisure'. In such circumstances the political responses have often been ineffective in the extreme; people have plumped for more pleasurable options, however limited their means.

For leisure has been conspicuous as an expressive form of pleasure, and often used as a form of consumer power. People have regularly ignored or appropriated the initiatives of worthy providers, choosing the hedonistic over the holy, the raucous over the respectable.

Even in financially straitened circumstances such choices will continue to persist. As Bill Martin and Sandra Mason put it:

... though financial stringency prompts consumers to review their

*Sociology of Leisure: A reader.* Edited by C. Critcher, P. Bramham and A. Tomlinson. Published in 1995 by E & FN Spon, London. ISBN 0 419 19420 7.

leisure spending across the board, . . . individual leisure activities are not willingly dispensed with when money is tight. Instead, it seems that the initial reaction to slowdown is for people to economize a bit on all their leisure activities. Only when there is a substantial cut in individual incomes, as with unemployment, do people contemplate a more radical change in leisure behaviour.

We have chosen the following piece by Ken Roberts because it captures a sense of both the most significant recent trends in leisure in Great Britain, and of the political economy of leisure culture throughout the modern period.

## REFERENCE

Martin, B and Mason, S. (1990) Current trends in leisure: leisure in a less buoyant economy. *Leisure Studies*, **9** (1).

# Ia Leisure in Britain

# 1

# Great Britain: socioeconomic polarisation and the implications for leisure

Kenneth Roberts

## THE ECONOMY: BREAKTHROUGH OR BREAKUP?

In 1987 the Thatcher government sought and achieved re-election claiming a record of proven economic success. Britain was then in her sixth year of continuous economic growth. The rate of inflation had been lowered from over 20 percent in the 1970s to 4 percent in 1987. The number of workers in employment had risen steadily since 1983. Wages and salaries had risen well ahead of inflation. Taxes on incomes had been lowered. Company profits were at historically high levels. The stock market had broken through former ceilings. The Conservative Party claimed that, until 1979, Britain was over-taxed, many firms were over-subsidised, and even more were overmanned. Too many were said to be controlled by indifferent managers who were intimidated by over-powerful trade unions. Hence the severe impact of the 1979–81 world recession, the deepest in postwar history. 'Lame ducks' had to be allowed to sink. Excess labour had to be shaken out to give firms any chance of survival. The medicine was admittedly unpleasant. It meant a dramatic rise in unemployment between 1979 and 1982. Subsequently, the government could claim, the leaner and fitter firms that survived the recession, together with new companies, had begun

*Sociology of Leisure: A reader*. Edited by C. Critcher, P. Bramham and A. Tomlinson. Published in 1995 by E & FN Spon, London. ISBN 0 419 19420 7.

winning larger shares of domestic and overseas markets. On all these counts the Thatcher administration could claim a breakthrough, and could present Britain's economy as a success story of the 1980s.

The opposition parties spread different 1987 election messages. They insisted that the 1980s had seen Britain sinking into an ever-deeper economic crisis. They deplored the seemingly permanent loss of manufacturing capacity that had occurred between 1979 and 1982 when many firms disappeared completely. In 1987 Britain's manufacturing output was still beneath its 1979 level. During the 1980s, for the first time in its industrial history, Britain was carrying a trade deficit in manufactured goods. In 1987 unemployment was still above 3 million, approximately 13 percent of the workforce. There had been no significant decline in these figures since 1982. The numbers living in poverty had increased substantially since 1979. The consumer boom of the 1980s was said to be based on credit and imports, the latter funded by the country's diminishing reserves of North Sea oil. By 1987 many families, communities and entire regions had already experienced years of crisis which, government critics claimed, would grip the entire nation eventually unless there was a radical change in economic management. Britain's economic base was judged in danger of total disintegration.

The health of the British economy has varied according to the observers' politics, but all parties have agreed on certain points, such as that the country has felt the full weight of recent worldwide trends. Unemployment in Britain rose following the 1973–4 oil price spiral. The level of joblessness subsequently declined, but lurched upwards again even more sharply during the 1979–81 recession. Firms and jobs were particularly hard hit in manufacturing sectors where the impact of recession was aggravated by the advent of micro-electronic technology. After 1982, despite the recovery of Britain's manufacturing output, employment in manufacturing continued to decline. Recent job creation has been mainly in private services – in financial and business services, hotels and catering, and sport and recreation.

Employment in Britain has shifted from manufacturing to services, and from manual to non-manual occupations. The proportions and absolute numbers of jobs at the professional, management and technician levels have increased. This is partly a product of the decline in manufacturing employment, but occupational restructuring within firms, especially by manufacturing companies, has also contributed. New technologies have generally meant fewer operatives, and more jobs in the design and management of the new systems. Britain's blue-collar jobs have declined in number, and changed in character. In the past male employees in manufacturing were rightly treated as the backbone of the manual working class. They are now outnumbered by a new working class based in service industries. Not all service sector jobs are white collar. These businesses employ thousands of sales assistants, cooks, cleaners and security staff. Many of these jobs are part time, and a high proportion are filled by women.

The destruction of old jobs and the generation of new employment have tended to occur in entirely different parts of Britain. Regional inequalities have widened. New jobs tend to be based in the south-east, the seat of government and where most of Britain's high-technology manufacturers and corporation headquarters are located. Industry no longer needs to be located close to coalfields. It makes better sense to locate amidst the largest domestic market, in the south-east, and close to Britain's main trading partners in continental Europe. Britain's provinces have suffered a net decline in employment, especially blue-collar employment. Hence the talk of two nations. However, there are equally dramatic inequalities within regions. The majority of would-be workers are still in employment even in Britain's most depressed areas, and many have good jobs in the public sector, or in successful manufacturing and private service companies. Conversely, there are pockets of high unemployment within the generally prosperous south-east. The unqualified and unskilled, and Britain's ethnic minorities, are heavily over-represented within these pockets.

Most people are inevitably concerned less about the performance of the economy in general than about trends in their own conditions and prospects, which have varied considerably. Britain in the 1980s has become a more polarised society. People's experiences have depended on the parts of the country they inhabit, their skills and qualifications, and the industries in which their experience and careers have been based. Over 3 million were unemployed in 1987. More people than ever were dependent on state benefits, and their standards of living were lagging further behind the average than in previous decades. Simultaneously, more people than ever were prospering. Some had made fortunes, while far greater numbers had simply seen their incomes and standards of living forging well ahead of price rises. Which of Britain's politicians appeared to be telling the truth in 1987 varied with the experiences of their audiences.


## GOVERNMENT POLICIES

Making sense of political responses to economic trends in Britain in the 1980s depends on recognising that the country's Conservative governments subscribed to the 'breakthrough', not the 'crisis' definition of the situation. Ministers acknowledged that the economy was severely battered by the 1979–81 recession. It was then government policy to expose firms and workers to the full rigours of market forces, thereby motivating all sections of the population to surmount their own problems. This meant ensuring that success was rewarded handsomely, and allowing failure to be penalised. The government endeavoured to revive enterprise by encouraging firms and individuals to stand on their own feet, and to accept responsibility for shaping their own prospects. Part of this strategy involved releasing businesses from political control, most spectacularly in the series of transfers of nationalised industries to the private sector – oil, telecommunications, gas, and Britain's main airline. Reducing taxes on earnings was a complementary strategy. The standard rate of income tax was cut in a series of stages from 33 percent in 1979 to 25 percent in 1988. Higher rates of taxation on top incomes were cut even more sharply and dramatically, from over 80 percent to 60 percent immediately following the 1979 election, then to 40 percent in the first budget after the 1987 election.

The government aimed to reduce its own spending, as a proportion of the gross national product, if not absolutely. However, the same government regarded the national interest as requiring higher spending on defence and policing. Circumstances forced increased spending in certain other areas – mainly on state pensions alongside the growth of the population in the retirement age group, and on unemployment benefits. This meant cut-backs in other programmes in order to prevent the rise of total government spending. The victims included most sections of the public dependent on state welfare. Britain's state earnings-related pensions scheme was dismantled. In the future the retired will receive only basic, flat-rate state pensions. New restrictions were imposed on the benefit entitlements of certain unemployed groups, including young people. Public housing subsidies were slashed. Homelessness increased. Even so, the government needed to raise other taxes in order to create scope for reductions in taxes on earnings. There were sharp increases in VAT, Britain's main sales tax, and in 'the rates', the property taxes imposed by local authorities. Rather than counterbalancing, these government taxation and spending policies tended to widen the inequalities arising from economic trends. As a result Britain's rich grew much richer in the 1980s, while the poor became relatively poorer. Critics accused the government of being uncaring and heartless. Ministers replied that their policies guaranteed a safety net for the weakest, while creating incentives for everyone to earn self-respect by supporting themselves in employment, even those who could obtain only low-paid jobs. Moreover, the government argued that its policies were building the incentives necessary to stimulate the enterprise which, given time, would generate higher living standards for all.

Spending on public leisure services was not actually cut by the Thatcher administrations. Grants to the main national agencies – the Sports Council and the Arts Council – did not decline, but any expectation that these agencies' incomes would rise inexorably was shattered. Sport and the arts were advised to tap other sources of sponsorship, meaning commercial advertisers. Central government experienced only limited success in its efforts to curb spending by Britain's local authorities. The latter's spending on leisure services continued to rise in the 1980s, though at a more modest rate than in the 1970s when new public sports and leisure centres were built throughout the land. 'Consolidation' became a keyword in the 1980s. 'Community recreation' also became fashionable. This meant greater reliance on voluntary associations to deliver leisure services, and using existing premises – schools, church halls or whatever – instead of planning new purpose-designed leisure buildings.

The government claimed agnosticism on the proper length of the working day, week, year and life. Efforts to reduce unemployment by work-sharing were minimal. A job release scheme allowed over 60-year-old males to retire on state pensions in order to free their occupations for younger workers. A job splitting scheme offered cash bonuses to employers who divided full-time jobs, thereby removing someone from unemployment. However, these measures made little impact on the level of joblessness. There was no general encouragement towards shorter hours of work all round. The government's view was that hours of work and rates of pay were best left to free bargaining, preferably between individual workers and employers, but otherwise by collective agreement. Average hours actually worked did not decline among Britain's manual or non-manual workers. By the mid–1970s, in Britain, the latter were working more hours per week, on average. Britain's professions have long ceased to be refuges for leisurely gentlemen.

The 1980s governments have not broken with British traditions in refusing to plan comprehensively for a growth of leisure. Britain has never hosted a domestic political debate on 'the leisure problem'. There has never been a central government ministry with overall responsibility for leisure or culture. Different government departments continue to support the arts, sport, broadcasting, tourism, services for young people, and so on, but without co-ordinating these efforts into overall leisure policies. Most local authorities now have departments providing leisure or recreation services. In the main, however, these departments simply deliver services that have historically been defined as their province. Once again, all this has happened without any conception of an overall way of life that might be desirable, or to which all citizens are entitled. Other countries' governments have formed definite views on the proper length of the working week, and amounts of free time in the form of annual holidays to which citizens are entitled. Britain has never had such a government. In some lands leisure time and opportunities to enjoy it have been defined as rights of citizenship, and the enjoyment of leisure may even have been elevated into a civic duty. Some governments have made no secret of their views that certain life-styles deserve public promotion. Some have sought to democratise culture so as to spread elite heritages, or to nurture and enhance the status of alternative arts and their publics. All these ideas remain foreign in Britain, where people's leisure is still treated as essentially a private, not a public, issue.

Of course, British governments have proscribed or discouraged particular pastimes, ranging from the use of certain drugs to enjoyment of sex movies. Other leisure activities, especially sport and the traditional arts, have benefited enormously from state support. But all this has been achieved without any overarching leisure or cultural policies, and without any conceptions of the overall ways of living that the state should encourage. Governments have intervened in leisure in the course of addressing a variety of health, crime and educational issues, and in their efforts to promote the well-being of children, young people, the disabled, the retired and so on. Despite all these efforts, the concept of leisure has never been politicised. Keeping politics out of leisure is one of the few stances on which Britain retains a broad political consensus.

## LEISURE

The significance of trends in leisure behaviour in Britain in the 1980s can be fully appreciated only when set in the above economic and political contexts. Many tastes and habits forged in previous years, including the popularity of television, have continued to flourish. A great deal of leisure in Britain throughout the 1980s has amounted to neither more nor less than 'business as usual'. Some of the main developments have been extensions of longer-running trends. For instance, work-free time and spending on leisure have continued to grow. However, even the same behaviour and trends can yield different experiences when surrounded by new economic and political conditions.

It is possible to distinguish four broad trends in British leisure in the 1980s.

### Home-centredness

The privatisation of leisure is a long-term trend in Britain. It is a product of a more mobile population, the decline of local neighbourhood communities, and the rise of the relatively independent nuclear family. The spread of car ownership has accentuated privatisation: families with cars can even go out in private. Radio and television have strengthened the home's position as most people's main leisure centre. In recent decades home-centred life-styles have been further strengthened by the spread of home-ownership. Two-thirds of Britain's dwellings are now owner-occupied. This has helped to promote the various forms of do-it-yourself. Home repairs, decorating, car maintenance and gardening are now the nation's main hobbies.

In the 1980s more time than ever is being spent at home, partly as a result of the declining proportion of lifetime claimed by employment. In addition, however, more money is being spent on in-home recreation, and this spending is mainly by the employed sections of the population. Britain's main growth areas in leisure spending in the 1980s have been on sound and vision reproducing equipment, telecommunications, and computer technology (Martin and Mason, 1986).

The proportion of employment in service sectors has increased, but much of this employment is in producer services such as banking and insurance. The proportion of consumer spending on services has actually declined. There has been a trend towards purchasing goods which are then used for self-servicing (Gershuny, 1978). Transport is a prime example. We are buying more motor cars to transport ourselves instead of purchasing bus and train journeys. For entertainment we are purchasing televisions, videos and music centres instead of attending live performances.

Participation has declined in most forms of out-of-home recreation that can be replicated or closely substituted by in-home entertainment. Cinema and theatre audiences, and paid admissions at spectator sports events are in long-term and continuing decline. In Britain they have now been joined by out-of-home drinking. We are consuming more alcohol per capita than during any previous period in twentieth-century history, but there is less drinking in public houses and more off-sales for home consumption. Drink, film and sports producers have survived by gearing to increasingly home-centred markets. Most films are now made for television and video distribution rather than cinema performances. Live sport is played to tele-viewing audiences. Commercially successful sports promotion now depends on television coverage. The presence of the media attracts sponsors, and attracting the media requires top-level performers. Hence the changing structure of professional sports occupations (Whannel, 1986). Stars command astronomical fees while the rank and file must be motivated primarily by the slender prospect of joining the elite.

Life-styles are generally home centred in all social strata, but homes vary tremendously in their comforts. Individuals in employment, who spend least time at home, can best afford large and well-equipped dwellings. Home has different connotations for most of the unemployed and retired, many of whom have become trapped in home-based life-styles by poverty, and as a result of local community facilities – cinemas, sports teams and pubs – either declining or disappearing completely.

## Out-of-home recreation

During the 1980s out-of-home recreation in Britain has grown in just two main areas. Participant sport is one. The spread of sports participation has been facilitated by new provisions, especially for public sector indoor sport, that have opened since the 1960s. However, this trend in supply largely reflects an independent growth in demand. The public has become more concerned with health and fitness. Hence the decline in cigarette smoking, and the popularity of health foods and diets, the development of jogging, and the transformation of marathon runs into mass participation events.

Tourism is the second main growth area in out-of-home recreation. More people are taking more holidays away from home. Overseas holidays have become more common, with Greece and Spain as the most popular destinations. There are also more main and second holidays being spent inside Britain. In addition, more day trips are being made to coastal and countryside destinations, and to visit historic buildings. Theme parks have been launched on the growing demand for places to go and things to do.

But it is necessary to stress that not everyone has been part of the growth of sports participation and tourism. Two-thirds of British adults do not take part in any sport, unless long walks and swimming during seaside holidays are counted. Two-fifths of households do not take a holiday involving even one night away from home. A fifth of British adults never visit the countryside from year to year. Non-participants in these different activities tend to be the same individuals. Households without motor cars, approximately two out of every five in Britain, suffer general recreational disadvantages. The decline of public transport has led to enforced home-centredness among these groups. The old and the infirm, together with the poor and the unemployed, are sharing neither in the enrichment of home-based leisure, nor in the growth areas in out-of-home recreation.

## Connoisseur leisure

The expert and committed minorities that are surrounded by much larger numbers of less frequent, often voyeuristic, participants in most leisure activities are growing in size. It is impossible to measure this trend precisely. Participation data rarely permit a clear distinction between the dedicated and the casual. However, sales of specialist magazines have risen, while membership of leisure-based voluntary associations is also growing (Bishop and Hoggett, 1986). More people are seeking special-interest holidays in preference to mass-marketed packages.

In virtually all leisure activities, whether pursued at home or outside, there are minorities of enthusiasts with finely tuned skills and exceptional knowledge who commit considerable cash, time and energy to their pastimes. Among the mass of sports participants there are dedicated minorities who make cultivating peak performance into a serious occupation. Most spectator sports attract core groups of dedicated fans. The arts, the countryside, wines and home improvements are further bases for minority enthusiasms. Collectively these leisure connoisseurs have little in common. Their interests are highly specialised. At the connoisseur level leisure tastes are fragmented. Nevertheless, it is possible to discern a general bifurcation in Britain's leisure markets, with the experts, who are growing in number, demanding a different standard of service to the larger armies of dabblers who are content with mass-marketed goods and packaged experiences (Darton, 1986).

Serious or committed leisure appears capable of performing some socio-psychological functions normally associated with employment such as structuring time, providing interests and social relationships, status and identity (Haworth, 1986). Yet the unemployed are rarely leisure con-noisseurs. Committed leisure seems most common among sections of the population whose current, past or future occupations provide the income, economic security and status on which to build leisure careers. Students in post-compulsory education are one section of the population where committed leisure is common. Early retirees, and some individuals who begin withdrawing from employment psychologically prior to officially terminating their working lives, often become connoisseurs in their chosen fields of leisure interest. Many middle-aged citizens in the post-parental life-stage for whom compulsory retirement is imminent, or earlier as an option, remain physically fit and active, and mentally alert. Their current or former occupations supply the status and economic security from which to build entire life-styles around leisure enthusiasms.

### The threat of the mob

Other sections of the population, including the unemployed and those financially impoverished for other reasons, have far less opportunity to become leisure connoisseurs. The leisure of impoverished adults and the ageing, however deprived, rarely surfaces as a public issue in Britain. Their life-styles and problems are usually privatised. Unemployment accentuates privatisation. Lack of income and loss of work-based social networks conspire to confine the victims indoors.

Young people are different. They are less likely than other age groups to become trapped in domesticity through lack of employment. Young people are an exceptional age group in so far as their life-styles are not normally home-based: the majority have no homes of their own. This is one reason why their peer groups and friendships tend to survive unem-ployment. Young people usually spend more time with friends when out of work than when in jobs. This is one reason, possibly the main reason, why *youth* unemployment in Britain has been defined as a particularly urgent problem. The young unemployed tend to be visible, on the streets and in other public places. Fears of the uncouth mob and of the devil making work for idle hands that have flickered throughout urban history have been rekindled and are settling on the young unemployed.

Unemployment among young adults in Britain has risen to well above average levels. In some neighbourhoods, especially within Britain's depressed regions, youth unemployment has become more common than youth employment. Yet while so many young people's job prospects have been receding, their education has become more, not less, vocational. The threat of unemployment prompts young people and parents to demand the kinds of education that seem most likely to boost their job chances. Young people are still being schooled to expect employment. Simultaneously, overt and hidden persuaders are continuing to train them to become consumers. The attractions of spending are flaunted daily in television adverts and shop displays. Hence the multiple frustrations of unemployed youth.

Of course there are plenty of recreational programmes aimed at young people, especially at the young unemployed. The twin aims of policing the age group and offering satisfying life-styles are usually uncomfortably interwoven, and equally unfulfilled. Wagelessness restricts young people's access to leisure while joblessness makes them more dependent than otherwise on leisure activities to establish independence and adult identities (Roberts, 1983). Officially sponsored, socially hygienic recreation seems less likely to supply the satisfactions that socially excluded young people seek than symbolic and sometimes physical warfare to claim space on streets and soccer terraces, among other places. Efforts to marshal and contain these young people are constantly liable to provoke outbursts of hooliganism, even riots. These are highlights in some young lives, and are currently contributing to a breakdown of law and order in some of Britain's high unemployment inner-city areas. The young unemployed are over-represented among the officially recorded perpetrators of crime; they are also crime's most frequent victims (Kinsey *et al.*, 1986). Lawlessness is currently exacerbating the deterioration in the quality of life in many of Britain's high unemployment neighbourhoods. Policing is one of the few public services in Britain on which expenditure has risen sharply in the 1980s. The country has more police than ever. They are also better equipped, and better paid than formerly. Yet the country also has a record crime rate. Hence the decline in public satisfaction with, and confidence in, the police. Certain sections of the public, especially the young, have grown increasingly hostile towards the police and the society they represent. This is just one instance of the benefits of economic growth being consumed by the costs of handling the attendant problems.

## A LESS LEISURELY SOCIETY

The 1980s trends in leisure become intelligible only when set in their political and economic contexts. The British government has defined economic trends as the 'real world' to which people should adjust, and has therefore allowed these trends to threaten or undermine many adults' former ways of life. These same economic trends have been allowed to thwart many young people's routes to the jobs, wages and consumer life-styles to which they aspire. The victims have certainly not welcomed their predicament, yet it has inspired neither demands that the government should protect, nor widespread communal efforts to defend, leisure oppor-tunities *despite* economic conditions. Britain's unemployed have marched for the right to work, not a right to leisure. They have protested at the government's failure to protect their livelihoods, not their life-styles. Conditions in the 1980s have not undermined Britain's consensus that life-styles are private, not public, issues. The two parties that have dominated British politics since the 1920s have been challenged by a centre alliance of Liberals and Social Democrats, but this new political force has joined the debates on familiar political issues – the rate of economic growth, the level of unemployment, the gap between rich and poor, and the condition of public education, health and housing services. Leisure has not been promoted towards the head of Britain's political agenda.

Some of the unemployed have responded pro-actively and devised satisfying uses of their spare time (Fryer and Payne, 1984). A minority have experienced gains in physical and psychological well-being on being released from the pressures of employment (Walter, 1985). However, the most common adaptations to unemployment in the 1980s are the same as in the 1930s and involve resignation and apathy, not self-fulfilment (Jahoda, 1982; Kelvin *et al.*, 1984). Intellectuals have debated the possi-bility of compensating for lack of jobs and wages by promoting leisure-based life-styles. Public service leisure professions have been anxious to 'do something' for the disadvantaged, and have pioneered special pro-grammes for the unemployed and other low participation target groups. However, these efforts have struck few chords, certainly among Britain's unemployed. The latter have sought escapes from, rather than means of adjustment to, the predicament.

Industrial capitalism has in-built contradictions. Hence the century of debate about alienation and anomie, the almost incessant talk of crisis and prophecies of collapse in the absence of some *fundamental* reform. The system has consistently defied these predictions and has demonstrated an enormous capacity to absorb tensions. People whose preferred ways of life are endangered may or may not experience personal crises. They can resort to a variety of socio-psychological games which modify their goals or definitions of reality. Some such games, especially young people's con-frontations with authority, inflict penalties on the wider society, but these costs are spread widely: private troubles are not automatically translated into public issues. Britain's political and economic systems have not descended into crisis during the 1980s. Certain contradictions identified in previous decades have actually lessened. For instance, it used to be argued that the costs of meeting their political demands and thereby integrating the economically disadvantaged into capitalist societies would become mounting and eventually crippling burdens for the wealth-generating systems (Offe, 1984). During the 1980s, in Britain, the tendency has been to roll back the frontiers of legitimate demands on state welfare.

Neither the kind nor the severity of the threats to preferred ways of life in the 1980s are unprecedented. Most victims of economic restructuring and unemployment have been from Britain's working class, not the middle classes, and the former have a history of coping with fluctuating earnings and other misfortunes. Blocked goals are traditional frustrations for working-class youth. The literature on their deviant and 'magical' responses began to accumulate long before the 1980s (Merton, 1938; Cohen, 1976). Even during the long postwar boom, working-class lifestyles endured repeated assaults – from rehousing, especially in high-rise flats, from the breakup of neighbourhood communities, and from the influx of ethnic minorities. The part of the United Kingdom where people feel that their ways of life are in the gravest danger in the 1980s is not mainland Britain, but Northern Ireland, where the majority fear that their Protestant culture could be overwhelmed by Roman Catholicism and Irish nationalism.

In the long run Britain's middle classes could prove the more effective cultural revolutionaries. New and growing social movements in the 1980s have mainly middle-class activists. The Social Democratic and Liberal parties have overwhelmingly middle-class memberships. So does the Campaign for Nuclear Disarmament which, in Britain, plays the umbrella role of green parties in other countries, drawing together a variety of crusades against threats to the environment and peace. The women's movements with their opposition to patriarchy in families and labour markets, and to the stereotyped treatment of women solely on grounds of their biological sex, offer further examples of collective efforts to change ways of life independently of underlying economic conditions. These movements are also, as yet, the work of mainly middle-class women.

In the 1970s Daniel Bell drew attention to the contradiction between the rational values of capitalist enterprises with their necessary stress on efficiency and disciplined toil, and the relatively expressive, even hedonistic, values of the surrounding cultural systems (Bell, 1976). People are expected to derive their main rewards for occupational success through consumption, in leisure time. Yet the stresses of earning success can poison its enjoyment. In Britain in the 1980s more people than ever have good jobs which support rising standards of living. These people are working as long and probably harder than ever. Membership of the 'harried leisure class' (Linder, 1970) is growing, and the predicament is becoming more acute. The people who possess the money to afford consumer goods and services often lack the time to enjoy and, in some cases, even to use

them. Leisure is becoming more home centred. Prosperous sections of the
population in particular are spending more money than ever in purchasing
and equipping their dwellings. Yet family life is less stable than formerly.
A third of recent marriages in Britain will end in divorce if current rates
continue. Many white-collar occupations are being proletarianised in terms
of the conditions of work, career prospects and salaries. In some cases this
is a straightforward consequence of the decline in blue-collar jobs, and
the increased proportion of employment in non-manual occupations. This
makes it impossible to reward the majority of white-collar employees with
status and incomes that set them well ahead of the national average.
Individuals who desire real success can no longer be content with simply
getting into, but must climb career ladders within, management, education
and other public services. During the 1980s this seems to have been the
most common middle-class response to economic trends. Dropping out
and experimenting with alternative life-styles look less attractive as the
risks increase of being unable to scramble back.

Even so, there are contrary indicators. Connoisseur leisure is most
common among the middle classes, especially among young people in
post-compulsory education, and among individuals who are enjoying or
anticipating retirement. These groups could lead a pincer movement
strengthening the role of leisure throughout the life cycle. The middle
classes make the greater use of commercial and public leisure services.
They derive the greatest benefit from access to the countryside, provisions
for sport and support for the arts. There could be a cross-fertilisation, or
alliances with environmentalist, feminist and other broader social movements. Slowly the benefits should filter into the working classes who, in
the 1980s, have become more preoccupied than ever with simply holding
on to or regaining employment and wages, and making the best of home-
centred life-styles.

All the trends contributing to the growth of leisure during earlier periods
in industrial history have continued in Britain in the 1980s. Work-free time
and leisure spending have continued to grow. If life has not become more
leisurely for most people this will be due entirely to the trends' separation.
Time released from employment has been given to the poorest sections
of the population, while spending power has increased mainly for those
with the least leisure time. A change of government could lead to a
quick redistribution of leisure time and spending. Even without political
intervention, working-class pressure for jobs and a more generous share
of the nation's prosperity, combined with middle-class concerns that
improvements in standards of living are not being matched in the quality
of everyday life, could become major forces governing the development of
leisure during the remainder of the twentieth century.

# REFERENCES

Bell, D. (1976) *The Cultural Contradictions of Capitalism*. London: Heinemann.

Bishop, J. and P. Hoggett (1986) *Organizing Around Enthusiasms*, London: Comedia.

Cohen, P. (1976) 'Subcultural Conflicts and Working Class Community', in M. Hammersley and P. Woods (eds) *The Process of Schooling*. London: Routledge.

Darton, D. (1986) 'Leisure Forecast 1986: the Leisured Society', *Leisure Management*, 6(January): 7–8.

Fryer, D. and R. Payne (1984) 'Proactive Behaviour in Unemployment: Findings and Implications', *Leisure Studies*, 3: 273–95.

Gershuny, J. (1978) *After Industrial Society?* London: Macmillan.

Haworth, J. T. (1986) 'Meaningful Activity and Psychological Models of Non-employment', *Leisure Studies*, 5: 281–97.

Jahoda, M. (1982) *Employment and Unemployment: a Social-Psychological Analysis*. Cambridge: Cambridge University Press.

Kelvin, P., C. Dewberry and N. Morley-Bunker (1984) *Unemployment and Leisure*, unpublished manuscript, University College, London.

Kinsey, R., J. Lea and J. Young (1986) *Losing the Fight Against Crime*. Oxford: Blackwell.

Linder, S. (1970) *The Harried Leisure Class*. New York: Columbia University Press.

Martin, B. and S. Mason (1986) 'Spending Patterns Show New Leisure Priorities', *Leisure Studies*, 5: 233–6.

Merton, R. K. (1938) 'Social Structure and Anomie', *American Sociological Review*, 3: 672–82.

Offe, C. (1984) *Contradictions of the Welfare State*. London: Hutchinson.

Roberts, K. (1983) *Youth and Leisure*. London: Allen and Unwin.

Walter, T. (1985) *Hope on the Dole*. London: SPCK.

Whannel, G. (1986) 'The Unholy Alliance: Notes on Television and the Remaking of British Sport 1965–85', *Leisure Studies*, 5: 129–45.

Reading taken from A. Olszewska and K. Roberts (eds), *Leisure and Life-style*, © 1989, Sage Publications Ltd. Reprinted with permission.

# Activities

1. Roberts cites 'community recreation' as a fashionable notion of the 1980s. Approach a local authority leisure officer in the town or area from which you come and ask him or her what is meant by that term. Report back in a one-page memorandum, trying to specify what the term means in principle and practice.
2. Ask four young adults – two female and two male – to each list their four main leisure activities. Write up to 250 words on your findings in the light of Roberts' points about major tendencies in leisure in the 1980s.
3. Collect up-to-date statistics on leisure spending published by leisure consultants (such as Mintel or Henley Centre for Forecasting) or government surveys such as Social Trends. What are the recent patterns and changes in leisure markets and leisure consumption?
4. What problems confront social science researchers wishing to measure UK employment during the past decade?
5. Why should the UK government be reluctant to accept the Social Chapter in the Maastricht Treaty? What are the main implications of this European legislation on those working in leisure industries?
6. What are the current annual budgets and patterns of expenditure for the following quangos – Arts Council, Sports Council, Countryside Commission? What is the overall budget of the Ministry of National Heritage?

## ESSAYS

1. Roberts argues that 'Britain in the 1980s has become a more polarised society'. With reference to evidence on leisure participation and trends, assess the validity of this statement.

2. Drawing upon your own observations and experiences in leisure, discuss recent trends in 'connoisseur leisure'.
3. What determines the place of leisure on the UK political agenda?
4. Roberts notes that 'Spending on leisure services was not actually cut by the Thatcher administrations'. Why should leisure expenditure be exempted by a government committed to controlling public expenditure?
5. What are the arguments for and against a 'Ministry of Leisure'?

# PART TWO

# Leisure and Common Experiences

# Introduction

As suggested by the title, Leisure and Common Experiences, this part is concerned with ways in which leisure is influenced by three experiences which almost everyone undergoes at some point in their lives. Most of us undertake paid work, live for a significant part of our lives in families and move through various phases of the life cycle, from adolescence to old age. Sociologists generally agree that all of these experiences affect how we view and exploit leisure but frequently disagree about their relative importance and the precise ways in which they affect leisure choice. As is often the case, these differences of emphasis arise not only because writers disagree about leisure. They also argue about how far and in what ways the organization, or 'structure', of society impinges upon leisure (a debate further pursued in Part Five).

Our first topic is work, more properly paid work. (For discussion of the role of – largely female – unpaid work on leisure, see readings 12 and 23.) The first extract, from Stanley Parker, is an updated version of an argument first published in 1972 as *The Future of Work and Leisure* (Paladin) – one of the books which first established a serious sociology of leisure in Britain. Parker attempts to show how the nature of paid work – and such related factors as education – structures experience of leisure. He develops a typology of work-leisure relationships which stem from the kinds of jobs people do. Roberts, in his extract, disputes this position, arguing that work is by no means as important as Parker believes. People have other roles, such as those in the family, which may be more important to their sense of self and their leisure motivations, than what they do for a living.

Part of the debate about the importance or otherwise of work centres on the countervailing influence of the family, which is the topic examined by our next two extracts. John Kelly stresses the importance of the family as the source and location of our most intimate personal relationships and thus a central influence on how and with whom we most wish to spend

*Sociology of Leisure: A reader.* Edited by C. Critcher, P. Bramham and A. Tomlinson. Published in 1995 by E & FN Spon, London. ISBN 0 419 19420 7.

our leisure time. Kelly's main emphasis is on interpreting how people experience and value family life. By contrast, Clarke and Critcher stress inequalities within and between families, seeing family leisure as resting on unequal leisure resources and opportunities. (More feminist views of the effects of family life on women's leisure can again be found in readings 12 and 23.)

Growing up in a family, leaving it, starting a new one as a couple or single parent, then emerging in later life without dependent children, are all phases of the life cycle. This is not the same as the simple process of ageing, since individuals may enter or leave stages of the life cycle at quite different chronological ages. The most influential statement of this model is contained in the extract from Rhona and Robert Rapoport. They suggest that the preoccupations, interests and activities of people change according to the stage they have reached in the life cycle and this will affect the satisfactions they seek to meet in leisure activities. Family formation is a crucial stage of the life cycle but there are other phases where the family appears less important. To illustrate this, we have chosen two deliberately contrasting examples: those of male, working-class adolescence and those of the elderly.

Paul Corrigan's interviews and observations of semi-delinquent boys in Sunderland lead him to analyse why pop music and football are more attractive leisure options than those advocated by school or youth clubs. They offer more exciting, adaptable and potentially disruptive opportunities for the kinds of enjoyment valued by the boys. At the other end of the life cycle, Abrams reports survey data on the leisure of the elderly. A combination of factors – low income, poor health, limited education and social isolation – tends to restrict the possibilities of leisure in the final phase of life. Older people appear to become progressively disengaged from society as a whole, including active leisure.

Like other parts in this reader, this one is designed to access debates rather than resolve them. The only safe conclusion to be drawn is that the experiences of work, family and the life-cycle may be common to us all but appear to be more complex than is commonly understood.

# IIa Work and Leisure

## 2

# Towards a theory of work and leisure

Stanley Parker

## LEVELS AND PATTERNS

There are two levels on which we may consider the various possible types of relationship between work and leisure: in the life of the individual and in the structure of the society in which he lives. This, in fact, oversimplifies the matter because there are levels intermediate between the individual and the societal (for instance, the group), but the analysis is clearer if confined to these two levels and to a general description of the type of relationship (see Table 2.1). These general descriptions are the broadest possible ways in which we can look at work and leisure, covering both individuals and the society of which they are part. *Identity* describes any situation where work and leisure feature similar structures, behaviour, or purposes. *Contrast* means a definition of the content of one sphere as the absence or opposite of the other. *Separateness* sums up a situation of minimal contact or influence between the spheres. It will be helpful to remember these general descriptions when considering the different types of relationship between work and leisure and the important question of whether there is a connection between the two levels.

First, however, I shall consider the proposition that there are three main types of relationship between work and leisure and that each of us tends to have one of these in his own pattern of life. I introduced the terms 'extension', 'opposition' and 'neutrality' to describe the various types of relationship between occupation and council work for local government councillors. Now we can see how far these terms may be used to group

*Sociology of Leisure: A reader.* Edited by C. Critcher, P. Bramham and A. Tomlinson. Published in 1995 by E & FN Spon, London. ISBN 0 419 19420 7.

**Table 2.1** Types of work–leisure relationship

| General description | Individual level | Societal level |
|---|---|---|
| Identity | Extension | Fusion |
| Contrast | Opposition | Polarity |
| Separateness | Neutrality | Containment |

together the patterns of work and leisure shown by the other types of people mentioned. The *extension* pattern consists of having leisure activities which are often similar in content to one's working activities and of making no sharp distinction between what is considered as work and what as leisure. With the *opposition* pattern, leisure activities are deliberately unlike work and there is a sharp distinction between what is work and what is leisure. Finally, the *neutrality* pattern consists of having leisure activities which are generally different from work but not deliberately so, and of appreciating the difference between work and leisure without always defining the one as the absence of the other . . .

First, work–leisure relationships at the individual level need careful definition. Then I shall look at the aspects of occupations and work involvement ('work variables') that seem to be associated with each of these patterns of relationship. Finally, I shall deal with the non-work (mainly leisure) variables that are also associated with the patterns. In this way it is possible to build up a total picture of what it means to have an extension, opposition, or neutrality pattern of work and leisure.

In Table 2.2 the details are set out in summary form. The various descriptions of values of the variables are based on research conclusions already noted in earlier chapters, but sometimes a certain amount of speculation is involved. Further research may require that some of the details be changed or qualified.

To put some flesh on the bare bones of Table 2.2 we may consider just what it means in human terms to have each of these patterns. With extension there is a similarity between at least some work and leisure activities and a lack of demarcation between what is called work and what is called leisure. The extreme cases of people having this pattern are those who are free from the necessity of earning a living but who do work of a kind and in circumstances of their choice. A larger group of people includes those whose lives show a strong tendency to extension of work into leisure but also some elements of opposition and/or neutrality. Thus some social workers feel that it is bad for them and for their clients if they are too work-centred, and their leisure accordingly has some elements of deliberate opposition to work. Having work as a central life interest is part of the definition of the extension pattern. This is because work, to someone who sees a continuity between work and leisure, is a much more embracing concept than just 'the job' or even 'the occupation'. Work signifies the

**Table 2.2** Types of work–leisure relationship and associated variables (individual level)

| | Extension | Opposition | Neutrality |
|---|---|---|---|
| *Work–leisure relationship variables* | | | |
| Content of work and leisure | Similar | Deliberately different | Usually different |
| Demarcation of spheres | Weak | Strong | Average |
| Central life interest | Work | – | Non-work |
| Imprint left by work on leisure | Marked | Marked | Not marked |
| | | | |
| *Work variables* | | | |
| Autonomy in work situation | High | – | Low |
| Use of abilities (how far extended) | Fully ('stretched') | Uneven ('damaged') | Little or no ('bored') |
| Involvement | Moral | Alienative | Calculative |
| Work colleagues | Include some close friends | – | Include no close friends |
| Work encroachment on leisure | High | Low | Low |
| Typical occupations | Social workers (especially residential) | 'Extreme' (mining, fishing) | Routine (clerical and manual) |
| | | | |
| *Non-work variables* | | | |
| Educational level | High | Low | Medium |
| Duration of leisure | Short | Irregular | Long |
| Main function of leisure | Continuation of personal development | Recuperation | Entertainment |

meaning and fulfilment of life, and in saying that it is also the centre of life such people are not necessarily denying the integrated role that leisure plays in it. Also, because of deep involvement in their kind of work it leaves a relatively great imprint on the rest of their lives – it is often an influence from which they are never really free.

The key aspects of the opposition pattern are the intentional dissimilarity of work and leisure, and the strong demarcation between the two spheres. The extreme cases of this pattern are those who hate their work so much that any reminder of it in their off-duty time is unpleasant. But paradoxically such people do not in one sense get away from work at all: so deeply are they marked by the hated experience of work that they measure the delights of leisure according to how much unlike work they are. Thus if work means submission to authority then leisure means 'having a go' at authority in some other way. A less pure type of opposition between work and leisure is shown by the person who has an ambivalent rather than a completely hostile attitude to work – he hates it because of the physical or psychological damage that he feels it does to him, yet he 'loves' it because he is fascinated by its arduousness or by its dangers (it is 'real man's work'). The strain of such work ensures that it is not carried over into leisure, from which it is clearly demarcated. With opposition, the source of central life interest is generally not clear; if work is viewed with unmixed hatred then presumably non-work is seen as the centre of life, but if there is a love–hate relationship to work then either sphere could be seen as central, or perhaps the very opposition and dissimilarity of the spheres renders the person incapable of making a comparative judgement.

The third pattern of neutrality is only partly defined by a 'usually different' content of work and leisure and by an 'average' demarcation of spheres. This pattern is in many ways not intermediate between the extension and opposition patterns, although it may at first glance appear to be so. The crucial difference between extension and opposition on the one hand, and neutrality on the other, is that the former denote respectively a positive and negative attachment to work, while the latter denotes a detachment from work that is neither fulfilment nor oppression. With extension and opposition the imprint left by work on leisure is relatively marked, in either a positive or negative way. But people showing the neutrality pattern are neither so engrossed in their work that they want to carry it over into non-work time nor so damaged by it that they develop a hostile or love–hate relation to it. Instead, work leaves them comparatively unmarked and free to carry over into leisure the non-involvement and passivity which characterises their attitude to work. In other words, detachment from any real responsibility for and interest in work tends to lead to detachment from any active and constructive leisure pursuits. Although some individuals are able to break out of this vicious circle, the tendency is to sit back and wait to be entertained. Since entertainment is more 'fun' than work, people with the neutrality pattern are likely to find their central life interest outside the work sphere.

## ASSOCIATED VARIABLES

Turning now to the work variables associated with the three patterns, we may note first the effect of degree of autonomy in the work situation. The study of social workers with relatively high autonomy showed that they were also very likely to exhibit the extension pattern. But the bank workers, who generally had little autonomy, typically showed the neutrality pattern. The conclusion for the opposition pattern is not so clear. Autonomy is probably low for most of these people, being accompanied by little interest in the work itself and hence a desire to escape from it. But a highly individualistic work situation, neither machine-paced nor closely supervised, could also be accompanied by opposition of work and leisure if the attitude to work were one of alienation.

The second work variable, use of abilities, needs to be analysed in terms of both amount and evenness of being extended or 'used' in the job. The social workers, who used most of their abilities in an intensive way, tended to show the extension pattern, while the bank workers, usually less extended in their jobs, tended to show the neutrality pattern. Those men and women who are unevenly extended in their jobs are likely to want to compensate for this by a counterbalancing type of non-work life that will help to repair the ravages of work. To sum up on use of abilities, we can say that extension is usually accompanied by a feeling of being 'stretched' by the work, neutrality by being 'bored' with it, and opposition by being 'damaged' by it.

To describe types of involvement in work we may draw upon Etzioni's (1961) types of involvement by 'lower participants' in organisations – moral, calculative and alienative. Since we are restricting our analysis to economic (employing) organisations and do not, as Etzioni does, include a comparison of economic with other kinds of organisation, the parallel is not an exact one; it may nevertheless be worth making. Accepting that economic reward is a motive common to all employees for participating in work organisations, we may describe as 'moral' the kind of involvement which produces a desire to go on working in that way even if freed from the necessity of earning a living. 'Calculative' involvement occurs where the work is done consciously as part of a transaction, that is, where economic reward is overwhelmingly the main motivation. 'Alienative' involvement occurs where economic reward is also important but is experienced less as a transaction than as a sense of being forced to do the job against one's will. These three types of involvement seem to be associated respectively with the extension, neutrality and opposition patterns of work and leisure, although there is some ambiguity between the last two patterns.

The likelihood of having some work colleagues among one's close friends is high among those with the extension pattern and low among those with the neutrality pattern. Again, the opposition people are not so predictable. If work is hated then presumably the thought of mixing with work colleagues off the job is also hateful (and this may help to explain the feeling among some factory workers that 'mating is not palling'), but it is also possible that the damaging experience of work is made more tolerable by a feeling of solidarity with workmates whose company may well be sought off the job. An 'occupational community' does not require that all members be positively involved in the work: all may be negatively involved, provided that they are conscious of sharing this feeling.

The degree of encroachment of work on leisure is high for those with the extension pattern and low for the other two groups. The extension people are likely to let their work carry over into leisure time because they find it interesting for its own sake. Where work does encroach on the leisure time of the neutrality group, it is likely to do so only as a means to an end, for example, to pass examinations in order to get promotion. Where work encroaches on the leisure time of the opposition group, it does so only in the sense that a person must first recover from the effects of this kind of work before he can enjoy leisure.

The above analysis of work variables in relation to types of work–leisure relationship has been based on the research reported in earlier chapters. This research has mostly been concerned with specific occupational groups, although the effects of certain variables within occupational groups have also been noted. I do not claim that certain occupations and certain types of work–leisure relationship always go together, but to round off the discussion of work variables the following tentative additions may be made to the typical occupations listed in Table 2.2. Extension may also include successful businessmen (perhaps they are successful because they have little or no time for leisure), doctors, teachers and self-employed workers; neutrality may include minor professionals other than social workers; and opposition may cover unskilled manual workers, assembly-line workers, oil rig workers and tunnellers (the last two being 'extreme' occupations in the sense both of high pay and physical working conditions).

We now come to three non-work variables – one of education and two of leisure. Concerning education, the child care officers, the majority of whom showed the extension pattern, also had, in the majority, attended university. The bank employees, the majority of whom showed the neutrality pattern, had mostly attended grammar schools but had not gone on to higher education. The large majority of the 'opposition' manual workers had had only elementary or secondary modern education. The question arises: is it type of education which determines the occupation which in turn influences work–leisure patterns, or does education exert an influence on work–leisure patterns independently of occupation? There are two clues to the answer to this difficult question. One is my own impression gained from the pilot interviews with business and service workers. Several of the people in business occupations who had a neutrality work–leisure pattern had been well educated (university or public school) yet seemed far less involved in their work than some of the less well-educated social workers who had an extension pattern. Secondly, the analysis of attitudes of local government councillors suggests that a number of manual-worker councillors had been so 'educated' by their experience of public work that they now felt capable of doing things which they felt they would have been prevented from doing previously by their low level of formal education. Both of these clues point in the direction of the influence of work experience on work–leisure patterns independently of the level of formal education.

There is ample evidence that professional and business employees have less time for leisure than the mass of routine and clerical workers (Linder, 1970). This suggests 'short' and 'long' duration of leisure time for those with the extension and neutrality patterns respectively. Again, the opposition pattern presents problems. The distant-water fishermen have about nine months of the year at sea and three months ashore, mostly as leisure time; the latter, therefore, is better described as 'irregular' rather than as either long or short. For others with the opposition pattern the lack of work encroachment on leisure may mean a relatively long duration of leisure, but a willingness to work long hours for big money would shorten available leisure time. There is, then, no general conclusion about duration of leisure time for those with the opposition pattern.

Finally, there is the question of the main function of leisure. Here it seems reasonable to borrow and modify slightly Dumazedier's (1967) three functions of personal development, entertainment and relaxation to apply to extension, neutrality and opposition respectively. For 'personal development' we may substitute 'continuation of personal development', since the work done by people with the extension pattern is usually of the kind that promotes personal development and the need is for leisure to continue it in a different or complementary way. 'Entertainment' has the right connotation of relief from boredom to describe the function of 'neutrality' leisure. 'Relaxation', however, is too similar to, and implies too much of the passivity of, entertainment to describe 'opposition' leisure, and the term 'recuperation' seems preferable. It should be understood that only in exceptional cases does any one of these three functions characterise the whole of leisure. For example, we may say that a person has the extension pattern because the general nature of the relationship between his work and his leisure is as outlined in Table 2.2, but that need not stop him from sometimes feeling the need for recuperation or entertainment.

## SUBSEQUENT CRITICISMS AND REFINEMENTS

Since my original formulation of the three work–leisure relationships there have been a number of critical assessments of these, which in turn have led me to some revisions to meet those criticisms which seem to be justified. In reviewing models, methods and findings in work and non-work research, Kabanoff (1980) sees our aim as

> to describe different work/leisure/family patterns, to discover the factors that determine these patterns, and to relate these patterns to other significant life outcomes such as general life satisfaction, work and leisure satisfaction, physical and mental health, and so on. (p. 74)

It seems that we are not so far advanced in this endeavour as to be able to be dogmatic about any statements we venture to make or to ignore constructive criticisms of those statements.

Clayre (1974) says of my typology that

> it leaves many questions open. It is a classification of people's activities only. But people do not necessarily find either the work or leisure they want; so their needs and wishes cannot necessarily be assessed from their actions. There may be more people seeking 'extension' or 'compensation' in leisure than actually finding it. (p. 198)

Although my typology certainly focuses on activities, it does so very much in the context of the functions of those activities in the life pattern rather than being concerned simply with the content of the activities. Clayre is right to claim that needs and wishes cannot always be assessed from actions – or even from personal statements. I am not even sure that it is valid to say that people are seeking extension or compensation. Many would no doubt like their work to be as interesting and creative as their leisure (and a few vice versa), while others are aware that mass-produced and passive leisure does not make up for work with the same limiting characteristics. If social scientists are to become social commentators and hence agents of social change, then they will have to find ways of encouraging people to regard as problematic and alterable what they now see as inevitable and beyond their control.

Bacon (1972), in the course of a critical review of concepts used in research on work–leisure relationships, suggests that these relationships may be examined on two dimensions: behavioural, which concerns the degree of fusion or polarity between the component elements of leisure and work; and normative, the degree to which values found in the work sphere complement or are opposed to values in the leisure sphere. Bacon's own research (1975) on hobbyist craftworkers and his assessment of other research of a similar nature leads him to conclude that there is little evidence of behavioural relationships between work and leisure but some evidence of normative relationships: 'To a considerable extent, the things that people choose to do in their free time are unrelated to the nature of their employment.' But he readily acknowledges that my types of work–leisure relationship (which he amends for measurement purposes to low, medium and high work-generated alienation) correlate well with various statements about fusion, opposition and neutrality between work and leisure. For example, 52 per cent of his craftworkers with high work-generated alienation, but only 15 per cent with low alienation, said 'I put up with my work and do the things that really interest me in my leisure' (Bacon, 1977). . . .

Roberts (1974) quite rightly insists that work–leisure relationships should be distinguished at the individual and societal levels and in behavioural and ideational terms.

At the level of individuals' life-styles, leisure interests are often only weakly related to characteristics of people's jobs, though types of work do have some bearing upon leisure interests ... But individuals with similar jobs can cultivate completely dissimilar leisure tastes. Conversely, people with quite different jobs may choose to spend their free time in similar ways. (p. 27)

This line of reasoning is consistent with Bacon's findings on craftworkers. Distinguishing ideas from behaviour is important because relationships discovered between work and leisure at one level will not necessarily be reflected at the other. As Roberts notes, leisure could be more potent than work in giving meaning to life, while job factors could be stronger in influencing leisure behaviour. In a similar vein, Mansfield and Evans (1975) suggest a distinction between the form and meaning of a person's activities both in and out of work.

We are still some way from being able to make confident and reasonably reliable statements about the complex web of different dimensions of the work–leisure relationship. As Near and his colleagues (1980) remark, in order to determine actual relationships between work and non-work thoroughly developed conceptual models must be devised and more sophisticated design and data analysis procedures must be used. We have so far assembled some fairly reliable statistical associations between attitudes to work and other domains of life, but we do not yet know much about the pathways underlying such relationships, their direction of causality, or relative strength.

## REFERENCES

Bacon, A. W. (1972), 'Leisure and research: a critical review of the main concepts employed in contemporary research', *Society and Leisure*, no. 2, pp. 83–92.

Bacon, A. W. (1975), 'Leisure and the alienated worker: a critical reassessment of three radical theories of work and leisure', *Journal of Leisure Research*, vol. 7, no. 3, pp. 179–90.

Bacon, A. W. (1977), 'Leisure and the craftworkers', in M. A. Smith (ed.), *Leisure and Urban Society* (London: Leisure Studies Association).

Clayre, A. (1974), *Work and Play* (London: Weidenfeld & Nicolson).

Dumazedier, J. (1967), *Toward a Society of Leisure* (London: Collier Macmillan).

Etzioni, A. (1961), *A Comparative Analysis of Complex Organizations* (New York: The Free Press).

Kabanoff, B. (1980), 'Work and nonwork: a review of models, methods and findings', *Psychological Bulletin*, vol. 88, no. 1, pp. 60–77.

Linder, S. (1970), *The Harried Leisure Class* (New York: Columbia University Press).

Mansfield, R., and Evans, M. G. (1975), 'Work and non-work in two occupational groups', *Industrial Relations Journal*, vol. 6, no. 2, pp. 48–54.

Near, J. P., Rice, R. W., and Hunt, R. G. (1980), 'The relationship between work and nonwork domains: a review of empirical research', *Academy of Management Review*, vol. 5, no. 3, pp. 415–30.

Roberts, K. (1974), 'The changing relationship between work and leisure', in I. Appleton (ed.), *Leisure Research and Policy* (Edinburgh: Scottish Academic Press).

Reading taken from S. Parker, *Leisure and Work*, published by Allen & Unwin, 1983. Reprinted with permission.

# 3 | Work and its corollaries

Kenneth Roberts

## WORK CENTRALITY

Work is another influence upon leisure, and an intention in this chapter is to explore how occupational differences account for variations in leisure behaviour. At the same time, the following argument warns against exaggerating the significance of work. The influence of work upon leisure is much less powerful than familial variables . . . , and just as analysis in terms of social networks and life-styles allows us to understand the family's importance, so it also reveals why the impact of work upon leisure should be relatively marginal; much less dramatic than suggested in some previous accounts.

In the past sociologists have tended to treat leisure as a subsidiary sphere of life with a character derived from more pivotal institutions, particularly work. As Giddens has noted, 'Leisure has in general been regarded as merely ancillary to those systems of economy, power and prestige which have been taken in sociology as crucial to the explication of social behaviour.' Historically, sociological research into leisure developed largely as an adjunct to the sociology of occupations. This was probably to be expected given that contemporary leisure owes its character to industrialism, coupled with sociology's continuing 'obsession' with social class. Nothing has seemed more obvious to many sociologists than that variations in uses of leisure will be attributable to individuals' occupations. Hence the volumes charting the significance of various aspects of work including income, prestige, career patterns and whether work is a source of interest and friendships. Literally scores of enquiries have sought to identify how work can affect leisure, conveying the impression that work is the central determining factor in individuals' life-styles. . . .

*Sociology of Leisure: A reader.* Edited by C. Critcher, P. Bramham and A. Tomlinson. Published in 1995 by E & FN Spon, London. ISBN 0 419 19420 7.

No one would wish to deny that leisure is influenced by work . . . investigators who have probed this area have uncovered many relationships. In social research, however, statistically significant connections are rarely difficult to unearth. Social life is an interconnecting web in which everything tends to be related to everything else in some way or another. The really important questions, therefore, concern exactly how powerful an influence work exerts, and the sum of the available evidence indicates that today this influence is rather weak – sufficiently so to justify talk of the compartmentalisation of leisure from the influence of individuals' work roles. . . .

Many of the influences of work upon leisure are permissive rather than deterministic, meaning that a pay rise, for example, may widen an individual's leisure choices, but it will not determine exactly how he uses the extra money. Many work-based 'causes' are translated into specific leisure effects only through independent mediating processes. Besides being workers, individuals are involved in other social relationships and immersed in other sources of values. Family, neighbourhood, educational and religious contexts translate opportunities such as accompany rising wage levels into particular uses of leisure. Likewise the additional free time offered by shorter hours of work is used in contrasting ways depending upon the life-styles towards which individuals are independently oriented. . . .

Querying the importance of work's effects upon leisure might appear to be quarrelling with common sense. Many leisure goods and services cost money, so surely income, for example, must make a big difference. Working class families simply cannot afford round-the-world cruises, private stables and paddocks for their horses, or regular weekends in luxury hotels. Focus upon such specific uses of leisure, and clear contrasts will be apparent between groups with different levels of income. What must be borne in mind, however, is that at all income levels a great deal of leisure is spent at home, doing nothing in particular, or watching television. Theatre-going is a mainly middle class pastime and rates of working class participation lag far behind. But theatre attendances account for only a minute proportion of all middle class leisure. A far greater volume of middle class leisure time is spent watching television which is also popular among the working class. Examining total life-styles enables some of the sharper social class contrasts that can be drawn to be kept in perspective. Although the majority of families cannot afford weekends at luxury hotels, they can usually devise uses of leisure time to perform similar functions in their life-styles, such as taking trips to the coast or countryside. Similarly, although the type of holiday must depend upon income, most families in Britain can afford a holiday away from home, and likewise most individuals can afford to participate in some sport. There are social class variations to uses of leisure, but these are by no means as clear cut as, for example, in politics, where the majority of middle class electors vote Conservative, while Labour is easily the most popular working class choice.

Work-related variables constrain some groups' uses of leisure more than others, but as constraints are eased, the opportunities created are mostly used to modify details within the basically unchanged life-styles that the individuals in question continue to prefer. Shorter hours of work, therefore, allow manual workers to spend slightly more leisure engaged in the social intercourse that, in any case, tends to be a prominent feature of their life-styles. Variations in hours of work and income levels do not produce really dramatic shifts in life-styles since in themselves they do not reshape the social networks upon which, as argued and illustrated earlier, uses of leisure are constructed. . . .

## THE AUTONOMY OF MODERN LEISURE

While work and leisure do not coexist in absolutely unconnected compartments of life, the sum of the evidence does not justify treating leisure purely as a dependent variable. Uses of leisure are certainly influenced by the nature of individuals' occupations. But when we ask how and to what extent, we see that rather than treating work as a determinant, it is often more appropriate to regard individuals as accommodating to the constraints that their working lives impose and using the resources that their occupations offer to cultivate whatever life-styles they prefer as a result of their personal tastes and the social relationships in which they are involved in their non-working lives. The effects of work frequently amount to no more than modulations upon constant themes. Work differences tend to produce deviations around but do not submerge independently recurrent patterns, and these patterns can rarely be explained principally in terms of work-related factors.

Workers are also people who are influenced by the other roles that they play, particularly their family roles, and can manage their leisure to sustain the life-styles they seek by accommodating to whatever distinctive constraints and opportunities accompany their types of employment. In the absence of friendly relationships at work, white-collar employees in particular draw upon kin, neighbours or other friends for social intercourse. Income may rule out expensive activities such as polo, but substitute forms of recreation can be discovered without exceptional ingenuity. Human beings are innovative creatures and are capable of building upon the opportunities that accompany their work to pursue their independently formulated preferences. In contemporary pluralist societies 'man at leisure' is subject to heterogeneous influences and opportunities within which the effects that in isolation would follow from work can be managed and assimilated into life-styles to which individuals are independently committed.

Of course, there are some individuals whose leisure is strongly influenced by their work, and in these cases treating leisure purely as a dependent variable can be appropriate. There are people who remain strongly motivated by a work ethic and for whom work is a central life interest that patterns their uses of leisure time. Today, however, such work–leisure relationships are exceptional . . .

In addition to charting the influence of work, therefore, the analysis of leisure must also stress the autonomy that this sphere of life has attained. Historically contemporary leisure may have been shaped by industrialism, but it is no longer just a minor by-product. This is the substantive conclusion towards which this chapter points, and uses of leisure have been released from the influence of work because individuals' social networks contain other and usually more potent bases. . . .

Work is important, but even its claims upon lifetime must be kept in perspective. At any point in time, one-half of the population is economically inactive. Without taking any account of the involuntary unemployed, the young and the retired plus full-time housewives account for approximately one-half of the total population. For individuals who are currently part of the labour force, work consumes less than a quarter of their time in any one year. Work remains an important activity, but it is less domineering than sometimes imagined. . . .

Treating work as *the* sphere of life containing men's major social obligations and hopes for self-expression discords with the autonomy that leisure has attained in the lives of most present-day citizens.

To say this is not to belittle work, which continues to account for a substantial block, even if not the greater part of lifetime. But work today is less than the central force still postulated in many texts. The value of a sociological perspective in a proper understanding of leisure is one of the recurrent themes in this book. Yet it is necessary to repeatedly protest the inadequacy of some favourite sociological perspectives when faced with the leisure phenomenon. Sociology's texts, journals and conferences stress politics, the economy and stratification as casting the macro-social structure. The family, neighbourhood communities, and leisure as well, are often dismissed as incidental and trivial – easy stuff suitable for those who fight shy from major theoretical and social controversies. . . .

There is now a wealth of evidence that the quality of life, individuals' well-being and happiness, depend mainly upon the quality of the primary social relationships by which they are surrounded. Self-rated happiness depends more upon social participation than income. When asked what *they* consider the main determinants of the quality of life, members of the public are more likely to talk about homes, friends and families than social class, the economy and politics. The macro-structure *does* impinge upon primary social relationships – to an extent. But contemporary societies are sufficiently loosely-knit systems to make the primary relationships amid which individuals experience life substantially independent of the larger political economy. Work centrality still reigns in much of sociology, but contemporary society is different. . . .

Individuals' occupations remain important elements in their self-identities. Men in particular, but women also to an increasing extent, require a work-role in order to enjoy a creditable social status. Take the work-role away through unemployment or compulsory retirement, and individuals' entire personality structures can begin to topple. In itself the growth of leisure contains no solutions to the problems traditionally associated with unemployment and retirement. Yet while it may be a basic prop, we do not need to regard work as the only source of identity for contemporary man. It is surely more realistic to regard individuals' work-roles as bases – essential bases, that people can add to and build upon in the course of developing preferred life-styles outside their workplaces. And in these life-styles it is possible for individuals to cultivate qualities and self-images that differ from and . . . are sometimes inconsistent with the demands of their jobs. Presuming work centrality neglects these aspects of social reality.

In addition to asking how uses of leisure vary alongside work-based differences, we also need to question how individuals accommodate to the constraints and exploit the opportunities associated with their particular occupations to construct and defend life-styles to which they are independently committed as a result of their family circumstances, other social relationships and resultant personal tastes. We need to explore how individuals manage and rationalise the sometimes contradictory pressures to which they are exposed in their working and non-working lives. To understand leisure we certainly need to recognise the implications of work, but without remaining transfixed within an assumption of work centrality.

Reading taken from K. Roberts, *Contemporary Society and the Growth of Leisure*, published by Longman Group UK Ltd, 1978. Reprinted with permission.

# IIb Leisure and the Family

# 4 Leisure and the family

John R. Kelly

The relationship of leisure and the family begins with a paradox. If leisure is defined as having an essential element of freedom, how can the most pervasive set of obligations in our social worlds not be in conflict with leisure? There are some social roles that are relatively discrete and segmented, carried out in social spaces cut off from other roles. Some work roles are quite segmented in time, place and associations. Some leisure roles are quite specific to an activity setting. But familial roles tend to pervade our allocations of resources – time, space, financial and personal; our modes of interaction; and our definitions of responsibility. How long can we ignore the expectations of the immediate others in our nuclear families? How often can we expend time or money without some consideration of the needs and obligations of home and family? The family is the *budgeting* unit of Western societies in relation to all resources.

It is no wonder that Joffre Dumazedier proposed that most family activity is at best *semi-leisure* and too laden with obligations to be leisure for its own sake.[1] Family activity is just not free enough to be authentic leisure according to this view. The other pole of the paradox is represented by the accumulated evidence that a high proportion of non-work activity is done with other family members as companions or is essentially familial in its substance. Further, such activity is generally valued most among all the range of leisure choices and investments.[2] How can family-related leisure be both constrained and preferred, least free and most valued? . . .

In a line of research carried out in the United States the author discovered a surprising anomaly. Even though freedom has been stressed as the central element of the meaning of leisure, complementary leisure with higher perceived constraint was found to rank higher in importance to adults than relatively unconstrained unconditional leisure.[3] In the univer-

*Sociology of Leisure: A reader.* Edited by C. Critcher, P. Bramham and A. Tomlinson. Published in 1995 by E & FN Spon, London. ISBN 0 419 19420 7.

sity town study, using a value scale, only 38 percent of the high-value activities were unconditional as opposed to 56 percent of the lower-value activities. In the mill town 68 percent of those activities ranked first by respondents were role complementary, 56 percent of those ranked second, 51 percent third, 46 percent fourth and 39 percent of those ranked fifth.

One possible explanation is that people really prefer constraint and place a lower value on relative freedom. They may find decision threatening and structure comfortable. However, there is a simpler and more plausible explanation. It is that the complementary kinds of leisure that are related to primary roles are valued more highly because of satisfactions attached to those relationships. Family leisure may be more constrained by expectations, but also be more satisfying. When we recognize that 64 percent of such adult activities are usually engaged in with other family members, the picture becomes more clear. It is not that we disvalue freedom, but that family interaction – even with somewhat less freedom – is valued more highly. For most adults, then, the most important leisure is relational, social leisure chosen because of the positive satisfactions anticipated. . . .

If nuclear family interaction is central to most adult leisure, does this reflect more than convenience or availability? If there is something more, is it a response to the expectations of intimates, a positive satisfaction found in the relationship, or some combination of the two?

The author's research is far from final or definitive. However, there are several consistent indications from the multicommunity studies.[4] First, in both the US and UK studies, positive 'relational' satisfactions ranked with relaxation as two of the highest three substantive reasons for selecting important leisure. Enjoyment of companions and strengthening relationships are primary orientations of adult leisure, each at least six times more often mentioned than family expectations.

Secondly, the primary content of considerable adult leisure is family interaction itself. Further, many activities serve primarily as a context for interaction, as social settings. Thirdly, situational factors are important in specific decisions about what to do at a given time. Therefore, the convenience of family companions is one element in such interaction. They tend to be most available, in the same residence and on parallel schedules.

Fourthly, building intimate relationships of sharing and communication is considered a central life concern and goal. Some leisure, then, is in part instrumental – a context for inaugurating, developing, enhancing, enriching and strengthening primary relationships. Fifthly, another element in such familial leisure may be 'role comfort'. All the attention given to role-testing, problematic outcomes and identity presentation should not obscure that on some occasions we prefer not to experiment, compete, or even refine identities. The relative acceptance within intimate communities may be a positive factor in choosing to spend time with others for whom identities are well established and interaction patterns relatively routine. Just as TV-watching may be relaxing and recuperative due to its low investment requirements, so some familial leisure may be valued just because it can be familiar and easy and responses accurately predicted. . . .

Leisure companionship is a major, if often overlooked, element in family life and marriage. It is far more complex than just responding to the expectations of others or meeting conventional role requirements. Fulfillment is found in the midst of life's ongoing relationships, not just in moments of ecstasy or transcendence. Who we are may be explored in a variety of settings, but is grounded in our intimate communities. Therefore, leisure companionship is a multidimensional phenomenon.

Family members are generally the most available companions for both informal and unscheduled leisure as well as for events that require planning. The family is thus seen as a primary resource for leisure. Enough adult establishment period leisure is organized by and for couples that being without this resource calls for a different set of opportunities for social leisure. The expectation of 'double occupancy' for vacation trips, the games that require pairs for participation and the customs of entertaining are only part of the expectation. Those who lack this resource, both for social events and for ongoing interaction, live in quite a different social world for leisure. The attention given to leisure as a resource for familial development should not be allowed to obscure the reverse, the significance of the family for leisure.

An issue that is only beginning to emerge is that of the expectations associated with the 'leisure role' in the family. Not only is a spouse, parent, sibling, or even child often expected to provide companionship for others in the family, but there are expectations as to the quality of the interaction. Members of the nuclear family are expected to listen, to give attention to the relating of events and attitudes so important to interaction. They are expected to give some priority to the priorities of others, to be ready to enter into conversation, adjust a schedule preference or even commitment, and share the interests of the other. In fact, the quality of leisure companionship may become more and more of an issue in marital stability or dissolution. The increase of divorces during and following launching of children suggests that for a husband to be an adequate breadwinner or a woman an acceptable mother and homemaker may not be enough to hold a marriage together. There is the further desire for companionship, for a sharing of interests and activities not only at home, but outside. The study by Lillian Rubin[5] documents the failure of some blue-collar husbands to meet the companionship expectations of their wives. One factor in meager communication may well be the lack of leisure interaction and sharing. . . .

The particular forms and settings of such leisure companionship change as roles change. Early marriage as an intensification of the courting period brings about a processual shift of leisure to what is shared with the partner.

The birth of children not only adds responsibilities, but breaks the simplicity of the dyad. Now a drastic new set of relationships, responsibilities and roles turn the couple into the more complex family of productivity and also may seriously erode the quality and quantity of dyadic leisure. However, more and more leisure for parents is found in the various support functions that attend childrearing. The transition that accompanies the loss of those support functions during launching does not mean that there is a simple return to preparental dyadic sharing. Rather, the leisure roles must be rebuilt during this latter transition if they are to take a more central place in the investments and allocations of the couple ...

The considerable emotional as well as economic investments in the nuclear family are made with the expectation of being given much in return. Among the aspects of return is leisure. What, then, are the leisure functions of the nuclear family?

First, leisure is a mutual interest for the family, a focus of interaction and communication. Generally, adult and youth members of the family join in deciding and planning a vacation trip. While relative influence may not be equal, the planning, anticipation and recollection of a vacation trip may be a common topic of conversation and medium of sharing.[6] In the same way, other common leisure events and investments – entertaining, visiting, a toy such as a boat or game, or any shared event – are concrete symbols around which communication and interaction are built.

Secondly, leisure is a social space for parenting. Not only one-on-one play with a child, but the various forms and locales of playful interaction are the context of considerable development of relationships. Family life that is all task and schedule, without leisure or spontaneity, would be lacking much of the joy and openness that break routine and add affective richness.

Thirdly, leisure is an opportunity for trying and developing new facets of family relationships. While there are values in routine sharing, even doing the dishes, leisure is the context of the unexpected and the novel. It is in leisure that we are most likely to break routine and discover something new in relationships.

Fourthly, leisure may also be an opportunity for autonomy and independence.[7] On the freedom side of the paradox, leisure legitimates independence from the family. Leisure, whether it is a ball game or an evening class, is an acceptable purpose for a spouse or child to go out on his/ her own. It is space for the development of non-familial identities that complement the family role identities. One important element of such autonomy, especially for adolescents, is sexual exploration and expression.

Fifthly, leisure is removed enough from the economic and maintenance functions of the family that it may serve as the context for role-enactment that alters and defuses the authority patterns of maintenance. The rigidity of breadwinner, banker, provider, schedule-keeper and teacher roles may be broken and emotional tension reduced through play that allows dominant family members to take less authoritative roles.

Sixthly, the expectation of mutual support in the family depends on some voluntary decisions as well as meeting social expectations and legal requirements. The companionship and trust developed and continued in leisure interaction contributes to the overall relationship that includes various kinds of support through the life course.

The other side of the investment–return issue is based on the significance of the family in the value schemes of adults in contemporary Western societies. Evidence that the family–home investments are most often of greatest salience has been presented. In the context of a fuller analysis of the family this central investment of self and resources may be re-examined. One approach is instrumental. Leisure is understood primarily in terms of what it provides to the stability and richness of family relationships. Leisure may be seen as at least some of the brightness and uniqueness in the overall fabric of family. Leisure is defined as good for the family, a necessary addition of variety and developmental opportunities. Leisure is approached as it makes significant contributions to that central investment of life, the family.

The second approach takes the family as a resource for leisure. Leisure is not defined just in terms of instrumental values, but also in terms of necessary expressivity. One element of the importance of the family is that it provides a social context for much leisure. Leisure, from this perspective, is a necessary space for freedom, expressivity and self-development. Enacting leisure roles has intrinsic as well as instrumental value. After all, in a family there are multiple roles and relationships. Among these is the role of leisure companion, enacted in many activity and environmental settings. Leisure roles are seen as an important part of the set of roles that make up the family institution. Further, family leisure roles enable portrayals that are needed to balance more structured role reciprocity and to facilitate possibilities of change through the life course.

In a society that requires so much from the nuclear family it should be no surprise that it is given such centrality in overall schemes of value. Nor should the close relationship between the family and leisure be considered surprising in a social system that has increasingly separated the workplace and residence, delegated a high proportion of time and other resources to the family, and been no more than ambivalent about the importance of social solidarity. As a consequence, those who remain outside the nuclear families for extended periods of their life course generally have to find some substitute.

## FORMS OF FAMILY LEISURE

Most of the forms of familial leisure have been mentioned. However, their variety can be seen more clearly by distinguishing three types.

### Informal leisure

In terms of the amount of time invested, the main kind of family leisure consists of ongoing interaction that takes place chiefly around the home. Evidence that this kind of leisure is most highly valued has been introduced. Such interaction consists of interstitial conversations, play with children, informal episodes in which dyadic interaction is the focus and various interaction sequences that are more processual than planned. They take place in and around the home, in transit to both tasks and events, and often in connection with meals. . . .

The meaning of much of the informal interaction is actually found in the communication that takes place. The lack of such communication may be defined as an acute and significant deprivation. Whether such communication takes place at the dinner table, before the TV, in the garden, or even in the garage and around the car is incidental. Such leisure is essentially one element of intimate interaction, perhaps the light side of the ongoing relationship.

Of course, the home is also the locale for a number of events such as entertaining, different kinds of celebration related to life course milestones and general holidays, and definitions that designate an occasion as important. Further, external schedules often enforce a timetable in informal and interstitial social leisure that give it a feeling of having to take place at a particular time or not at all.

### Scheduled events

From one perspective, scheduled family leisure becomes the punctuation in the run-on sentence. Events are the designated high points of family interaction that lend meaning and excitement to the rest. They are the events that require some planning and anticipation as well as a specific allocation of at least one resource, time.

Some such events are regular. They include participation in church worship and organizations, other voluntary organizations, activities that require collecting certain people at the same time and place such as a sport contest or choral concert, and all the special events selected as worth this attention and resource allocation. Some events are related to the social roles taken by family members such as a mother's participation in community theater, a brother's track meet, or a school-related convocation. Such events may be clustered in weekend periods or be routinely scheduled on the 'fourth Friday evening'. Others are seasonal or related to the school or church calendar.

The decision processes related to such events are often complex. In some families the mother becomes the keeper of the social schedule and arbiter of conflicts.[8] In other families the responsibility is shared or delegated according to convenience or salience. There seems to be a close connection between transportation needs and resources and such schedule arbitration in the modern metropolitan family. Juggling all the priorities, schedules, changes, losses and contingencies can be a demanding and complex task in a family with children over 10–12 years old.

Another issue is the extent to which leisure events separate or integrate the family. Some community agencies which claim to serve the entire family actually segregate their activities quite rigidly by age. Activities and events that allow for or require immediate interaction of family members may be relatively rare in many churches, clubs and community recreation programs. It is the self-organized events that are most likely to provide a frame for intimate community-building.

### Vacations

Although vacations do not all involve trips, some special use of the time is common. Even in Brent, almost three-quarters of the sample had been away from home on holiday in the previous twelve months and a third more than once.[9] Most of the other 25 percent had been on vacation during the previous three years. Further, such trips are found to have an important place in leisure and life satisfaction.

Such trips have many dimensions.[10] Not only is there the anticipation and recollection as well as the experience itself, but family vacation travel is more than getting someplace. Some parents report finding that just being together in the car with no distracting tasks or interference provides a singular opportunity for communication, especially with older children. Trips themselves are frequently more than transportation. A case study of a California family found that a single summer trip combined interaction on the way, camping in transit, visiting relatives and friends, sightseeing and even routines of eating at restaurants previously found attractive.[11]

Similar analysis of outdoor camping suggested that a variety of activities are contexts for many different role portrayals at a single campsite.[12] Activities such as chopping wood, erecting a tent, and preparing and gathering food, as well as hiking, boating and swimming, are opportunities for the symbolic presentation of various aspects of the identities of different family members. While this may be true for any event of sustained and varied interaction, the possibility of playing out sequences of role identities in company with others of the nuclear family seem especially evident in the vacation trip.

## TRENDS AND TRANSITIONS

We may continue to distinguish between structural elements of social institutions and those of style. Just as the stylistic 'how' of leisure may be more differentiated than the more structural 'what', so changes in the family are also both those of form and style.

### Structural trends

The analysis that follows is based on an analysis of structural trends in household composition and women's employment in the United States. The trends are common to other Western countries, but the rates and baselines differ. In general, the following trends seem well established:[13]

- The major increase will be in households composed of single persons and single heads rather than those headed by married couples.
- Fewer households will have children living at home.
- The trends toward lower birth rates and a slight increase in those who do not marry as well as higher divorce rates are actually consistent with the trends of the 1920s and 1930s. The 1940s and 1950s can now be seen as war-inaugurated deviation from long-term changes.
- More women will be employed and more of the employed married.
- As a consequence, there will be more two-worker families, decreased fertility and more continuous full-time employment for women.
- Single-women-headed households, with and without children, will continue to increase dramatically.

These are changes in structure. They may be summarized negatively: the traditional two-parent, single-worker with children family is expected to make up less than 15 percent of households in the USA by 1990. This means that at any given time, 29 percent will be female-headed, 16 percent male-headed and over half will have no children at home. Further, dual-worker couples are expected to be twice the number of single-worker couples. Later marriages and more divorces will increase the number of adults taking roles in work and community without a marriage partner. More persons, at any one time, will be in some stage of transition – in or out of a marriage, employment, or parenting. Further, those transitions can no longer be identified as associated with a particular age segment of the lifespan. At any age people can be single, courting, or separating; beginning or leaving parent responsibilities; and so on.

What does this imply for leisure? First, of course, the 'normal' family life cycle cannot be taken for granted. The Rapoports recognize this change as well as different ways of enacting roles in their analysis of the leisure of traditional and non-traditional families.[14] However, the structural changes alone are highly significant:

- The decrease in the proportion of the adult population engaged in childrearing lessens the resource constraints, but also provides longer periods in which that focus of leisure is absent. The possibility of more discretionary income and time means that adult leisure will incorporate most satisfactions other than those of fulfilling parental roles.
- The life course will involve more change. Transitions in and out of marriage, parental obligations and residential contexts mean that leisure will be called on to contribute to adaptation to such changes. Evidence that the transition periods, such as separation, are especially critical and difficult suggests that leisure can play a major part in providing continuity of associations as well as exploring possibilities for new intimate communities and strengthened identities.
- The common context of adult leisure – the nuclear family – will be an available resource for less of the population. More leisure provisions and occasions will have to be adapted to participation by those who do not come in couples or whose aims are different from those with a nuclear family waiting at home. Along with the missing resource, there comes some freedom. The orientation of complementary leisure with the need to integrate schedules and equitably allocate resources is sharply reduced, especially for those who do not continue as single parents. On the other hand, when all parenting is concentrated into a single unsupported role, then both freedom and resources may be severely limited.
- Two-worker families would presumably have greater schedule constraints combined with increased economic resources. The impacts of rising housing costs and consumption expectations on the allocation of those resources remains to be measured. However, we do know that employed wives and mothers engage in both efficiency and lowered expectations for homemaking and parenting. Further, employed married women, while spending 40 percent less time on homemaking than those not employed, also continue to carry the major responsibilities for housekeeping, meal preparation and the care of young children. They may have greater autonomy due to having an independent income, but there are tradeoffs in time. One aim may become an increased efficiency in time use for leisure as well as in child care and household management.
- Parental responsibilities are a crucial variable. Ninety percent of single employed parents are women who suffer under the typically lower incomes received by women. Their time is constricted by parenting tasks and the lack of a partner with whom to share them as well as by the job timetable. Their leisure resources are often acutely scarce in time and money. On the other hand, changes in women's roles can be expected to have impacts on leisure orientations and contexts. Women will have less time, and the time available will be more competitive

with men. Weekday programs will miss most adult women. However, fewer women will have their leisure dominated by their secondary support roles and by the expectations of their husbands. There will be both new opportunities and constraints. . . .

## LEISURE AND INTIMACY

One important step in the study of leisure has been to recognize that it is understood better in the context of family roles and contexts than as the second half of a 'work and' formula. In the light of structural and stylistic changes in the family, a next step may be to begin to address 'leisure and intimacy' rather than 'leisure and the family'. Family, especially the adult family of productivity, may be only one context of the development of intimate communities – for both children and adults. . . .

From this perspective, leisure is an interaction environment more than a set of activities. Some of the activity in this environment is explicitly instrumental – directed toward the development of intimate communities. Leisure is a social space in which the relative freedom allows us to concentrate on relationships as well as experiences, on intimacy as well as role identities. Leisure is not *the* environment for anything. Rather, leisure has characteristics that permit and even facilitate personal and social development that is most central to who we understand ourselves to be in relation to our social environments.

Cheek and Burch are correct, then, in proposing a significant social function for leisure.[15] In our social environments we build from the center outward, from intimate communities to the complex social system. This means that intimate communities are the primary building-blocks of the social structure, the first element in social cohesion. In a mass society we are connected first of all by our immediate communities. We escape alienation because of intimacy more than because we know ourselves to be contributing to some grand purpose or overall design. The family is the first primary group connection for most of us. However, other immediate communities may be developed through the life course, based on commonalities of family, religion, ethnicity, work, or even leisure.

And, since leisure is a major element in family interaction, in the development of intimacy through the life course, then it has a significant place in the overall scheme of social cohesion. It is not only opportunity and freedom, but the locus of considerable personal investment. When leisure is given a high priority in the allocation of resources and in self-definitions the investment is not entirely misplaced. In so far as leisure provides a context for intimacy as well as the expression of personal identities, it is critical rather than trivial.

## REFERENCES

1. Joffre Dumazedier, *Toward a Society of Leisure* (New York: The Free Press, 1967), p. 19.
2. J. R. Kelly, 'A revised paradigm of leisure choices', *Leisure Sciences*, vol. 1, 1978, pp. 345–63.
3. Kelly, 1978, op. cit.
4. J. R. Kelly, 'Situational and social factors in leisure decisions', *Pacific Sociological Review*, vol. 21, 1978, pp. 313–30.
5. Lillian Rubin, *Worlds of Pain: Life in the Working-Class Family* (New York: Basic, 1976), p. 311.
6. Dennis Orthner, 'Patterns of leisure and marital interaction', *Journal of Leisure Research*, vol. 8, 1976, 98–111.
7. Chad Gordon, C. Gaitz and J. Scott, 'Leisure and lives: personal expressivity across the life span', in *Handbook of Aging and the Social Sciences*, eds. J. Binstock and E. Shanas (New York: Van Nostrand Reinhold, 1976), pp. 405–533.
8. J. R. Kelly, 'Parents have problems too', *Swimming World*, March 1975, pp. 11–12.
9. Rhona Rapoport and Michael Dower, *Leisure Provision and Human Need* (London: Institute of Family and Environmental Research, 1978), p. 11.
10. J. R. Kelly, *Leisure* (Englewood Cliffs, NJ: Prentice-Hall, 1982), ch. 16.
11. ibid.
12. William Burch, 'The play world of camping: research into the social meaning of outdoor recreation', *American Journal of Sociology*, vol. 69, 1965, pp. 604–12.
13. George Masnick and Mary Jo Bane, *The Nation's Families, 1960–1990* (Cambridge, Mass.: Harvard MIT Joint Center for Urban Studies, 1980).
14. Rhona Rapoport and Robert N. Rapoport, *Leisure and the Family Life Cycle* (London: Routledge & Kegan Paul, 1975).
15. Neil Cheek and William Burch, *The Social Organization of Leisure in Human Society* (New York: Harper & Row, 1976).

Reading taken from J. R. Kelly, *Leisure Identities and Interactions*, published by Allen & Unwin, 1983. Reprinted with permission.

John Clarke and Chas Critcher

## COMING HOME TO ROOST

The family is the cornerstone of contemporary leisure analysis. All survey data show an accelerating trend towards home and family based leisure. The interpretation of this pattern has stressed the actual or potential cultural uniformity it induces. Different social classes appear to have a common aspiration towards a leisure style based round an ideal home and family. Other sources of division are similarly defused by the family. Age groupings exist mainly through the life cycle, which in turn largely depends on the stage of the family the individual has reached. The persistence of gender inequality may be only temporary as more egalitarian relationships filter down from the middle classes. Some rough edges remain, but the basic pattern is one of symmetry.

Earlier we suggested this interpretation involved a blinkered perspective, seeing neither the connection of the family with other social institutions nor the complexities of its internal dynamics. It is now time to extend that argument.

The family, we suggest, has to be understood in its basic characteristics, of which there are at least three. It is a structure, reflecting and absorbing influences from the social context. It is an ideology, a set of ideals about what could or should be achieved. It is a culture, where individuals find their way through the family as a structure and ideology to create their version of family life. These are our starting points; to understand the family at leisure, we must first see it in its other guises.

The form of the family is not wholly determined by economic factors but it bears their imprint. The ideal family for modern capitalism is one which is a mobile unit of consumption and cultural reproduction. The role

*Sociology of Leisure: A reader.* Edited by C. Critcher, P. Bramham and A. Tomlinson. Published in 1995 by E & FN Spon, London. ISBN 0 419 19420 7.

of consumer unit follows from the historical tendency of the economy to depend on mass demand for goods and services. That demand can and does take forms other than the family but few markets are as durable or as predictable as that of the family: a guaranteed source of continuous demands for comfortable and labour-saving environments, accessible and novel entertainments. The more so, since the home base is continually being remade. Especially for the high-consuming middle classes, the family is constantly on the move, housed on estates no more than temporary settlement camps on the road of social mobility. The system of production, from which the family seems a retreat, here bears heavily on where and for how long a family shall dwell, for such decisions are at the behest of employers. For those unwilling to uproot themselves and their families and follow where employers beckon, economic and political leaders have harsh words: 'on your bike'.

The consumerism and mobility of the modern family are necessary complements to the system of economic production. There is another way in which the family, no longer a significant unit of economic production, contributes to the conditions necessary for such production to take place. The family reproduces not only a new generation of potential recruits for the process of production but also the habits and assumptions which legitimate such participation: the divisions of time and space between work and leisure, the divisions of responsibilities between breadwinner and home maker.

To achieve this, the family embraces a sexual division of labour if anything more exaggerated than that which prevails outside it. The evidence suggests that, despite some marginal changes, gender roles within the family remain mutually exclusive and unequal. Who goes out to what sort of work, who has the most interests outside the family, who performs which daily menial task around the house, who takes primarily responsibility for the care of children, are not allocated on the basis of ability or choice but on the basis of gender. That we may choose and feel most able to carry out those tasks appropriate to our gender, is not proof of biological programming but the successful education of our personalities into gender roles. Inevitably so, since they are learnt initially in and through the family. There we learn not only specific social roles ('that's what daddies do') but also sets of relationships ('that's how daddies talk to mummies'). Individuals and groups make innovations in these practices, otherwise there would be no social change, but such change is limited to those details which can be accommodated within existing social arrangements.

For the family is arranged, in ways we are too commonly unaware of. These arrangements become visible most clearly when the family ceases to function 'properly' and becomes dependent for its income on the state. The social security system is particularly notorious for the assumptions it makes about relationships of dependency which should prevail between the sexes inside and outside family life. Most obviously, the cohabitation rules for supplementary benefit still (despite cosmetic change) take as their premise the idea that a woman ought to exchange her sexual services for economic maintenance by a man. Like many norms of behaviour, these are implemented most harshly against the unsupported and the unemployed but even those in work will encounter a tax system operating a set of categories in which sex and marital status are the most important characteristics.

Thus the state – here subtle and indirect, there brutal and direct – enforces a set of regulations arranging family affairs. Such policies are the material consequences of ideas about the family. The family as a structure, a social institution, produces and is produced by an ideology of family life. The ideology has its apologists. A whole phalanx of pedagogues – politicians, sales directors, social workers, agony columnists – endorse the normal, average family as being what politics/selling/case work/real life are about. Ideologies work most effectively as common-sense images, in which the media trade. In advertisements, advice and exhortation, appeals to the common interest, the family, subcategorised as the family man or the housewife, is the natural reference point. And the point about these images, together with those about gender from which they are indivisible, is that they are conveyed during and about leisure activity. As the family, together or separately, relax and enjoy themselves they will soon encounter distortions of their own images, as others would like them to be, perhaps as they would themselves like to be, but rarely as they actually are.

But what is this thing that families actually are? We have been insisting on the need to understand the family as both social institution and moral ideal, since these aspects have been consistently underrated by leisure analysts. Yet these only provide the structural and ideological context in which the everyday culture of family life is lived. They furnish both frame and canvas, but do not of themselves define the outline or the texture of the finished portrait. Many have tried to enhance our appreciation of family life. Treatises have been written on the biology of sex, the psychology of love, the sociology of marriage. Handbooks are provided on how to find and keep a mate, achieve sexual satisfaction, avoid neuroses in your children. Yet for all the theorising and occasional empirical analysis devoted to it, the family remains an enigma. It is by definition (and perhaps fortunately) impenetrable to social science. It cannot be observed from the inside, except as autobiography. Observation from the outside is limited by the resistance of its members to revealing what they consider to be the most private and personal parts of their lives. How families live is something on which we are all individually expert and collectively ignorant.

Common-sense is, by and large, an obstruction to the kind of understanding we are advocating in this book but there are times when appeal to our common experiences can usefully serve as a bench-mark for theory and argument. We are all perhaps more familiar with the intensity and ambiguity of family life than is much of the literature. Relations between a wife and a husband can, as all married people know, be loving, fulfilling, mutually respecting; they can also be hateful, cramping, domineering. Children can, as all parents know, fuse a relationship, provide a common goal, be a continuous source of wonder and pleasure; they can also bitterly divide adults, be constantly tiresome and make unremitting demands. Our own experience of family life enables us to recognise such potentialities and the ways in which our particular families have managed to cope with these inherent contradictions of family life.

We must insist again that harmony and stability are not the natural outcomes of family life; they have to be worked at. One index of the difficulties involved may be found in the divorce statistics, evidence for the familiar projection that one in every three new marriages will end in a decree. If crisis may occur in individual families, there is no crisis in the institution of the family. Most of those divorced will eventually marry again (though being female and/or old decreases this probability). The project of marriage and family life retains its attractiveness. Even those who have had good cause to count the costs involved still assess them to be outweighed by the potential benefits. . . .

We have emphasised how much of family life is in actual practice hard work. We work at our marriage partnerships, at bringing up children, at providing a safe and secure physical and psychological environment. Thus some members of the family undertake one kind of work, selling their labour on the open market, to provide the conditions and resources which make family work more viable. Some of this family work may have little or no inherent interest. Doing the washing, hoovering the floor, cleaning the windows, are jobs which simply have to be done: an endless cycle in which, even as the job is being finished, the need to do it again reappears.

Yet at least some family work has visible results and perceptive purpose. To use one psychological model we do find useful, such work is as much 'expressive' (providing some intrinsic satisfaction) as it is 'instrumental' (undertaken for extrinsic, normally financial, reward). A neatly dressed child, a carefully arranged garden, a rust-free car, cannot be achieved without hard work, some of it arduous. But these achievements may belong to us more closely and more permanently than anything we can produce outside the family. Thus the family restores a sense of meaningful endeavour, tasks which fit into an overall project we ourselves design, plan and execute. It may not be much but it is all our own work.

This gives point to our earlier scepticism about the usefulness of categorising such activities as 'satisfying physiological needs' and 'non-work obligations', or trying to place them on a continuum between the externally imposed and the freely chosen. In making families, we choose to enter into a set of mutual obligations, in which caring and being cared for are inextricably mixed.

Such obligations are built into the networks of which the individual family is part. The rituals of family life draw the 'whole family' together around key points in its cycle: birthdays, marriages, christenings, anniversaries, funerals. Such ceremonies integrate the nuclear family with its extended kin, symbolically reaffirming the unity of this one family and the universality of the family as a basic human institution.

There is work here too, before, during and after the event: invitations to be sent out, catering to be arranged, interactions to be managed. Who should sit next to who is a matter of some import in such a fragile enterprise, if potential disunity is to be kept in check. Each family has its own folklore of disasters, featuring at least one spectacular family row threatening and sometimes succeeding in ruining the whole occasion. If forgotten and thus not a possible source of future rows, their import fades with time. When the family next meets, to commemorate the birth or death, maturation or marriage, of one of its members, codes of behaviour will have been reestablished.

Both the work of family life and its rituals deserve, in at least some of their aspects, to be included in a review of leisure and the family. Their ambiguous and contradictory nature may remind us that the definition and model of human activity offered by 'leisure' has severe limitations. Family life is a complex mix of work and play, tension and relaxation, constraint and choice. To see the part called 'leisure', we must see the whole called 'family', if its core, the capacity to make us feel human when so much else does not, is not to remain elusive.

What we call family leisure is part of this total pattern but it has its own distinctive attributes. To explore these a little further we have chosen the instance of the family holiday.

## Getting away from it all

Statistics show the holiday to be one of the most favoured areas of leisure expansion. Here surely the economic functions, sexual politics and psychological strains of family life are least evident: the family seems at its best. Well, it all depends, not least on the weather. They may not last long in the memory but some holidays are disastrous – sunburn, rain, illness, food poisoning, transport which does not arrive, hotels lacking basic facilities. . . .

These are some of the known hazards of holidays which careful planning (and the necessary luck) can help avoid. This is one reason why the annual holiday is a major family project; it may only last two weeks but its influence pervades the whole year. Planning begins immediately after that other highpoint of the family calendar, Christmas. Prospect starts with retrospect. The family photograph album is retrieved and memories of people, places and activities from past holidays are recounted. Brochures are obtained and pored over, the costs and benefits of alternatives compared in detail. Some may wish to try something new, the experiment being part of the excitement. Others may prefer repetition – 'let's go there again' – which can eventually become a holiday tradition – 'we go there every year'. The decision to be made has to be negotiated: different family members have their own preferences. As children grow up, their wishes may be difficult to accommodate. It is perhaps one of the few decisions genuinely made by the whole family, even if some opinions carry more weight than others. Once the choice is made and the deposit (having been carefully protected from the ravages of Christmas) has been paid, the waiting and the saving begin. Eventually holiday time arrives. And it is a special sort of time. If not actually timeless, holidays replace the rhythms of paid and domestic work obligations with potential choice over the use of time. Some may choose to have others restructure their time for them, by opting for holiday camps or package tours – 'the coach will leave in twenty minutes'. Handing over control of your own time is not without its compensations – 'we didn't have to worry about a thing; it was all laid on for us'. Less highly organised holidays have the attraction of improvisation: 'what shall we do today?' Time does not cease to exist. Every holiday has its own schedules. But its meaning and its use are different: it is yours to dispose of as you wish.

Complementary to an altered sense of time is a different sort of place. It is not a real holiday to spend it at home; a change of environment is required. We must get away, above all out of town or city to the country or the seaside. This may sometimes be less of a difference than it appears: high street is merely exchanged for promenade, the crowds of the city centre for those of the beach. There may even be a loss of space, holiday accommodation rarely allowing the family to spread itself about. Still, exploring a new if temporary habitat, of woods and fields or beaches and cliffs, even shops and restaurants, remains a source of pleasure. Perhaps the ideal is a balance between the known, familiar, relied on, and the novel, strange and untried. Holiday resorts abroad aim at this kind of balance: enough which is familiar to reassure visitors, enough which is exotic to convince them that they really have 'seen Spain'.

Time and place: two of the constraints of everyday life from which the holiday offers relief. Another is self-restraint, replaced by self-indulgence. The pay-off for the saving of innumerable yesterdays is to spend as if there were no tomorrow. Food and drink are consumed to excess, known trivia purchased and treasured for their worthlessness. For a couple of weeks life is a funfair; being taken for a ride and not caring an essential part of the pleasure. Not only money can be wasted; so can time. Lying about, that primaeval Protestant sin, becomes on holiday a virtue. Time and money have been carefully hoarded to be carelessly squandered.

Holidays thus reverse, or at least modify, those influences which structure our everyday existence. Family relationships similarly undergo a partial transformation. The rigid roles which normally provide the base of family life become blurred. Men, for example, are more available to wives and children than at any other time of year. Depending on the type of holiday chosen, the woman may be relieved of her usual domestic duties (though some, like the washing, may simply be stored up for later). Child care is more shared and relaxed. Children experience a greater freedom in where they go, what they do, when they go to bed. The sharing of a holiday acts as confirmation that the members of the family exist for and through each other. Perhaps as a result, relationships with other families are easier. Friendships are made instantly by children and adults alike, sealed by the recognition of a common interest – 'we're all here to enjoy ourselves'.

## High days and holidays

Holidays are lived fantasies. The elements of the fantasy have been described as the four S's: Sea, Sand, Sun and Sex. It is possible to interpret these features as the reclamation of a self in communion with nature, in direct contrast to the artificial self of civilised society. Our own preference is for a more low level explanation. One, and only one, way of understanding not just holidays but family leisure in general is through the concept of play. In our discussion of the spatial and temporal realignment of the holiday, its concentration on self-indulgence and self-confirmation through the family, we may have been talking about no more than how holidays provide playtimes, playgrounds, playthings and playmates.

We think of these terms and indeed of play itself as something confined to childhood. The process of achieving adult status is one of learning to forsake play, suppressing childish impulses and channelling those which remain into activities for which we have names other than play: sports, hobbies, leisure interests. The family disguises its retained forms of play under the heading of games: party games, board games, card games, video games – 'games for all the family'. It is no accident that these are often the first way to cope with bad weather on holiday. For the basic point about our sense of play, and why it fits so well with the general ethos of the holiday, is that it needs no rationale, no purpose other than its own intrinsic satisfaction. That sense is present in less intense and visible forms in a whole range of family leisure activities: watching television, visiting the park, having a day out. The incorporation of much of the new technology into family life, from computers to video-cassette recorders, depends upon its convertibility into items of and for play.

Play is a necessary illusion. It is necessary because our pleasures must appear to lie out of the reach of social and economic influences: in their very 'otherness' is their appeal. It is an illusion because play is not and cannot be beyond their reach. The interaction of child and adult around play of all kinds is, for example, a powerful instrument of socialisation. The acceptance of rule structures, the pitting of skill against chance, the acknowledgement that some must lose in order for others to win, are all ways of preparing the child through the unreality of play for the 'realities' of adult life. Adults, while teaching the child to play, may also indulge in that sense of anarchy – 'behaving like a child' – which maturity has untaught them.

The antithesis of work and leisure may, then, more usefully be understood as that of necessary labour and unnecessary play. Yet opposition is itself a kind of relationship. The positive is defined and structured by the negative, play and holiday by what they are not: labour and workaday. Society does more, however, than provide the context and thus the meanings for the significance we attach to the holiday experience. It also influences who gets access and under what conditions to which sort of holiday experience, a specific example of what we called earlier the distribution of leisure opportunity.

### 'You don't know what you're missing'

Acknowledgement of the political, economic and social shaping of access to, and enjoyment of, an annual holiday needs to be more than skin deep. In our history chapter we noted how paid holidays were an integral part of the claim to leisure made by working people and their families from the end of the nineteenth century. At the present time (at least until the onset of recession), there is a preference for any extra free time to take the form of longer paid holidays rather than a reduced working week. For the mass of the population, holidays away from home are a relatively recent innovation. The leisure industries have responded by providing a range of holiday possibilities, differing in location, cost and appeal. Travel is a profitable if high risk business, backed by increasingly sophisticated marketing techniques, the mainstay of television advertising in the early part of the year. Holidays are thus political and economic in origin. The culture of the holiday, its otherness in time, place and activity, is not less bound to the prevailing social order and its routines of paid and domestic labour.

Even this does not exhaust the social influences upon this 'freest' of leisure activities, for the holiday reproduces all the social divisions we have been discussing in this chapter. First, that between social classes. In 1979, 40 per cent of the British population took no holiday away from home; an estimate three years earlier was that eight million had enjoyed no holiday away in the previous five years. The deepening recession will not have improved these figures. Containing as it must, the elderly, the sick and the poor, this group remains as deprived of holidays as it does of most other things. If this is leisure democracy, a substantial minority remain disenfranchised. Not for them the naked egalitarianism of the beach, since they cannot afford the price of admission.

Such egalitarianism is in any case misleading. There are different beaches in separate locations for particular social groups, defined as much by income and social status as by personal taste. Some resorts are reserved for the affluent (skiing in St Moritz). Other holidays, in guest house or chalet, cater for those who can only just afford the whole enterprise (a week in Scarborough). There are also different kinds of holiday, fitting into the overall leisure style of particular groups. Two weeks at Butlins and a month in a French villa might look like equally viable alternatives; in practice, they require different levels of resources and rest on contrasting cultural affiliations. For those whose class or social status is denoted by their colour, the holiday is paradoxically a chance to go home to visit friends and relatives left behind as a result of emigration. For them the end of the holiday means leaving home once again; for their children, possibly an increased uncertainty as to just where home is.

Age is no less an influence than class and colour. The leisure market has recognized and institutionalised its significance, the most obvious examples being holiday packages aimed exclusively at the under twenty-fives or over-sixties. Adolescence may be no less problematic here than elsewhere. Tussles over participation in family holidays or the attraction of going away unsupervised with friends are its minor manifestations; more major ones are evident in the sporadic confrontations between the police and male working-class youth, when and where else but on Bank Holidays and at seaside resorts. Meeting someone of the opposite sex for a holiday romance is not the least adolescent aspiration; it also underlies the holiday experience for a wide range of ages. In a more relaxed form, the gender relations dominant in leisure generally prevail on holiday too. Discos, bars, beaches and promenades hold the potential for sexual adventure, possibly without the complications and consequences normally attendant.

If that potential is primarily for exploration by the young and unattached, gender relationships on holiday do not cease to be of significance after marriage. The trend emergent amongst the middle classes to eschew fixed holiday accommodation for caravans and tents may suggest that some families want more autonomy and flexibility in their holiday schedules. Their designation as 'self-catering' may raise the question as to which 'self' does the catering. Facilities for cooking, cleaning and washing have to be part of the essential equipment carried by itinerant holiday-makers. Responsibility for these tasks has to be parcelled up too. The luggage of gender roles may not be declared at customs, labelled his and hers in hotel rooms, or insured against loss in transit, but it is as present as if it were strapped to the roof rack on the car.

Reading taken from J. Clarke and C. Critcher, *The Devil Makes Work*, published by Macmillan London, 1985. Reprinted with permission.

# IIc Leisure and the Life Cycle

# 6 | Leisure and the family life cycle

Rhona Rapoport and Robert N. Rapoport

## FIRST PRINCIPLES

We are concerned with the key problem of the link between individual and society, microsocial intimate small groups and macrosocial bureaucratic large-scale organizations. The large organizations – in this case, directors and staff members of leisure centres, pools, parks, libraries and local government departments of leisure and recreation – are not concerned with the same issues as the people who use them. . . .

Our argument is that there is a gap between the institutions of leisure-facility providers and the wishes, 'needs' and requirements of people seeking to develop meaningful whole-life experiences. It is necessary for society to attend to both levels (organizations and people). How do we proceed to think about them systematically in relation to one another? We suggest the life-cycle framework as a useful (not the only useful) one, and one that has been insufficiently understood or applied. We are particularly concerned with the influences of the family in the individual's 'life line' of development, and in the way different spheres of influence interact at different times in the cycle. Individuals develop their lives along three lines – work, family and leisure. Individuals integrate influences and experiences in all of these life spheres as they create and live out a life career. This is the 'enterprise of living'. While the three separate planes are conceptually distinct (as suggested in Figure. 6.1), individuals combine them in characteristic ways to form whole life-style patterns.

*Sociology of Leisure: A reader.* Edited by C. Critcher, P. Bramham and A. Tomlinson. Published in 1995 by E & FN Spon, London. ISBN 0 419 19420 7.

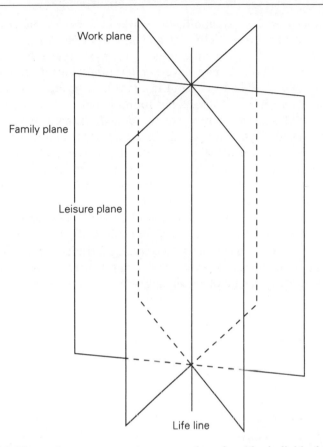

Work plane

Family plane

Leisure plane

Life line

**Figure 6.1** Three planes representing sectors based on the individual life line.

Each life-line strand is thought of as a helix because at each critical status transition (such as getting married) people go back psychologically over ground covered earlier. The life revision that occurs, consciously or unconsciously, as each new stage is entered into and a new integration brought about, gives the process a spiralling or helical character. Because each of the points at which there is a necessary turning involves fairly fundamental revision, we think of each as a 'life crisis'. Together, the three strands form a 'triple helix' rather than three distinct spirals because of the way each of the strands interacts with the others, an effect particularly notable at critical transitions. At the time of these critical transitions there is an 'unfreezing', a disorganisation during which established patterns are loosened. Then reorganisation follows. In the period of disorganisation a revision occurs which provides a potential challenge to develop new patterns for all strands, not only the one in which the transition occurs. For example, when an individual marries, his patterns of heterosexual and family relationships, his orientation to work and career, his pattern of involvement in peer group activities and his other life interests are all likely to be affected. Changes in jobs, changes in life interests (such as in sailing or a second home) may have similar ramifying effects not only within the specific life-line strand, but in the other strands as well. . . .

Influences from diffuse macroscopic sources such as the mass media, the larger institutional structures like the church (shown in Figure. 6.2) to the more specific influences assignable to actual people known and interacting with one are at play throughout the life cycle. 'Normative agents' express attitudes of approval or disapproval, and provide both substantive content for what can be done and sanction as to what ought to be done by the individual in specific situations.

Most people try, less or more consciously, to locate or create congenial experience and environments. There are many difficulties in achieving this; there are barriers and frustrations; sacrifices and trade-offs, conflicts and struggles that occur in the process of evolving satisfying life styles. The construction of life styles involves dealing with resistances and constraints

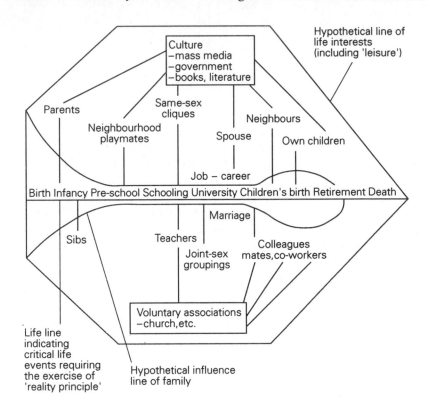

**Figure 6.2** Influences on the development of the life line.

as well as taking advantage of opportunities and potentials. Figure 6.2 centres on the development of the life line. At critical transition points, influences from different spheres impinge on the individual and he interacts with them to give a structure to his involvement in those spheres. Experiences in each of the strands affect decisions and subsequent developments in the other strands. Interests can arise in any of the strands and either be contained within it, or diffuse to others.

Our thesis is that underlying observable life-style patterns there are socio-psychological dimensions of motivations that are important to appreciate if one is to understand people's life requirements. At the most fundamental level, rooted in psycho-biological development, are people's *preoccupations*, changing with growth in the course of the life cycle. Preoccupations may be manifested in *interests*, which may change or remain constant (perhaps with changing meaning for the individual) and a given interest may be channelled into various *activities*.

Any particular *activity* – say walking in the park – has different meanings for different kinds of people in relation to the *interests* they are pursuing. It may be a way of being alone for a young courting couple; a way of exercising a pet for an old lady living alone; a way for a middle-aged man to fend off the coronary at which he is at risk, and so on. Similarly a given *preoccupation* (for example with a sense of excitement and stimulation) may be expressed differently by different individuals: through sports cars, drugs, sexual adventures, or in mountain-climbing. Some may experience similar stimulation by visiting art galleries. For many tycoons 'making a deal' provides excitement and the addiction to work of some businessmen and professionals can be better understood in these terms than in terms of economic drives. For a poet it may come by finding the right words to match his feelings, and for a scientist the right experiment to demonstrate a scientific principle. Is there any pattern in this, or is it all a matter of individual variation?

Variations observable in the life styles of individuals and groups while ultimately individual in detail have underlying patterns. These are determined by influences which can be systematically described. The variables which have been productive in social research for detecting and analysing patterns have included age, sex, social class, type of residence and education. Each of these, and clusters of them, are capable of explaining observable behaviour. It seems to us, however, that they are losing power as predictors to the extent that age, sex, social class, standards of housing and education become less socially divisive.

To the extent that static categories are indeed losing relevance for understanding people's behaviour and values, one requires a framework that is amenable to the analysis of change and variation. We want to explore the utility of the family life-cycle framework for this purpose. Individuals have life cycles, according to which they change their preoccupations, interests and activities as they develop – maturing and ageing in the course of the life cycle. But individuals vary systematically not only according to their biological drives, but to their social roles in relation to the family life cycle and family structure. The events of marriage, child-birth and all the subsequent critical transitions as children develop and eventually leave home are in and of themselves important as foci of interest and activity. In addition they signal reorganization of life style, determined by social class and other influential factors indicated in the overarching framework presented above.

The family life cycle is geared both to age and sex variables but it encompasses something more. It implies a changing organization of roles and value orientations (for example in child-rearing) which partly reflect the large social environment, and partly the particular people. The key concepts reflecting the developmental nature of the changes that occur in the course of the cycle are the following:

1. *Preoccupations* are mental absorptions, less or more conscious, which arise from psycho-biological development, maturation and ageing processes as they interact with social-environmental conditions.
2. *Interests* arise in people's awareness as ideas and feelings about what they want or would like to have or do, about which they are curious, to which they are drawn, through which they feel they might derive satisfaction.
3. *Activities* are spheres of action – such as driving, dancing, participating in or watching sports, attending clubs, etc.

As we have indicated, there is no one-to-one relationship between preoccupations and interests, and a given interest may be fulfilled through different activities with a similarly non-specific link. The way in which activities and interests are matched affects the level of satisfaction that different individuals derive.

Preoccupations arise at a relatively 'deep' motivational level in 'human nature' as the individual develops through psycho-social stages of maturation. Given preoccupations may be present all through the life cycle but they tend to become particularly salient at a given phase, and to effloresce at critical stages. Interests take form out of the interaction between an individual with his felt preoccupations and his social environment. Aside from providing (or failing to provide) the content and structure for the cultivation of interests, society through its various providers of facilities offers channels through which interests may flourish and provide satisfactions.

Reading taken from R. Rapoport and R. N. Rapoport, *Leisure and the Family Life Cycle*, published by Routledge, 1975. Reprinted with permission.

# What do kids get out of pop music and football?

## 7

Paul Corrigan

## COMMERCIAL ORGANISATIONS

### Pop music

It is interesting if we turn from looking at the school concert to the boys' attitudes to their own music, pop music. Whilst I have never felt competent to analyse the deep meaning of pop music for these boys (or indeed for myself since I *do* find that I 'just like the beat') it is easy to see it as important to them. As I have said before, much of the sociology has oversimplified some of the complex relationships involved. Pop music has an existence for all these boys, not simply those who went to dance halls.

Whilst it may be very difficult to speak with any certainty about the deeper meaning of individual sets of music to the boys, it did become clear that there was a set of experiences which could be talked about, and this was going to a pop concert and going to a dance hall. Obviously such experiences are linked with the nature of the music (the differences between rock concerts, folk concerts and jazz concerts do relate to the music, though they are never totally *caused* by it) but they do not neces- sarily spring totally from it. The rock concert and the dance hall represent somewhere to go for those who not only enjoy pop music but want something else too.

> *Question*   Do you listen to much pop music?
> *Ian*   Well, I stay in on a Thursday night to watch *Top of the Pops*.

*Sociology of Leisure: A reader*. Edited by C. Critcher, P. Bramham and A. Tomlinson. Published in 1995 by E & FN Spon, London. ISBN 0 419 19420 7.

Then I'm back on the streets again about half-past-eight.
*Question*   Do you ever go down the Mecca?
*Ian*   Well, I used to go down the Rank on a Saturday night but I used to get into trouble so I stopped going.

*Question*   Do you and your mates listen to pop music when you go round each other's homes?
*William*   Aye, we've got all the L.P.s.
*Question*   Do you go down the Mecca?
*William*   No. We get kicked around by the skinheads.
*Question*   Don't they have special nights with skinhead sort of music?
*William*   No, they're down there all the time.

So the dance halls are not simply places where music is played, but where fights and trouble take place. Not surprisingly, the fights and the troubles become more important than the music, even though both of the boys specify their interest in other ways of listening to music.

For others, the dance hall provides *both* a place to listen to music and a place either to chat up the lasses or to have a fight. These boys seem very committed to pop music of a specific kind and in fact they would appear to be using the dance hall in a very different way.

*Question*   What do you do on an average Saturday evening?
*Bert*   Don't usually go out on a Saturday. Go out on a Sunday. Last Sunday we went down the Mecca and saw The Free and Amazing Blondel.
*Question*   Do you and your mates go down there every Sunday?
*Bert*   Yes
*Question*   What do you do down there?
*Bert*   Listen to the music and chat up the lasses.
*Question*   Do you ever get involved in any kind of trouble?
*Bert*   Sometimes with a couple of skins. Sometimes when the skins come we have a scrap ... sometimes.

*Question*   Do you like pop music?
*Doug*   It's hellish great.
*Question*   Where do you listen to it?
*Doug*   On telly, but we go down the Mecca on Tuesday. Tuesdays they have special music for skins.
*Question*   Why?
*Doug*   Well, they don't let us in other nights. Any case, the music is best on a Tuesday, and the lasses too.

These boys seem a lot more selective about using the institution of dance halls. In a way, they are pushing the autonomy of the buyer in the cash-nexus situation as far as possible. They say we are here not only for the music that you offer us, but also for the social institutions that we can create out of the freedom that we are allowed. We come for the music that you sell us AND we come for the lasses and the trouble that we can make.

All these impressions of the importance of these group experiences can be backed up by any visit to a rock concert. In really trying to come to grips with this aspect of the kids' lives I went to a number of rock concerts in different parts of the country (well, also because I enjoy rock concerts!). The most striking example of the experience was in visiting a Slade concert in Earls Court. Slade only became a national group after I had finished my research, but it would seem likely that to the kids at Municipal School, at any rate, they would have represented their favourite group. The experience of this concert, though, starts long before the music starts; long before you enter the hall; for when I joined the District Line tube train at Sloane Square I was already among the pop crowd. My immediate impression was confused because the train was full of West Ham fans decked in scarves, rosettes, and occasionally singing 'I'm forever blowing bubbles'. Being a West Ham fan there seemed nothing odd about this except that the District Line train was heading in the wrong direction, it was a Sunday evening and several of the fans had large top hats with silver circles pasted on them (the hat that the lead singer of the Slade, Nobby Holder, wears). This immediate impression of a football crowd became more significant at Earls Court; here the Shed from Chelsea, the North Bank from Arsenal, the Rough End from Spurs, Millwall and even Fulham were all massed in one space. The music and the audience participation made this all the more obvious; it was a football crowd with no game. The experience of going to this concert obviously *depended* upon the Slade playing their music (as any Slade fan will agree); but the concert was a total group experience of a certain kind that went on both before and after the music.

Therefore, when we try and make sense of rock music for teenagers it does nothing simply to try to understand the music itself; it must be seen as relating to a whole range of working-class group experiences many of which are outside the normal music itself and all of which are a group-experienced phenomenon.

**Football**

This can be directly linked with the nature of the experience of going to a football match . . .

Over the past few years there have been claims about the increasing violence by teenagers both at dance halls and football matches. But the question arises of whether this violence IS actually increasing or, as is more likely, there is now a different sort of experience involved.

What *is* violence at football matches and dance halls?

*Question*   Do you watch much football?

*Derek M.*   We chant, have a scrap with some of the lads. Perhaps have a crack at other supporters. Keep away from coppers. Watch the match too (laughs).

*Question*   Do you get into trouble?

*Derek M.*   Aye, but not real trouble and it's great.

Football is being offered to these boys by Sunderland F.C., or rather the right to stand and watch a football match and to shout for Sunderland. Rather than simply accept it, they take part in a complete and different set of experiences called 'going to footy'. This *includes* watching the football, and in fact is pervaded throughout by what is happening on the field in front of them, but is a collection of experiences that are not simply watching a game of soccer. Such experiences are difficult for me to articulate, let alone the boys. To be at your team's ground in the middle of a good game of football is *more* than watching a game of soccer. To go with your mates to the Fulwell End is to take part in a collective and creative experience that starts at about half-past-one and finishes at about six o'clock. This experience may lead to violence either of a verbal (chanting) or of a physical character, but is not *necessarily* an experience characterised by violence.

Similarly in a dance hall. The music, like the football, pervades the experience but does not limit that experience to a spectator one. . . . Any visitor to football or dance halls over the past four years could not have failed to notice the attempts by those who run these institutions to limit that freedom to create their own non-spectator experience with the introduction of more bouncers, more stewards and, of course, more police.

The participation of these boys in the experience of a football match is a group experience with their mates. It represents a challenge to the mere spectator role of the sport and represents a possibility of the group *creation* of action. The action created – chanting, fighting, singing on the terraces, fighting, having a laugh in the dance hall – is action that represents the cultural background of the boys. There is none of the quiet appreciation of the skills of football or music that might characterise a more intellectually-inspired audience. Instead there is involvement and creation of their own kind of action. With regard to pop music this would also cut across the simplistic generational boundary drawn by the concept of 'teenage culture', since the experience of going to a dance hall would be difficult if one's own concern was the perception of the music, or the feeling of the physical dance. If it's the fights and the lasses that are important, then the structure of the music cannot be the main reason for going. Similarly with football. This represents a distinctive attitude to the total experience of these spare-time activities; a way of understanding them that does not see them as a means to an end, but rather as a *total experience*.

What role, then, do commercial institutions play in spare-time activity? The young people of the working class cannot command the resources and power to build their own institutions (in terms of bricks and mortar). This can be contrasted with the student union facilities at universities which can provide an alternative to the commercial institutions of the capitalist society around the university. Consequently the working-class boys must use these organizations, all of which are run primarily for profit. Nevertheless, the question of who controls these facilities is vital for them; it is important to try to understand that control, and their reaction to it.

These differences in the type of control experienced by the boys are directly related to the type of aims that the institutions have, and to what they are trying to do 'with' or 'for' the boy. The difficulties of, say, the youth clubs are immense in that they are attempting to change the boys' attitudes and behaviour, yet do not have the compulsory powers of attendance that the schools have.

Yet this differs from the nature of the control exercised by commercial institutions. The *aims* of commercial institutions are, primarily, to make money. As far as the boys are concerned, for a certain amount of money you can buy a certain amount of freedom, since the aim of the institutions is not primarily to interfere with the behaviour or ideas of those that enter them.

Thus if we were to compare the formal control structure of a dance hall and a youth club, it would be found that both are dominated and run by non-working-class adults. Nevertheless, if you were to look specifically at the way in which the organization attempts to interfere with boys' behaviour, it is easy to see the way in which boys experience a greater amount of freedom in the dance halls. While they are limited within the dance hall, no one is trying to get them to *think* about something that they don't feel like; they can come as often or as seldom as they like. Both sides of the *commercial* contract respect the autonomy of the other, with the single and vital proviso of all capitalist institutions that the seller can refuse the buyer if he has not got the cash to fulfil the relationship.

The increasing economic power of the young has provided individual boys with some economic power, and this enables them to gain access to these institutions. The extent of this economic power in the hands of these particular boys who have not yet left school can be grossly overestimated, since they exist for the most part on pocket-money and part-time earnings. For these boys, dance halls are expensive places, and do not necessarily enter the realm of possible realistic choices on a Saturday evening. For *those* boys the street corner is the most likely institution open: it is cheap and always accessible. . . .

The nature of both of the major institutions used by boys – the dance hall and the football ground – is changing. In the very recent past these institutions have tightened up on the amount of freedom that they allow their customers. Anyone who stands behind a goal at football matches at a first division club will realise that the increase in police activity in recent years has been enormous. Football programmes and statements in the local and national press show the clubs' dislike of the bad publicity given to them by the 'small minority of fans' that have been labelled soccer hooligans. This fear of 'public' reaction has led to a tightening up in social control in football grounds culminating, at the time of writing at any rate, in a member of the Football Association calling for the banning of all under 18-year-olds from football grounds. In dance halls recent years have seen the closing down of a number of smaller halls and the tightening of control within the two major chains, Rank and Mecca, which now try and exclude 'unruly' elements. In both institutions the amount of freedom open to the boys has been limited. This has increased the general importance of the street as an institution for youth spare-time activity.

Nevertheless, in terms of the boys' actual experience there is still an important difference between commercial and evangelical institutions. . . .


## WHY, THEN, DO BOYS GET INTO TROUBLE?

We are left, therefore, with a very different way of understanding 'getting into trouble' at football matches. The whole experience for the boys is a lot less instrumental than I at first thought: the getting into fights and so forth is also intelligible only in a different way. We must see it in relation to the *structured* leisure activities that are imposed upon the boys at youth clubs and schools. Within *these* structures activities occur for instrumental reasons. The boys reject those structures, and those organisations; when they take part in activities that they choose they create very different sorts of structures which allow them much greater possibilities of involvement. Once more, as in the educational system, it is of no use offering these boys involvement in the *content* of the activity; of itself this is rejected as a sham participation. It is essential for the boys to be allowed to create their own *structure* of activity. This is true in the fields of playing and watching sport, as well as music.

Footy and pop provide for these boys degrees of freedom from interference as a participator and a spectator. It provides them with an identity separate from those groups that are trying to mould their behaviour into more acceptable forms. Consequently, the Fulwell End at Roker Park, and all the equivalents all over the country, are playing a vital role in the maintenance of the boys' counter-culture at school and on the streets. What goes on in those 'ends' is intelligible to and experienced by only those involved. Teachers and policemen go along to watch football; but their interest and involvement are totally different. For the young supporter it represents a much more separate experience which he *knows* is only his own. He *knows* that a crowd of teachers chanting 'We hate Nottingham Forest . . .' is just not on. He also knows that he enjoys taking part in that. Therefore it reinforces the separate world of working-class youth; a separateness which becomes of political importance every Monday morning in the classroom. Without experiences such as these the boys would be much 'easier' for the teachers. If they did all take part in purely structured leisure activities, they would be able to accept the structures of work at school much more easily. The battles in the classrooms are therefore made fiercer by the 'aggro' on the terraces.

Similarly with pop music. Teenage working-class boys experience it very differently from their teachers. A visit to a Slade concert, where thousands of kids treat the auditorium much as they treat the rough end at the football match, shows the difference between the way they experience pop music and the way that their teachers do. Everyone at most concerts sings along with the music, has an involvement beyond the comprehension of anyone outside the culture. I've been to a Slade concert and learnt a lot about enjoying pop music, but I was there as an outsider looking in. These experiences, like football, provide 15-year-old working-class youth with a background which they play a part in creating. Pop music, even on the radio, is listened to in an entirely different way; lyrics and music are not separated out and dissected; different sorts of music are used for different sorts of 'background'. All of these experiences provide the boy at school with a culture that he can draw on in the conflict and, as such, both pop and footy are of political significance far beyond the simplistic way which we usually view the politics of pop.

Reading taken from P. Corrigan, *Schooling the Smash Street Kids*, published by Macmillan Press Ltd, 1979. Reprinted with permission.

## 8

# Leisure time use by the elderly and leisure provision for the elderly

Mark Abrams

As far as available statistics permit, I shall regard 'the elderly' as the $8\frac{1}{2}$ million men and women aged 65 and more who today constitute 16% of the total population of Great Britain. All of them have reached pensionable retirement age and indeed all except 5% of the men and 2% of the women are no longer part of the nation's active labour force.

It is often assumed that the retired elderly, having withdrawn from the time-consuming necessity of earning a living, have at their disposal an abundance of free time to be used on any of the leisure activities so lavishly available in modern Western society. However, their use of this 'free time' for leisure activities is subject to a variety of constraints. For many elderly, the most limiting constraints are the inevitable consequence of the decline in income that follows immediately on retirement. This is well documented by the Government's annual 'Family Expenditure Survey' (F.E.S.). The report for the year 1986 presents the information collected over 7000 households; in 26% of these the head of the household was aged 65 or more.

In households where the head is aged 65 or more the weekly household gross income at £121 was less than half the £258 received by households where the head was aged 50–64. Part of the latter's larger gross income went in taxation and savings, and what was left was spent on meeting the needs of a larger household – one of 2.35 persons as compared with the 1.62 persons in households where the head was aged 65 or more.

*Sociology of Leisure: A reader.* Edited by C. Critcher, P. Bramham and A. Tomlinson. Published in 1995 by E & FN Spon, London. ISBN 0 419 19420 7.

**Table 8.1** Weekly household income and expenditure (£) by age of head of household (Family Expenditure Survey, 1986)

|  |  | 50–64 £ | 65–74 £ | 75+ £ | All 65+ £ |
|---|---|---|---|---|---|
| Gross household income | Total | 258 | 133 | 104 | 121 |
|  | Per head | 110 | 78 | 72 | 76 |
| Expenditure | Total | 198 | 121 | 87 | 107 |
|  | Per head | 84.4 | 71.1 | 59.6 | 66.0 |

Largely as a result of these adjustments, the average person in households where the head was aged 65 or more had to 'make do' by spending 20% less than the average person in households where the head was aged 50–64 (see Table 8.1).

The average household headed by a person aged 65 or more achieved the inevitable economies by reducing sharply its expenditure on goods and services which play a large part in the leisure activities of those in non-elderly households; they cut back substantially in their expenditure on meals out, transport and vehicles, services (e.g. hotel and hotel expenses, club subscriptions and theatre and cinema admissions), and expenditure on what the survey classifies as 'other goods' (e.g. sports goods, gardening materials, cameras). Expenditure on these goods and services by the average retired household of two people (one man and one woman) is less than half that of the average non-retired middle-aged couple; this inevitably reduced their range and quantity of leisure activities, but it makes it possible for them to maintain their expenditure on fuel and on food at home (see Table 8.2).

However, the financial constraints on the use of 'free' time do not bear equally on all sections of the elderly population, since the distribution of income among the elderly is almost as unequal as it is among the non-elderly. According to the Family Expenditure Survey (F.E.S.) carried out

**Table 8.2** Weekly household expenditure of two-person households (1 man, 1 woman) (Family Expenditure Survey, 1986)

|  |  | Retired households 72 years £ | Non-retired households 46 years £ |
|---|---|---|---|
| Expenditure on | Meals out | 2.40 | 9.02 |
|  | Transport/vehicles | 13.50 | 33.65 |
|  | Services | 19.37 | 30.85 |
|  | 'Other goods' | 9.35 | 16.48 |
|  |  | 44.62 | 90.00 |
|  | Food at home | 25.23 | 24.18 |

in 1986, nearly 30% of all households where the head is aged 65 or more have a gross weekly income of less than £60. At the other end of the spectrum there were 8% of elderly households with weekly gross incomes of £275 or more. These relatively affluent elderly households were found mainly among the younger elderly; thus households where the head was aged 65–69 constituted less than one third (32%) of all elderly households, but they accounted for 45% of all elderly households with gross weekly incomes of £275 or more. The higher average gross income of the younger elderly household (aged 65–74) made possible a weekly household expenditure that exceeded that of the older elderly (aged 75 or more) by 40% (F.E.S., 1986, Table 19).

This additional income enabled the younger elderly to follow consumption and expenditure patterns more frequently associated with the resources of the non-retired. Table 8.4, derived from the National Readership Survey of 1987, indicates some of the consumer areas where younger elderly men and women tend to be closer to those aged 45–64 than they are to the older elderly. Like those in the former age group, but unlike the older elderly, they live in households which own a car, a deep freezer, a lawn mower, a record player or music centre. They have credit cards, take holidays away from home, and take these holidays abroad.

In short, the financial restraints on the leisure activities of the elderly affect almost all of them, but limit most deeply the possibilities available to the older elderly.

A second source of constraint on the leisure activities of the elderly is ill-health – not only their own but also of a spouse. Ever since it was launched in 1972, the Government's Annual General Household Survey has devoted a section of its questionnaire to health. The usual opening question was: 'Do you have any long-standing illness, disability or infirm-

**Table 8.3** Income distribution among the elderly (Family Expenditure Survey, 1986)

| Gross weekly household income | 65–69 % | 70–74 % | 75+ % | All 65+ % |
|---|---|---|---|---|
| Under £60 | 17 | 26 | 36 | 28 |
| £60–99 | 29 | 32 | 32 | 31 |
| £100–149 | 23 | 18 | 13 | 17 |
| £150–199 | 11 | 8 | 8 | 9 |
| £200–249 | 8 | 7 | 4 | 6 |
| £250–374 | 8 | 7 | 3 | 6 |
| £375–549 | 3 | 2 | 2 | 2 |
| £550 or more | 1 | 1 | 2 | 1 |
| Total | 100 | 100 | 100 | 100 |
| Median income | £110 | £ 85 | £ 70 | £ 86 |
| Sample size | 589 | 521 | 744 | 1854 |

**Table 8.4** Consumer goods and services of the elderly, 1987

| Age: | Men | | | Women | | |
|---|---|---|---|---|---|---|
| | 45–64 | 65–74 | 75+ | 45–64 | 65–74 | 75+ |
| | % | % | % | % | % | % |
| *Household* has: | | | | | | |
| Car | 79 | 61 | 37 | 72 | 41 | 20 |
| Washing machine | 90 | 82 | 66 | 91 | 77 | 57 |
| Deep freezer | 75 | 62 | 48 | 76 | 55 | 35 |
| Lawn mower | 75 | 71 | 59 | 74 | 63 | 49 |
| Record player/ music centre | 83 | 65 | 45 | 82 | 57 | 29 |
| *Respondent* has: | | | | | | |
| Credit card(s) | 44 | 32 | 18 | 36 | 24 | 10 |
| Taken holiday* | 63 | 56 | 39 | 61 | 57 | 40 |
| Of which, taken abroad | 38 | 23 | 13 | 35 | 33 | 10 |

* Defined as sequence of 4 nights away from home in past 12 months.

ity? By long-standing I mean anything that has troubled you over a long period of time or is likely to affect you over a period of time?'

Throughout the 1980s, an average of 58% of those aged 65–74, and 66% of those aged 75 or more, said they had a long-standing illness. Of all elderly respondents, 30% said that because of ailments of one kind or another they had during the two weeks before the interview been forced to cut down on some of the things they usually did around the house in their spare time. . . .

In a survey carried out by myself among 1650 persons aged 65 or more, respondents were taken through a list of ailments and symptoms of illnesses and asked, for each one, whether or not they suffered from it. Only 15% of them claimed to be free of all the 21 health problems on the list. Some of the highest claims were for arthritis/rheumatism (53%), poor eyesight (36%), unsteadiness on feet (33%), hardness of hearing (25%), backache (34%), attacks of giddiness (35%), high blood pressure (20%), and, among both men and women, 8% said they were troubled by urinary incontinence. All these figures relate to elderly people living at home, (and exclude the incidence of health impairment among the 400 000 elderly who on the average day are resident in hospitals, homes for the old and disabled, nursing homes etc. (approximately 6% of all elderly people).

A third limiting factor on the leisure activities of the elderly of today is related to their educational background: 70% had left school at the age of 13 or 14, and another 20% had left before reaching the age of 17. No more than 5% of the men and 3% of the women had been exposed to any form of higher or further education. As school children in the 1920s, at least half of them had been taught in classes that contained over 40 children. Currently less than two-thirds of them read one of the national morning newspapers and half of these readers are concentrated on the two picture tabloids: *The Sun* and *The Daily Mirror*. . . .

A fourth constraint on the elderly person's use of leisure is his or her isolation. Currently 20% of all men aged 65 or more live alone and 45% of all women in this age group also live alone. And of all elderly people living alone 40% have never had any children, and another 5% have outlived any children they had had. One third of all elderly respondents in this survey had outlived all their siblings, and those who had not rarely saw any of their surviving brothers and sisters. Of all respondents aged 75 or more, less than 30% had been visited by any family member at any time during the weekend before the interview. Among those aged 65–74, 31% had received a visit from a family member during the previous weekend (Abrams, *Beyond Three Score and Ten*, Part Two). Both age groups had received even fewer visits from non-family people either at the weekend or during the week. Indeed, one of the most striking features of the lives of elderly people, especially those aged 75 or more, is the large proportion of their 'free time' that they spend in isolation. . . .

The avoidance of isolation and of low social interaction usually necessitates going out – and here we come to the last restraint on the leisure activities of the elderly that I wish to mention: their fear of going outside their dwelling, especially at night. On the average day, over half of all elderly people do not go outside their dwelling and two-thirds say they are afraid to go out at night. According to a recent Harris Research Centre survey in this country, 'Among people aged over 55, 38% had not been out at night for more than a year' (*The Times*, Feb. 15, 1988).

So what do the elderly do with their 'free time'? To begin with, a considerable part of it goes on housework, shopping and self care. It would be inept to describe these as 'leisure activities'. Making beds, cooking, shopping, washing up, hoovering the floors, should certainly be described more accurately as 'unpaid work', and for elderly people, slow and exhausting work.

In one survey it was found that significant minorities of the older elderly said they had difficulty with various self-care tasks such as taking a bath, getting around the house or flat, putting on their shoes and stockings, getting in and out of bed etc., but less than a quarter of those with any difficulties said they received any help from anyone with these tasks: they managed either by doing them very slowly or else by doing them badly – sometimes both slowly and badly.

In spite of, or because of, their heavy consumption of sleeping tablets, tranquillisers and 'night caps', elderly people spend a large slice of the daily 24 hours in bed or dozing in a chair. In its mammoth survey 'Daily

Life in the 1980s', the BBC found that, in winter on an average weekday, 30% of people aged 65 or more were already asleep by 10.30 p.m., and not until 9 a.m. the next day were as many as 94% awake. In short, the typical elderly person spends between nine and ten hours every night in bed. Of the remaining fourteen hours, substantial chunks are taken up by watching television (2.9 hours), listening to the radio (1.5 hours), reading (1.3 hours), just resting or dozing (1.8 hours), going for a walk (0.6 hours) and 0.9 hours on a wide range of time-consuming activities that can be regarded as pastimes and hobbies. The remaining five hours were spent doing housework, shopping, doing the laundry, cooking, eating, washing up, sitting in the doctor's waiting room, collecting prescribed medicines etc. The low level of average participation by the elderly in genuine leisure activities is documented by the findings of the Government's Annual General Household Survey.

In most years the Survey records respondents' participation in any kind of leisure activity during the four weeks before the interviews; for figures published on the year 1983, the claims by both men and women and by both younger and older elderly were extremely modest. For example, among the elderly the most likely to engage in outdoor activities (i.e. men aged 60–69) less than a quarter (22%) claimed that over the four weeks they had taken a walk of two miles or more, and 1% had gone swimming. Among those least likely to spend any time on outdoor activities (i.e. women aged 70 or more) only 6% had taken a walk of two miles or more and less than 1% had undertaken any outdoor swimming.

Rates of participation in indoor leisure activities were even more modest. Among men aged 60–69 the most widespread of such activities were snooker (5%) and darts (3%); and among older elderly women the most widespread activity was attendance at 'keep fit' classes: 1% of the women attended such classes and they accounted for half of all attendances by women aged 70 or more at all forms of indoor leisure activities (see Table 8.5).

The BBC's survey on the use of time by people is presented in a different form and is much more detailed. The recently published report ('Daily Life in the 1980s') lists people's main activity for each quarter hour, starting at 6 a.m. until the quarter hour starting at 9.45 a.m. and then for each half hour of the day from 10.00 a.m., through the day and night, until the half hour starting 2.30 a.m. In Table 8.6 the day is divided into four time sectors:

a.  Early morning: the 16 quarter hours between 6 a.m. and 10.00 a.m.
b.  Late morning: the nine half hours between 10.00 a.m. and 2.30 p.m.
c.  Afternoon: the nine half hours between 2.30 p.m. and 7.00 p.m.
d.  Evening: the eight half hours between 7 p.m. and 11 p.m.

In each of these sectors the activity of respondents aged 65 or more has

**Table 8.5** Participation rates in sports, games and physical activities in four weeks before interview: 1983, Great Britain

| | Men | | Women | |
|---|---|---|---|---|
| | 60–69 | 70 or more | 60–69 | 70 or more |
| *Outdoor* | | | | |
| Walk, 2 miles or more | 22 | 13 | 17 | 6 |
| Golf | 5 | 2 | – | – |
| Fishing | 1 | * | – | – |
| Swimming | 1 | * | 1 | * |
| Cycling | 1 | 1 | 1 | * |
| Bowls | 2 | 2 | – | – |
| Camping | 1 | * | – | – |
| At least one activity† | | | | |
|    excluding walking | 12 | 6 | 4 | 1 |
|    including walking | 31 | 18 | 20 | 7 |
| | | | | |
| *Indoor* | | | | |
| Snooker/billiards | 5 | 2 | 0 | 0 |
| Darts | 3 | 1 | 0 | 0 |
| Swimming | 2 | 1 | 3 | * |
| Bowls/ten pin | 2 | 2 | 0 | 0 |
| At least one* | 11 | 5 | 7 | 2 |

\* Less than 0.5.
† Includes all activities not listed separately in the table.

been averaged over the several time units (quarter hours or half hours). The results in Table 8.6 deal with the behaviour of all respondents aged 65 or more on Fridays in winter. In the early morning period the average quarter hour is almost entirely taken up with washing and dressing, preparing and eating food and doing the housework; the only substantial 'leisure' activity would appear to be 'listening to the radio' – an activity enjoyed by over 20% in the average early morning quarter hour.

The average late morning half hour is still dominated by preparing food, eating and drinking, housework and listening to the radio. However, these new 'activities' now take up just as much time: watching television, talking (e.g. to one's spouse), and resting.

In the average half hour in the afternoon, more time is spent on these new 'activities' (watching television, talking and resting); this apparently is made possible by cutting back sharply on listening to the radio and housework, but not on preparing and eating food.

The average evening picture is dominated by one activity – watching television; in the average half hour, two-thirds of all elderly people spend their time watching the box. Talking and resting still hold their afternoon levels.

Throughout the day and evening, negligible proportions of the elderly have as 'main activities' gardening, bingo, visiting a pub or restaurant,

**Table 8.6** Use of time by respondents aged 65 or more, 1983–4, average Friday, winter

|  | Early morning % | Late morning % | Afternoon % | Evening % |
|---|---|---|---|---|
| Personal care | 8 | 2 | 1 | 6 |
| Preparing food | 10 | 14 | 16 | 7 |
| Eat, drink | 17 | 19 | 17 | 13 |
| Housework | 17 | 19 | 7 | 3 |
| Shopping | 3 | 4 | 5 | * |
| Gardening | 1 | 2 | 1 | 0 |
| Bingo, betting | 0 | * | * | * |
| Pub, restaurant | 0 | 1 | * | 2 |
| Theatre, cinema etc. | 0 | 0 | 0 | 0 |
| Entertaining someone | 1 | 4 | 7 | 4 |
| Taking a walk | * | 1 | * | 0 |
| Hobbies, games | 1 | 2 | 4 | 4 |
| Tending pets | 1 | 1 | 1 | * |
| Resting | 4 | 10 | 12 | 12 |
| Reading | 6 | 8 | 12 | 7 |
| Talking | 7 | 17 | 18 | 19 |
| At classes, lectures | * | 1 | 1 | 0 |
| Listen to records, cassettes | * | * | 1 | 1 |
| Listen to radio | 21 | 20 | 9 | 3 |
| Watching TV or video | 4 | 20 | 34 | 67 |
| Out at work | 2 | 5 | 2 | 0 |

\* Less than 0.5.

visiting a theatre or cinema, entertaining visitors, taking a walk, tending pets or attending classes or lectures (see Table 8.6) . . .

For the early morning periods the difference between winter Friday and summer Saturday is negligible: a little more gardening is done in the latter, a little less resting and a little less listening to the radio and watching television. In the late morning period, summer is the time for a little less household work and for much more shopping and gardening. But this apparently leaves appreciably less time in the morning for watching television and listening to the radio. . . .

In the afternoon period fewer elderly are engaged in cooking (but there is no decline in eating and drinking) in the summer, and more carry out some gardening; in the summer there is appreciably less reading and more talking. Watching television remains, as on winter Fridays, the main afternoon activity of the elderly.

In summer Saturday evenings a handful of addicts continue gardening. Higher proportions go out to pubs or stay at home entertaining friends and kin. The main casualty of summer Saturday evenings is watching television; in the average evening half hour no more than 47% of the elderly are watching television – a mere two-thirds of the 67% recorded for winter Friday evenings.

What is distinct for both seasons and for all four periods is the very low proportion who in the average half hour spend any significant part of their time at theatres or concerts, taking a walk, pursuing hobbies, or attending classes or lectures. The 'free' time that comes to them from no longer working for a living would seem to be largely absorbed by the passive activities of watching television and the arduous tasks of housekeeping and looking after themselves. Extremely small minorities favoured by income and education take stimulating holidays and read books that engage their minds.

Yet firms that specialise in holidays for the elderly will for £800 provide them with a seven day tour around 'Classical Greece' during the less pleasant part of the British winter, and those whose addiction has been neglected because of poor eyesight need no longer delve among the large-print rubbishy novels stocked by public libraries: they can now, through an Oxford-based entrepreneur buy, but not borrow, large-print copies of books by Rebecca West, Graham Greene, Scott Fitzgerald, Doris Lessing, Bernard Malamud, Tennessee Williams, Isaac Bashevis Singer etc.

Some people, concerned with the well-being of elderly people, and aware of their lack of social interaction, try hard to counter this lack. But so far they have had little success. The statutory services make contact with very small minorities of the elderly population. The General Household Survey carried out in 1983 found that in the month preceding the interview only 10% of all aged 65 or more had received the service of a home help; 3% had received 'meals on wheels'; 4% had had lunch at a day centre; 5% had attended a day centre; and 7% had received a health visitor.

The voluntary services have not been much more successful in providing social intercourse for the elderly: 12% claim to be members of a church/chapel/synagogue etc., but only half these claimants attend these groups at least once a week. Only 10% belong to any club for the elderly, though three-quarters of these members attend their club once a week or more.

The lack of social interaction and the abundance of empty 'free' time experienced by many of the elderly, largely due to constraints discussed earlier, not only induce in many of them acute feelings of loneliness, but may also seriously affect their longevity. . . .

There is much to be said for Freud's conclusion in his old age:

Against the suffering which may come from (the loss) of human relationships, the readiest safeguard is voluntary isolation, keeping oneself aloof from other people . . . There is another and better path: that of becoming a member of the human community . . . One gains

the most (from this) if one can heighten the yield of pleasure from sources of intellectual activity.
(*Civilisation and its Discontents*, London, Hogarth Press, 1930: p. 14.)

A population in which nearly 40% of all elderly people live alone and are acutely aware of loneliness had clearly not yet found how, through their leisure activities, to add re-engagement to retirement on any significant scale – except for a small minority with large incomes and with some experience of further or higher education.

Reading taken from A. Tomlinson (ed.), *Leisure and the Quality of Life*, published by Leisure Studies Association Publications, 1990. Reprinted with permission.

# Activities

## INTERPRETATIVE EXERCISES

1. Make a list of the arguments forwarded by Parker to support his claim that work influences leisure. Make a further list of the arguments against the influence of work forwarded by Roberts. What emerge as the main points of contention? What kinds of evidence might help resolve these issues?
2. Choose any three popular leisure activities (e.g. watching television, going on holiday, eating out). Illustrate diagrammatically how the different phases of the life cycle might affect how often, where and with whom these activities are undertaken.
3. What are the main leisure functions of the family? Illustrate the different arguments offered by Kelly, Clarke and Critcher and the Rapoports by referring to your own personal experience.
4. What do you understand by the term 'life cycle' as coined by the Rapoports? Take one leisure form (e.g. dance and dancing) and illustrate its significance for different age groups in the UK.
5. Make contact with four 'elderly' (two 'new' old and two 'old' old). Interview them to find out what are the major constraints and opportunities on their leisure time.

## ESSAYS

1. Of the three influences on leisure – work, family and the life cycle – which one do you consider exerts most influence and why?
2. Kelly suggests that 'family interaction is itself the dominant form of leisure for adults living in nuclear families'. Outline the evidence supporting this statement and discuss its implications for leisure policies and practices.

3. How useful is the concept of play in understanding leisure within family networks?
4. What key issues confront social science researchers interested in the leisure life-styles of the elderly in the UK?
5. The task of the 'sociological imagination' is to link people's individual experiences with wider common structural processes. Is it accurate then to argue that the choice of leisure life-styles is simply a private matter?
6. How do gender relationships find their expression in family leisure?

# PART THREE

# Leisure and Social Relations

# Introduction

The previous part has looked at the common contexts and experiences facing people growing up and growing old in both the private worlds of the family and in the public worlds of paid employment and work. In contrast, this section introduces some of the major divisions within society – those of class, gender and race. It draws upon literature which highlights the diversity of experiences in UK society and warns against simple stereotypes and cameos of a mass leisure society.

It is now conventional wisdom in social theory and in a wide range of professional practices to acknowledge that people's experiences – within the family, at school, in health care, in local communities, at work and at play – differ. People carry with them important identities – male/female; black/white; working/middle class – which significantly affect both the ways people see themselves and how other people see them.

The stereotypes of gender, class and race have their own complex histories which exert a powerful influence over individuals, groups and social institutions. The first step is to acknowledge that class, gender and race are crucial ingredients in social relations, both as resources and as constraints. The next step is to try to explain how these differences of class, gender and race are in turn mediated by people's experiences and social practices. It is worth stating from the outset that these historical processes cannot be treated simplistically or in isolation. The patterns of inequality, of racism and sexism, provide both the context and the content of people's experiences. However, the patterns of experience demand detailed attention. For example, institutionalized racism at work may (or may not) exhibit different features and processes from those evident in the worlds of sport, recreation and leisure.

Class divisions have been central to understanding the development of sociology. Marxist analysis has emphasized the importance of class and class struggle in shaping the nature of capitalism and its cultural expression

*Sociology of Leisure: A reader*. Edited by C. Critcher, P. Bramham and A. Tomlinson. Published in 1995 by E & FN Spon, London. ISBN 0 419 19420 7.

within civil society. Some writers, however, have expressed reservations about attributing too much significance to class as an influence on leisure. The first two extracts which open this part highlight the enduring importance and vitality of class and class relations. Jeremy Seabrook maps out some of the changes taking place within the UK and the increasing polarization between the affluent 'service' class and the unemployed. Indeed, more recently, the traditional debates about class differences in the realm of production and work have shifted towards debates about class differences in terms of life-style and patterns of consumption. The second contribution has been taken from a classic 1950s study of a mining community, which was seen as an exemplar of a proletarian occupational community. The whole book raised many crucial issues about doing community studies, the importance of work and class in everyday life and the sexual divisions within work, family and leisure.

During the past decades, a new generation of feminist researchers have challenged the assumptions of the conventional wisdom in leisure sociology, for example that 'work' means paid employment. They have argued this to be but one instance of the ways in which concepts, models and theories deployed in the sociology of leisure have privileged male rather than female experience. Feminist researchers have shown how women's leisure opportunities are structured by their distinctive position and roles in society – in school and at work, in the home and the street, in relation to child care and in terms of sexuality.

Sheila Scraton sets out to discover why adolescent women are so resistant to school PE. They object to its implicit attempt to define their bodies as muscular and sweaty, its invasion of their bodily privacy in changing and showering facilities, the unstylish design of PE kit. Scraton argues that the need is less for girls to have the opportunity to do the same physical activities as boys than for time, equipment and space in which to develop their own sense of bodily potential.

Green, Hebron and Woodward undertook a major study of how women spent and saw their leisure time in Sheffield. The extract emphasizes that women's experience of leisure is complex and varied. Like other feminist writers (see Deem later in this volume) they identify both structural and cultural constraints on women's leisure. Three key leisure resources – time, money and transport – are more available to men than women. Equally important are expectations about how women ought to behave in their leisure time. Such expectations are enforced by men, who control the leisure activities of their partners and express hostility towards the presence in public of women 'unaccompanied' – that is, by a man.

Green, Hebron and Woodward are very careful to emphasize how little is known about leisure amongst women from ethnic minority cultures. Much of the literature on ethnic minority leisure has concentrated on the apparent over-representation of Afro-Caribbean males in organized sport.

Carrington and Wood explain this prominence in terms of processes at school. White teachers tend to 'channel' into sport Afro-Caribbean males who they see as having little aptitude for academic work. Success in sport is seen by the youths themselves as one of the few areas in school with which they can identify and in which they can succeed. Thus sport is not an arena of equal opportunity but one which reproduces ethnic inequality and stereotyping.

Parmar shows how similar processes operate in the quite different ethnic context of young Asian women. Her attempts to provide leisure opportunities for this group were distorted by the mainstream youth service. It was assumed that they were trying to resolve social problems in the Asian community, attributed to a largely stereotyped view of ethnic cultures. The need to provide innovative and flexible places, times and foci for Asian girls was regarded as threatening conventional youth work practices and their assumptions. So little does white society understand the experiences and aspiration of young Asian women that it cannot begin to reach or acknowledge them.

Taken together, the extracts in this part demonstrate the dangers of leisure ideas and practices which take as their norm the leisure of white, middle-class males. Those who fall outside these categories are not a deviant minority but a substantial and often unrecognized sector of the leisure public.

# IIIa Class and Leisure

# From leisure class to leisure society

## 9

Jeremy Seabrook

With the rise of the service industries, the prominence of banking, merchandising, credit, insurance, retailing, tourism, travel, catering, we are dealing with far more nebulous activities than when it was a question of the stern materialities of mining, manufacture or engineering. So much of present-day economic endeavour is connected with impalpables – consultancies and public relations, the making and changing of images, the play of appearances, the adding of value, the selling of ideas, the marketing of abstractions, the importance of 'invisibles' – that labour, sheer hard work, becomes something not to be scorned by the privileged, but rather to be appropriated by them. And there is considerable evidence that this is the case. The work ethic, far from having been discarded, has merely been re-shaped by the rich for their own purposes; not this time, to serve as a model of iron discipline to the workers in industry, but as a kind of decoration, an impressive and plausible façade for themselves, which will conceal the uselessness or even the downright noxious nature of their avocations. They proclaim themselves dedicated to work in such a way as to maintain the fiction that the distribution of labour in the contemporary world falls most onerously upon them.

It may well be that the work to be done – the significant work or at least that which can be presented as such – has become both too important and perhaps too scarce to be left to the working class. It is no accident that in this age the rich have developed a hitherto well-concealed talent for making great public display, not of the idleness and vacuity of their pastimes, but of their own functional and indispensable role in society,

*Sociology of Leisure: A reader.* Edited by C. Critcher, P. Bramham and A. Tomlinson. Published in 1995 by E & FN Spon, London. ISBN 0 419 19420 7.

their exhaustless devotion to work, the seriousness of their purposes, their service to the nation. Princes are no longer playboys, but hard-working and energetic servants of the people. Prince Andrew, for instance, is not only a war hero, but has an important naval career to pursue; and his bride expressed her desire to continue her work in publishing despite her elevation to the position of Duchess of York. Princess Anne regularly demonstrates her dedication to the poor of Africa by means of her work for the Save the Children Fund; the Prince of Wales' concern for the fate of the inner city, the deprived and disadvantaged is deeply felt, something far more than a piece of astute public relations; and this is before any of the burdens of official duties which claim so much of their time and energy.

These illustrious public activities are only the most dramatic efflor-escence of a far more widespread and deeply rooted assumption of a burden of labour by minor royals and major celebrities who leave their names on all those tablets commemorating ceremonial openings of mainly undistinguished modern buildings – new civic centres and shopping pre-cincts, stretches of motorway and sheltered accommodation for the elderly. The same commitment to work may be seen in the conspicuous 'punishing schedules' of business people and executives, those unwearying commuters of transnational corporations whose budgetary responsibilities are said to exceed those of many sizeable nation states, in the ills attendant upon the disorientation induced by a series of identical luxury hotels, the jet-lag and hang-overs from the unavoidable intensity of that hospitality which is part of their duty of selling British, showing the flag, boosting exports, chasing up orders, opening up markets, clocking up sales. Their weary attendance at expensive restaurants where so much vital work is done; the obligatory nights in the opera boxes which their company reserves for the season; the millions of pounds for which they are personally accountable to the last penny; the entertainment of irksome and mannerless foreign buyers on their yacht and in their mansion behind screens of rhododendron and conifer in the Thames Valley; the indulgence of the whims of potential customers on rain-swept golf courses or in discreet and expensive sex parlours; the vast expenditure of energy in the futures and commodity and stock markets which burn people out before they reach 35; the six-figure salaries justified only because nobody can work at that pitch for more than a few years and which must compensate for the long years afterwards spent nursing the heart condition or in the vain search for relief from the disordered digestive system – all this amounts to an oppressive excess of labour, a sacrifice to command the awe and the compassion of those called to perform no such exalted task in the world. Perhaps most glaringly of all, the new votaries of labour are the pop, TV and movie stars, discussing their 'work' in breathless media interviews, as they extort public sympathy for their high-speed, coast-to-coast appearances, for a life that is no longer their own, pursued as they are from pillar to post by both fans and journalists; an unstinting giving of themselves to insatiable audiences that can lead only to nervous exhaustion and collapse. It is perhaps only to be expected that politicians should also have surrendered themselves to the same gruelling surfeit of labour. Their busy attendance at summit meetings, is only the most visible aspect of this – the sessions prolonged into the early hours, the rumours of tensions and irreconcilable differences, the breakthrough at the eleventh hour, the officials working on an agreed communiqué, the press conference at dawn delivered in the insomniac style of those celebrated for needing no more than four hours of sleep a night; how taxing, yet how selfless it all is.

Nor is this remarkable weight of function confined to those in whom it has been traditionally to a remarkable degree absent. A clamorous and aggressive self-justification penetrates quite deeply into the employment structure. Never in the history of labour – so much of it backbreaking and destructive of life and limb, so much of it that drained the last ounce of energy from muscle and sinew – has there ever been such a competitive claim for recognition, for the tribute due to such feats of toil as are undertaken today. We have only to consider all the voluntary 'workaholics' in our society, those who don't know what to do with themselves when they're not working, those striving to wrench or coax a sense of purpose out of the most unpromising circumstances: the self-important and the inflated self-worth of the media people, the performers and the journalists, as well as those devoted to 'working with people', and whose work in consequence is never finished, the social and community workers, the architects and planners, all those experts and professional people committed to the running of other people's lives, the teachers and academics, not to mention the salespeople and advertisers whose mission it is to rouse some slumbering whim and elevate it into insatiable desire for some commodity; those on crusades and quests to promote some supremely marginal and dispensable product; those processors of words and generators of ideas and masters of information and possessors of knowledge, the custodians of the labyrinths of impenetrable but vital bureaucracies – all those whose lonely and unacknowledged self-immolation to labour means that at the end of the day they find it impossible to turn off, to wind down, to relax, to sit down and take stock, and who spend their leisure time colluding with each other that theirs is the most supremely exigent and necessary contribution to the work of society. One result of all their efforts is, of course, real suffering. These are the people most liable to tension, worry and stress, to heart disease, ulcers and breakdown, as they valiantly brave intolerable tube journeys and interminable tailbacks on the M25, with nothing but the cassette of Nina Simone or *Carmina Burana* for company and the endless newsflashes telling them to avoid the congestion they are trapped in. They struggle into work even though they have a temperature of 103° and have been told by their doctor that he or she will not answer for the consequences if they don't take a couple of weeks' complete rest. Their heroic commitment to customers, clients, employees or colleagues is perhaps prompted by an obscure sense that their absence, even for a day, might not only fail to result in the collapse of the firm, company or department but, on the contrary, might not even be noticed; indeed, an even greater worry, that the whole enterprise might actually proceed more smoothly without them underlies the defensive insistence that they must at all costs put in an appearance. Cynical friends sometimes strike a painful chord by pointing out that if they fell under a bus tomorrow (always a bus, never the more likely agent of their annihilation, the car), this would not be the end of the world for those who employ them.

Many of these people are part of that group identified by Galbraith as members of the New Class, often in origin far from anything resembling a leisure class. They 'take it for granted that their work will be enjoyable. If it is not, this is a legitimate source of dissatisfaction, even frustration. No one regards it as remarkable that the advertising man, tycoon, poet or professor who suddenly finds his work unrewarding should seek the counsel of a psychiatrist.' Galbraith points out that 'the New Class is not exclusive. While virtually nobody leaves it, thousands join it every year.' But what he didn't mention – or perhaps it was too early in the 1950s to perceive one of its distinguishing traits – was its defensive self-importance and self-attributed heroics: 'I have to be in Brussels on Tuesday, then I've a meeting in Manchester, and there's the conference in Stockholm next weekend'; the fluttering of the leaves of diaries, the frowns and bitten Faber-Castell pens and the adamant declaration that it is impossible to fix up anything before the end of November. 'I can't make it, I'm busy, I haven't a free moment, I've got meetings, engagements, commitments.' People book appointments with each other at many months' distance that call for the movement of sheaves of papers across the city – or even across continents – by document-bearers on motorcycles called Hermes or Mercury, delivering scripts, outlines, plans, blueprints, briefings, portfolios, curricula, drafts, agendas that are required to have reached their destination yesterday. They engage upon campaigns and strategies to discuss market research at solemn, even portentous, meetings, where projects of vast triviality take on the allure of a major military manoeuvre: 'For many long-standing advertisers, television advertising has been transformed from a matter of saturation bombing to something resembling guerrilla warfare' (*Campaign* magazine.) There is a deep displacement of emotion poured into the committee meeting, the planning group or the advisory panel, where the question 'Well, what is it all for?' must never be asked in all the hyperactive intensity that goes into discussions about the promotional merchandise or the layout of a new magazine, the format of the half-hour programme that involves such a vast expenditure of energy and money in order to attract a few stray moments of attention in off-peak time from a jaded and indifferent public. They invoke the regrettable necessity of living in the real world, that increasingly eccentric construct of fantasy. Many women are expected to find satisfaction in the borrowed lustre of those they serve in the guise of personal assistant or person Friday to the big white chief, the managing director, the principal, the king pin, he who must be obeyed. They spend whole days talking things through, looking at a project from all angles, sleeping on it, wrestling with problems of presentation and differences of emphasis, deciding whether a re-vamp or a shake-up is required, making lightning raids, planning mergers and take-overs, pooling resources, exchanging views, acting as a sounding-board, floating an idea, thrashing things out, getting hyped up to meet a deadline, to land a contract, to deliver on time, to make a killing, to go for broke. If so many people admit, in their less defensive moments, that what makes their work worthwhile is the people they work with, this may be because these have often become the primary purpose, and the ostensible reason for their labour is seen for what it is – an elaborate and collusive suspension of disbelief.

In support of their heroic role, the new martyrs to labour can often be heard wishing they had a humdrum nine-to-five job, expressing their envy of those who work merely for the wage-packet at the end of the week and can forget all their worries the minute they walk off the premises. Such carefree employees do not lose sleep fretting about some particularly intractable problem of office management, wondering how on earth they are going to tell the most recent employee that her contract cannot be renewed when you know she is a single parent with three small children; *they* don't wake up in the early hours with parched throat, trembling with responsibility of having to face all those people in the morning; *they* aren't up at dawn, writing down a few notes, an outline of a lecture, a few selling points, some ideas on a new creative thrust that will keep some brand fresh, relevant and motivating; and *they* don't get up feeling like nothing on earth, but knowing that they must be at their sparkling best in time for that 10.30 meeting, and ransacking an inadequate wardrobe for some-thing to give them that extra lift, that little touch of distinction.

Sometimes these people go even further, using their exploited and disregarded substance in order to lay claim to self-administered rewards and treats as an extra consolation for salaries which are, in general, not inconsiderable, but are never quite enough to compensate for the stresses and strains that go with the job. 'I must get some sun', they say passionately, leafing through the brochures that advertise discreet private villas in Tuscan hill-towns; or, more regularly, 'I need a drink.' 'I must have some space, some time, some room to think', 'I must have a break,' 'I shall have to get away', 'I must get out from under', 'I can't stand the pressure.' And the self-pity which is never far from the surface seems to be allied to a gnawing and subjective feeling of poverty, in spite of a parallel awareness of great privilege. They are always hard up, regretting the things they can't afford, wondering how they are going to get through to the end of the month, snowed under with bills and demands, terrified of facing the bank manager, wondering how on earth they will survive without the phone-answering service or the domestic help; and because they are, on the whole, so well-rewarded, their sense of impoverishment must be taken as metaphor, and as arising from causes other than insufficient money. If they dwell at such length on their unique importance, their vital role, this is perhaps less because of the indispensable nature of their specialized and infinitely subdivided labour than because they suspect its marginality, its expendability and, above all, its growing remoteness from any detectable human purposes. As Veblen observed in 1899:

> The strain is not lightened as industrial efficiency increases and makes a lighter strain possible, but the increment in output is turned to use to meet this want [i.e. that of conspicuous consumption], which is infinitely expansible, after the manner commonly imputed in economic theory to higher or spiritual wants. It is owing chiefly to the presence of this element in the standard of living that J. S. Mill was able to say that 'hitherto it is questionable if all the mechanical inventions yet made have lightened the day's toil of any human being.'

It is perhaps the further development of this process that makes the rich societies of the late twentieth century create an artificial busyness (claimed by the most privileged), which is sometimes more akin to the make-work tasks of the occupational therapy ward than to the more direct service of human need (the therapy in question being, of course, the servicing of autonomous economic processes to which our interests are increasingly subordinated). It is perhaps the fatigue that comes from spinning fantasies around a ruined sense of function that makes such a real burden of so many forms of contemporary labour which are, in themselves, much mitigated. Murray Bookchin described this development almost 20 years ago:

> Much of the social 'complexity' of our time originates in the paper-work administration, manipulation and constant wastefulness of the capitalist enterprise. The petty bourgeois stands in awe of the bourgeois filing system – the rows of cabinets filled with invoices, accounting books, insurance records, tax forms and the inevitable dossiers. He is spellbound by the 'expertise' of industrial managers, engineers, stylemongers, financial manipulators, and the architects of market consent. He is totally mystified by the state – the police, courts, jails, federal offices, secretariats, the whole stinking sick body of coercion, control and domination. Modern society is incredibly complex, complex even beyond human comprehension, if we grant its premises –

property 'production for the sake of production', competition, capital accumulation, exploitation, finance, centralization, coercion, bureaucracy and the domination of man by man. Linked to every one of these premises are the institutions that actualize it – offices, millions of 'personnel' forms, immense tons of paper, desks, typewriters, telephones, and of course, rows upon rows of filing cabinets. As in Kafka's novels, these things are real but strangely dreamlike, indefinable shadows on the social landscape. The economy has a greater reality to it and is easily mastered by the mind and senses, but it too is highly intricate – if we grant that buttons must be styled in a thousand different forms, textiles varied endlessly in kind and pattern to create the illusion of innovation and novelty, bathrooms filled to overflowing with a dazzling variety of pharmaceuticals and lotions and kitchens cluttered with an endless number of imbecile appliances. If we single out of this odious garbage one or two goods of high quality in the more useful categories and if we eliminate the money economy, the state power, the credit system, the paperwork and the policework required to hold society in an enforced state of want, insecurity and domination, society would become not only reasonably human but also fairly simple.

In the interests of maintaining the fiction that we still live in a society of scarcity, and must therefore continue to produce more of everything that makes money, the rich have breathed new life into a work ethic which serves their purpose of concealment. But there is another element in their resuscitation of a defunct ideology of work. For they have also appropriated the heroic myth of labour, a myth belonging traditionally to a working class that has, to a considerable extent, recently been relieved of its sustaining purpose. The refurbishing of this collective myth is, as must be expected in its new guise as the property of the rich, in the form of individual and personal achievement and enterprise. Listening to the new bearers of Herculean workloads, it would seem that the rigours of mill or mine were not more oppressive than the pressure of that perpetual mobile of constant travel, of boardroom marathons, of conquering new markets, of a restless life fuelled by a 'potent mixture of adrenalin and high-octane energy' (*Campaign* magazine), of rushing all over the globe to the joyless interchangeability of Holiday Inns, in which you can discover exactly where you are only from the motif embossed on tasselled menus in the curtained and sequestered enclosures of the restaurants. The vast and self-protective activity which surrounds the contemporary rich occurs in the wake of the departure of much productive and necessary labour from the heart of Western industrial societies, labour which for 200 years had been their primary purpose. The work that has been suppressed in the rich countries has not disappeared from the face of the earth. Much of it has merely been transferred elsewhere, following a new international division of labour, whereby a great deal of manufacture can be carried out more cheaply and more efficiently in the slums of the cities of Asia and South America or in the industrializing countries on the rim of the Pacific. The vacuum in which all the talk of 'leisure societies' is possible in the West is that left by the removal of a great deal of essential work; it depends upon the extent to which the poor of the earth are willing to – or can be coerced into – underwriting the declining sense of function of the people in the West, notably of the Western working class. The politics of fantasy readily springs up to occupy the evacuated spaces; and this is how the privileged can plausibly project themselves as the true embodiment of necessary labour while, paradoxically, at the same time promising the millenarian coming of the leisure society to the people. In the meantime, leisure – not the easy opulence that is associated with past aristocratic castes or that which is to be achieved in an indefinite future, but actually existing leisure, leisure as a full-time activity (if that is not an indelicate word in the context) – devolves chiefly upon the most dispossessed in society, the unemployed, the retired and the young adults for whom no work is available.

Reading taken from J. Seabrook, *The Leisure Society*, published by Blackwell, 1988. Reprinted with permission.

# Leisure in Ashton

Norman Dennis, Fernando Henriques and Cliff Slaughter

**10**

## PRINCIPAL LEISURE INSTITUTIONS

The trade union, the colliery and the Miners' Welfare Institute have already been shown to appeal to only a few Ashton people as centres of leisure activity. This is not because the miner likes to spend his leisure time on his own, and refrains for that reason from joining these organized activities. On the contrary, the possible explanation is to be found in the fact that the Ashton miner has developed organized leisure institutions which adequately meet his requirements quite apart from the facilities these other organizations provide.

### The Working Men's Club

The leisure institution which appeals to more Ashton miners than any other is the Working Men's Club. There are six of these in Ashton, which, together with two small similar 'social clubs', have a total membership of 6844.

The Working Men's Clubs are predominantly male institutions. Only one of those in Ashton admits women as members. The others absolutely forbid by rule the admittance of women into the club except for the concerts on Saturday evening and Sunday midday and evening. Membership is open to all males aged 18 and over who have been proposed and seconded by any two members, and accepted by the committee as being suitable. As there are only 4824 males aged 18 and over in Ashton, and the total membership of the clubs is 6844, it can be seen that their appeal is widespread. The club membership is half as large again as the total male adult population. (This is possible because many men are members of

*Sociology of Leisure: A reader*. Edited by C. Critcher, P. Bramham and A. Tomlinson. Published in 1995 by E & FN Spon, London. ISBN 0 419 19420 7.

more than one club.) The membership is not restricted to 'working men'. Of those who work at the colliery the deputies as well as the workmen are club members. This is not so in all colliery towns in Yorkshire. At some there is a separate 'Officials' Club' and deputies are discouraged from joining any Working Men's Clubs. In Ashton even overmen are members of these clubs, and one of the three undermanagers is a member of two of the clubs, both of which he regularly visits.

Many of the men who do not work at the colliery are members of these clubs. Here again in addition to the ordinary workmen, many of the tradesmen are active members. Nevertheless, the miners are in a great majority. The prosperity of the clubs fluctuates with the miners' prosperity. Thus in the 1930s when there was unemployment and low wages, membership stood at less than half its present level, largely due to the fact that membership of more than one club became a rarity. The increase in miner's earnings in the last few years has led to a great increase in the membership of the clubs. New members have joined, and existing members have joined more clubs.

The objects of all the Ashton clubs are set down in the following terms: 'The Club is established for the purpose of providing for working men the means of social intercourse, mutual helpfulness, mental and moral improvement, and rational recreation.'

The reality is somewhat different. The means of social intercourse are certainly provided, and there is a certain amount of mutual helpfulness, but the clubs can scarcely be said to be seriously concerned with either 'mental and moral improvement' or 'rational recreation'.

At all the clubs the bar is '. . . the centre and support . . . the pole of the tent'. It provides first the financial basis. The balance sheet of a typical Ashton club (with a membership of 920) for the financial year 1951–2 shows a total income of £12500. Of this, £12200 was 'bar takings', under £40 came from members' annual subscriptions, and the balance consisted of cash in hand.

It can be seen that the clubs are vigorous centres of 'social intercourse', but are hardly active in 'mental and moral improvement'. With regard to 'mutual helpfulness' the clubs' achievements in this respect are not at all impressive. This is apparent both at the level of the formal mutual helpfulness organized by the club, and at the level of informal aid between the members.

In essence the Working Men's Club is a co-operative society for the purchase and sale of beer. The elected officers of the club purchase beer, spirits, tobacco, etc., on behalf of the members. These commodities are then sold to the members at the ordinary commercial price. This 'profit' from these sales is then available for the benefit of the members – it is in fact a 'mutual helpfulness' fund. The main use to which the funds are put is that of periodicals, providing members with their free beer or beer below cost price. Thus it is customary for each member to receive, say, 8 pints of free beer during each of the following holidays: Christmas, Easter, Whitsuntide, and August Bank holiday. The second use to which the profits are put is providing ... concerts ... Thirdly, the profits are used in providing games equipment, newspapers, and when necessary, such things as a television set. The members of the club who do not spend a lot of money at the club are in that way 'helped' by those who do. There is no suggestion of 'mutual helpfulness' on the basis of need.

The Working Men's Clubs can therefore be seen to reflect in their behaviour as organizations the thriftlessness of their members. The clubs' funds are spent as quickly as they are accumulated, just as the members' wages are spent as quickly as they are earned. To take one example: an Ashton club with a membership of over 1000 and an income of just under £15000 in 1944 possessed a total investment income of just under £15 from Defence Bonds. The result is that in the event of industrial depression the clubs have always been forced to borrow to meet their necessary costs. In 1926, for instance, Ashton's largest club borrowed £1000 from a large brewery company.

The funds are, however, used to a slight extent to help needy members, or members who are presumed to be in need – namely the old age pensioners. Every year each club gives the old age pensioner members one or two 'treats' – either in midsummer or at Christmas or both. The old men are entertained to a meal free of charge, to free drinks, and each is usually given about 10s pocket money. There are also 'treats' for the members' children, and sometimes a party at Christmas. The cost of these 'treats' is borne by the income from lotteries organized for the purpose, supplemented by a subvention from the general funds of the club. ...

Both these institutions – club and public house – which are so very similar, continue to exist separately and retain their individuality. This is possible because each has advantages that the other lacks. The profits of the clubs are used to provide the club members with cheap or free beer regularly. Of course this does not happen at public houses. On the other hand the publican is more sensitive to the wishes of his clientele than are the club committee men to the wishes of their members, because the publican's livelihood depends upon his relations with his customers.

## Sport

There are only two other leisure activities which regularly bring large numbers of Ashton people together. They are sport and the cinema.

Those activities connected with sport in Ashton resemble the club and public house in being primarily the domain of the male. The most important of the 'sporting' activities is that of supporting the Ashton Rugby League team. The term 'supporting' has been used advisedly. It is meant to signify that the activity is not a mere passive process of watching and taking pleasure in the display of a particular skill. Each game is an occasion on which a high proportion of Ashton's males come together and participate in the efforts of Ashton to assert its superiority (through its representatives) over some other town (through their representative). The Lynds expressed the same view in connexion with the part the basketball team played in the life of Middletown. The team's victory, the Lynds said, gave each supporter the sense of being 'a citizen of no mean city, and, presumably, no mean citizen'.

Whatever else members may do at the club, they spend a good deal of their time simply conversing over their beer. Conversation is notably free and easy. The men conversing have often been life-long acquaintances; having been at the same school and played together as children, they now, as adults, work at the same place and spend their leisure together in such places as the clubs. The clubs do not provide much variety from one to another in respect of the topics which are discussed. Within each club, however, there is considerable differentiation between the groups. A description of one of the clubs in this respect can be taken as typical.

The great majority of men who frequent this club spend most of their time at the bar, drinking and talking. The topic which surpasses all others in frequency is work – the difficulties which have been encountered in the course of the day's shift, the way in which a particular task was accomplished, and so on. A whole series of jokes are based on this fact. It is said that more coal is 'filled off' in the clubs than is ever filled off down below and that the men come back exhausted from a hard shift at the club. . . .

Apart from drinking and talking the most popular activity at the clubs is the concert. At the three largest clubs free concerts are held each Saturday and Sunday evening and Sunday midday. For these professional artists are engaged. The performances generally consist of a succession of songs, often taken from popular musical comedies of many years ago. The spectators sit at small tables drinking beer during the performance, and there is a 'Master of Ceremonies' to call for order. Women are admitted to the concerts and do come in considerable numbers. The exclusion of women from the clubs except on these occasions results in the women having an ambivalent attitude towards the clubs. In a conversation at one of the clubs a miner laughingly said:

> If all the women's wishes for the club had been granted, it would have been blown into the middle of the Sahara desert long before now. Except on Saturday and Sunday! Oh, the club's all right then! . . .

Those clubs which do not have concerts have in their place what is called a 'housey-housey session'. This is a lottery in which each player is given a card bearing a selection of fifteen numbers from 1 to 90. A 'caller' then picks tokens marked from 1 to 90 out of a hat at random, calls them out, and the first player to have all the numbers of his particular selection drawn is the winner. At these clubs women are admitted for the housey-housey sessions on Saturday and Sunday evenings, and Sunday midday in just the same was as they are admitted at the others for the concerts. Six or eight 'games' are 'played' in the course of a session, and there are usually about 70 to 80 players in each game. Each player pays 6d. for his or her selection of numbers and the winner wins the sixpences of all the other competitors, apart from a certain proportion which is deducted by the club for some charitable purpose – for instance to provide an annual outing for the old age pensioner members of the club. The prize for each game is usually somewhat less than £2. Sometimes the 'card' (i.e. the selection of fifteen numbers) will cost 1s. and the prize is then correspondingly larger.

Though the rules of some of the clubs specifically prohibit gambling – for example, Rule 17 of one of the clubs which hold 'housey-housey sessions' states that 'no gambling, drunkenness, bad language or other misconduct shall be permitted on the club premises' – there is gambling in all of them. . . .

Another form of gambling which takes place at all the Working Men's Clubs is that connected with the playing of cards, dominoes, and darts. The stakes are nearly always small, not usually more than 3d. or 6d. Also each club has during the football season one or more 'sweeps' – each participant pays 3d. or 6d. for a team (he can of course 'buy' several teams) and the winner is the holder of the team which is first to score the requisite number of goals.

Each club also has its own 'bookie's runner' – someone who is available at the club and with whom horse-racing bets can be placed. The 'runner' then takes the bets to the bookmakers for whom he is working, and receives a commission on the amount of money he has collected.

Equipment for other games, notably billiards and snooker, is provided at most of the clubs, and each game which is played has its handful of regular players. A small fee is charged for the use of equipment. It is very noticeable that today, as compared with the years of depression between the wars, games are not much played in the clubs. . . .

In 1953 the attendances shown in Table 10.1 at the home matches of the Ashton team were recorded. It must be pointed out, however, that a variable proportion of these attendances was accounted for by supporters of the opposing team and supporters of the Ashton team living in places near to Ashton. The magnitude of these attendances can be placed against the fact that the total adult population (male) of Ashton – i.e. males aged 18 and over – is a little over 4800.

That the interest in the game is not based upon the desire to witness a display of skill was well demonstrated in November 1953. In that month

**Table 10.1** Attendance at the matches in which Ashton Rugby League team played at Ashton in 1953 (i.e. the latter half of the season 1952–3 and the first half of the season 1953–4)

| Home match | Attendance |
|---|---|
| 1 | 3 300 |
| 2 | 2 800 |
| 3 | 4 000 |
| 4 | 4 200 |
| 5 | 5 000 |
| 6 | 10 000 |
| 7 | 3 500 |
| 8 | 3 200 |
| 9 | 6 100 |
| 10 | 7 700 |
| 11 | 7 800 |
| 12 | 3 500 |
| 13 | 3 500 |
| 14 | 4 500 |
| 15 | 3 700 |
| 16 | 3 400 |
| 17 | 4 400 |
| 18 | 3 500 |
| 19 | 3 800 |

the whole of the international Rugby League match between England and France was televised. In the television room of one of the clubs there were never more than nine men watching the match. There were 3400 at the match in which Ashton was playing at home.

With regard to the importance which the defeat or victory in these matches assumes for the supporters, it is a joke in Ashton that when the Ashton team is defeated 'two thousand teas are thrown at t' back o' t' fire'. The men are said to be too distressed to eat. A miner said of his colleagues in the concert-room of a club one Saturday evening when Ashton had defeated a leading team in the Rugby League: 'We beat ... today. Look at everybody! They would still have been happy tonight if the worst turn in the world had been on the stage!' ...

**Betting**

There are two forms of sport which while they find neither players nor supporters in Ashton, yet assume a considerable importance in one respect. The sports are Association Football and horse-racing. Their importance consists in their use as media for betting.

The descriptions of Ashton leisure activities given so far show that gambling is not confined to football pools and horse-racing. It dominates almost every form of leisure activity. The primary reason put forward for this domination has been discussed above in connexion with the general influences which determine the pattern of social life in Ashton. It is that the miner, because of the various forms of insecurity which beset him, cannot hope to escape the limitations of the miner's existence by saving. He can only escape the heavy, dirty and dangerous work by 'luck' in a big way.

A second reason for the popularity of gambling is that the increase in miners' earnings in the last few years has given him a large margin of income available for free spending. It has been already explained that the miner prefers to have a large proportion of 'free income' – income, that is, which is left after what are regarded as being necessities have been purchased. He is liable to be deprived of this margin due to injury or demotion, and therefore avoids becoming too dependent upon it. Gambling is under these circumstances a very attractive way of spending money and the miner becomes an easy prey for those who wish to engage in what the 1933 Royal Commission on Gambling called 'the mass exploitation for private financial gain of the . . . propensity to gamble'.

Other reasons which appear to give gambling its appeal – and these apply to gamblers in all occupations, not only mining – are the desire for self-assertion and the satisfaction derived from being 'lucky'. The satisfaction derived from 'assertion' and 'luck' are logically speaking contradictory, yet it is clear from observation that many people who gamble in fact derive satisfaction from both sources. The desire for self-assertion finds satisfaction in the belief that someone with knowledge of the intricacies of the sport has a better chance than someone who lacks first-hand knowledge. A winner feels that his superior skill has received its just reward. The belief in luck, on the other hand, ignores the question of merit, and the winner feels that his success is in some sense proof that he is a favoured son of Providence.

Of the two main types of gambling (football pools and horse-racing) which are not subsidiary to membership of some club, or indulged in merely to add spice to a game of cards or dominoes, football pools is the most widespread. During the football season in an average week 6000–7000 football coupons are delivered in Ashton. There are very few adult miners who do not participate in this form of gambling. Many who take part, however, do not consider themselves to be gambling at all. The reason for this is that the chances of winning a considerable sum are very slight – though very few participants realize just how slight they are. There is not therefore that feeling sometimes found among people who bet on the results of horse-racing – a confidence in their ability to back a succession of 'certainties' and thus solve all their problems. For most Ashton people who fill in football coupons the feeling is rather that 'I am just giving myself the chance, if it was to come to me.' They find it hard to understand why anyone should throw away the possible chance – however remote –

of £75 000 just for the sake of 1s. Generally this practice involves an hour or so one evening a week during the football season, and an outlay of a few shillings – 'just so as we have a chance'.

The second type of gambling is that which is centred on the bookmakers' offices in Ashton, of which there are five. The smallest of them is in a hut attached to the proprietor's private house. The other four are all dingy premises on Ashton's main roads. They have ordinary shop fronts, the windows of which have been painted. Inside each of the shops the scene is bleak and dusty. . . .

Although regular gambling on the results of horse-races is not as wide-spread as gambling on the results of a selection of football matches, it is probably more important in the life of Ashton. The bookmakers have a weekly turnover which resembles in magnitude that of the Working Men's Clubs. Thus the turnover of one of the bookmaker's shops in Ashton is known to be in the region of £700 per week in the 'flat season'. The separate sums which comprise this total are composed in the great majority of cases of bets under £1. Usually the bets are from 2s. to 10s. though one may take several such bets in the course of the afternoon. . . .

Though most of the individuals who frequent the bookmakers use them like they use other shops – they *purchase* their chance of winning a certain amount of money and leave the shop – the great majority of bets are wagered by the 'regulars'. Each of the four main bookmakers in Ashton has his forty or so regulars and these constitute the core of the gambling community. Only about five or six of these are women. The male regulars use the shop as a kind of club. The women, even if they are regulars, never use it in this way. They place their bets and leave. When one of the regulars is on afternoon shift he may spend the morning in the shop – that is even when there is no racing – with others like himself.

### Cinema-going

Clearly the leisure activities so far described bear out the generalization with which this discussion commenced. Life in Ashton, if it is to be judged from these activities, is undoubtedly vigorous and frivolous, in the sense given to the term frivolous in this context. These activities have also been shown to be predominantly the concern of the males.

When the cinema, the only other activity which brings Ashton people together regularly in large numbers is considered, the position is seen to be somewhat different.

In the first place, women are admitted on an equal footing with men, and audiences are in fact composed or roughly equal proportions of the two sexes. Women preponderate when certain types of film are shown – for example, musical romances – and men when certain other types are shown such as war pictures and 'westerns'. It is not at all unusual for women to attend the cinema unaccompanied. For many women with young children the cinema is the sole relaxation outside the home and they often come alone while the husband looks after the family.

Secondly even large attendances at the cinema are not evidence of 'vigorous social life'. The relationship subsists not between the different members of the audience but between each separate member of the audience and the film being shown. J. P. Mayer states in his *Sociology of the Film* that 'the atomized type of cinema-goer and the autark pair form the majority'. The majority of people who attend any sort of club or meeting *go* singly or in pairs. In the course of the meeting, however, there is a coming together of the individuals and pairs – they cease (to continue to use Mayer's terms) to be atomistic and autarkic. The account of the Working Men's Clubs Saturday concert given above describe this happening. In the course of a cinema performance on the other hand there is no such coming together. Even the relationships between the people who attend the cinema together are virtually suspended during the performance.

The cinema differs from other Ashton leisure institutions in that it is not predominantly a male preserve, and it is not vigorously 'social'. What the audience at the Ashton cinema requires is above all – action. The most popular types of film are therefore the coloured 'western', the spectacular adventure story, and the slapstick comedy. Pictures about the 1939–45 war are also popular. Musical romances appeal to the women. All these films resemble one another in their irrelevance to the problems of the day – they are escapist in that sense – most of them quite blatantly and unashamedly so.

Similar considerations apply to the influence of the cinema as . . . apply to coach trips to places outside of Ashton. There is in both cases a selection from the environment of those aspects which least disturb the Ashton pattern of life. When Ashton people visit other places they protect themselves from alien influences by searching out those activities which most resemble the familiar. When they visit the cinema they protect themselves by attending only those films which portray events so utterly remote from any they know that their portrayal has no real impact on their lives. An exception to this is that among young people such things as personal appearance, clothing and make-up, are affected. In this respect, the influence of the cinema is reinforced by that of commercial advertisements. . . .

## NON-INSTITUTIONALIZED LEISURE PURSUITS

One other category of leisure remains for consideration – that which is primarily individual or familial. The description of Ashton . . . made it clear that no one in Ashton is far away from the countryside. There is therefore ample land within easy reach of Ashton – indeed, at the end of each street – suitable for allotments. Many Ashton families do in fact cultivate allotments. In 1953 there were 3837 private households in Ashton; 1100 of these had allotments covering a total of 119 acres. There are in addition the gardens of the council houses and of a few of the non-council houses. Among men who have allotments there are those, a minority, who spend so much time there as to separate themselves from their families for considerable periods.

More strictly within the circles of the family, the leisure activity of reading is carried on. Nearly all the books which are read are borrowed from the public library, an amenity of comparative recent standing, for Ashton did not possess a public library until 1925. The existing library building was not erected until 1934 and then the total stock of books was 2300. Ashton's first full-time librarian was not appointed until 1942. In 1953 the book stock stood at just under 7500 of which 2700 were non-fiction books, 3700 were adult fiction and 1100 were junior fiction. There were 2188 registered borrowers in March 1953, and of these approximately 1500 used the library regularly, the monthly issue of books fluctuating between 5000 and 6500. Reading must therefore be ranked with the clubs, the public houses, sport and gambling in respect of the number of people concerned.

Only one-quarter of the library books issued were non-fiction. In general it can be said that Ashton's reading serves the same purpose as its cinema-going. That purpose is to convey the reader into a world quite different from his own or her own, and remote therefore from his or her problems.

Among books read by the men, 'westerns' are markedly the most popular. Partly the appeal of this type of book is that of all escapist literature, partly also their appeal is based on the close adherence to a formula, so that the reader feels at home, so to speak, in the strange country he has entered. Many readers are so reluctant to lose that feeling of being on familiar territory that they specialize in the novels of a particular writer. The desire for the 'formula' is perhaps further shown by the popularity of authors who use the device of writing a series of books about the exploits of a particular character.

The only other type of book which is demanded by Ashton males in large numbers is the so-called detective-thriller. In Ashton the book which is more of the 'thriller' type – i.e. which depends upon the action of the plot – is preferred to the 'detective' type of novel – the novel which depends upon the problems to be unravelled.

In Ashton women are predominantly the readers of the light romantic novel. There is some demand for 'westerns' but this is partly because in recent years the 'western' has tended to become also a 'romance'. The light romantic novels, however, are rarely read by the men. Among those authors whose works unfailingly appeal to Ashton women are Kathleen Norris, Margaret Pedlar, Simon Dare, Bertha Ruck, and Ruby M. Ayres.

The other main leisure activity centred on the home, the radio, has not proved a sufficient counter-attraction to the leisure facilities provided outside the home. Listening to the radio is much more a woman's than a man's pastime in Ashton. The word 'listening' in this context can, however, be misleading. It is common to find in Ashton households that the wireless is put on in the morning and remains on until there is a programme being broadcast which is disliked. If suitable programmes cannot be found as an alternative then the radio is switched off. Selection is then a negative process of switching off what is not liked rather than the positive process of tuning in to a programme which is desired. The radio accordingly tends to provide a background to other activities rather than to be the basis of a separate activity. In this Ashton does not, of course, differ from most other areas. . . .

Women's leisure activities in general (apart from cinema-going and week-end visits to the club and public house) are not so rigorously separate from work as they are for the men. The radio is a constant background of recreation while the women are working in their houses. Work is suspended intermittently when neighbours and friends come 'callin' ', come that is, to gossip. In the time spent on it 'callin' ' is the main leisure activity for women in Ashton.

There is evidence to suggest that leisure time is spent in Ashton today in much the same ways as it has been spent since the 1920s. (Before then the churches exerted a very much stronger influence on the way leisure time was spent.) The *mechanism* by which change is minimized is that of avoidance. Those agencies which would tend to induce change — for instance, the cinema, road transport, and literature — are neutralized to a large extent in the way which has been shown.

Furthermore the evidence suggests that the home in Ashton is considerably less important than places outside the home as a centre of leisure activity. And as the leisure facilities outside the home are for males rather than females, the husband and wife move for the most part in different spheres. The results of that separation belong however to a detailed discussion of the family in Ashton.

Reading taken from N. Dennis, F. Henriques and C. Slaughter, *Coal is our Life*, published by Tavistock Publications, 1956. Reprinted with permission.

# IIIb Gender and Leisure

# 'Boys muscle in where angels fear to tread' – girls' sub-cultures and physical activities

## 11

Sheila Scraton

## INTRODUCTION

This paper considers the relationship between PE in secondary schools and young women's sub-cultures. For many years PE teachers have been concerned with the apparent loss of interest and 'dropping out' of many adolescent young women from the PE lesson. This paper attempts to relate PE teaching to the sub-cultural experiences and resistances of young women and thus move beyond a biologically determined position which traditionally has explained young women's responses to PE as 'natural' and inevitable. . . . The analysis in this section draws on eight years' teaching experience in secondary school PE and qualitative research carried out in Liverpool secondary schools during the 1983–1984 school year. In conclusion the paper looks forward to possible initiatives which could help move towards a more positive and challenging approach to PE for adolescent young women. . . .

*Sociology of Leisure: A reader.* Edited by C. Critcher, P. Bramham and A. Tomlinson. Published in 1995 by E & FN Spon, London. ISBN 0 419 19420 7.

## PHYSICAL EDUCATION – WHAT IS ON OFFER?

PE in the majority of secondary schools is taught to single-sex groups even when part of a co-educational school system. My own research in Liverpool schools demonstrates the existence of a core curriculum in the first three years of secondary schools consisting of team games, gymnastics, athletics with some schools including swimming and/or dance. Within this core component half of the total PE time is taken up by competitive team games with the other activities sharing the remaining time. A programme of 'options' including more individually based activities (e.g. badminton, trampolining) or less competitive situations (e.g. keep fit) is offered, in most instances from the fourth year upwards. The extra-curricular programme offers team games in specific age groupings, gym, swimming, and/ or dance clubs for the younger girls with a badminton club a usual addition from the age of fifteen years. PE is theoretically compulsory up to the school-leaving age and is taught in mixed ability groups apart from extra-curricular representative-year team practices.

The notion of 'good practice' and 'standards' in PE has been at the forefront of PE teaching throughout its history and development. 'Good practice' centres around discipline, neatness, good behaviour, appearance, etc. It is stressed by PE teachers today as one of the most important features of their work. . . .

Today PE continues to stress discipline. Lining up in the changing rooms in silence, entering the gym quietly and responding without question to rules and regulations of games, are an essential part of contemporary PE lessons. In many schools the 'success' of PE is still measured by the achievements on the sports field or netball court. PE often provides the 'public face' of the school when it represents them at tournaments, inter-school matches, swimming galas, gym displays, etc. Even the discipline and behaviour of the girls when outside, playing hockey, tennis, etc. is on view to the rest of the school in their classrooms and the local residents as they walk past. In many respects what occurs in PE is under far closer scrutiny than teaching in the classroom.

The continuing emphasis on appearance for teaching practice in schools today demonstrates both its importance for teachers of PE and the values of subsequent transmission of such values to the pupils. The wearing of PE uniform is still compulsory throughout Liverpool schools. In most instances the uniform is regulated to a specific skirt/shorts/top of a defined colour. Even where this has been relaxed, which was only evident in three situations, there is an insistence on 'suitable' clothing as defined by the PE teacher. A considerable amount of time is taken up in the PE lesson by the enforcement of correct PE uniform and neatness of appearance.

While 'good practice' and 'standards' inform the teaching of PE, the primary aims and objectives are dependent also on economic, social and political forces. In my own research in Liverpool schools I found that in 1984 every girls' PE department placed leisure as their main or second objective for the teaching of PE especially from the third year upwards. The emphasis was on enjoyment and preparation for participation in post-school leisure time. Most teachers recognised this as a changed emphasis throughout the 1970s and early 1980s because of economic changes which they identified as producing increased leisure time, both in terms of shorter working hours, and most importantly through the reality of probable unemployment or part time work. The validity of these points will be discussed later.

The PE on offer to adolescent girls is therefore influenced, both structurally and ideologically, by a number of interrelated factors. In order to consider the relationship of PE to young women's sub-cultures, it is important to turn to the influences which impinge on the young women's responses to the PE experience.

## Young women's responses

It is obvious that young women experience biological changes during puberty, and which therefore usually occur between the ages of nine and thirteen. These changes are often dramatic with changed body shape, related to the onset of menstruation, happening over a short period of time. How far these biological changes influence young women's responses to PE remains questionable. . . .

What would seem more important is the social construction of young women's biology, the ideology of biology, i.e. the expectations placed on young women as to how they *should* be reacting to these physical changes. It is reasonable to assume that for some young women the changes of puberty produce such distinct changes in body shape that they find it awkward to move physically in the same way as in the past, for example in gymnastics or in athletics. It is, however, the social and ideological pressures linked to sexuality and body physique that produce the inhibition rather than a biologically determined restriction on movement. . . . Young women's experiences at adolescence centre around the culture of femininity. In terms of the 'physical' the expectation is one of inactivity, passivity, neatness (reinforced through socialisation, media, schooling, etc.). Young women are not expected to run around, get dirty or indeed sweat. The old adage that young ladies 'glow' as opposed to sweat remains firm in today's thinking.

Peer group pressure intensifies the culture of femininity. Whereas an individual may still be interested in playing netball or swimming in the team, it is often pressure from friends, which encourages her to 'drop out' or, certainly diminishes her enthusiasm. Option lists in the PE department often show names erased because a 'best friend' does not want to take part in that particular activity. Certainly many potential senior team members are lost, not necessarily through a loss of interest by the individual, but more often because of the sub-cultural influences that surround her.

So, what happens when the PE on offer encounters the young women it is intended for? The meeting place is the lesson and it is here that the relationship between secondary school PE and young women's sub-cultures becomes either a 'problem' for the teacher, or a subject for negotiation and resistance by the student.

### Teacher and student: the meeting of PE and adolescent young women

Figure 11.1 shows the centrality of the PE *lesson* and the resultant effects for both PE teacher and student.

First, PE teachers attempt to explain why young women tend to lose interest in physical activity during and immediately after puberty. This 'loss of interest' of adolescent young women is confirmed by the majority of heads of PE interviewed during my research.

> In the second or third year they just lose interest but not just in PE. They lose interest in everything at this time.

> Girls at this stage are going through . . . they're changing fairly rapidly. They get embarrassed very easily. They change shape more and feel more self-conscious than lads do. They just lose all interest in physical activity at this time – it's just natural.

> I've talked to my girls and they always say 'we're just beginning to be interested in outside.' They lose interest in PE at school. If they go to a disco they expend more energy than they ever would in a PE lesson.

The explanation is given as 'natural' – an inevitable problem inherent to

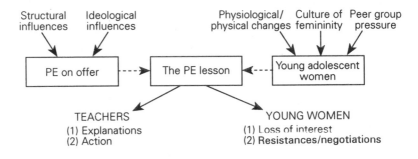

**Figure 11.1** The centrality of the PE lesson.

adolescent young women. In general, PE teachers see young women at this time as less interested in physical activity, lethargic and inactive. . . .

However, for many PE teachers the problems faced with 3E or 4X on a Thursday afternoon are real and, in general, result in one or two coping strategies. First, many teachers, identifying the 'problem' as biologically constructed and/or individually based, tackle the solution by reiterating their belief in the value and ideals of the PE on offer. They attempt to enforce participation through disciplinary means. Obviously this has minimal 'success' for even if the young women involved continue to participate in theory, in practice they remain uninterested and unmotivated. The value of 'enjoyment' placed so highly by *all* PE teachers on their list of aims and objectives cannot be achieved by use of hierarchical disciplinarian methods. Second, teachers have attempted to alleviate their difficulties by adapting the curriculum and making it more relevant to young women's needs and requirements. During the past decade and a half this has included the introduction of a scheme of options for the upper school age group. (These options have been introduced also for economic reasons where shortage of staff, facilities, etc., affect organisation. However, the primary justification given for 'options' is that they are more 'suitable' for adolescent young women.) These 'option' activities whilst retaining the compulsory element of PE allow more choice of content. The options offered tend to be individually based since this is recognised as being more 'appropriate' for older girls. The emphasis is on indoor activities which provide 'an activity which won't mess up their hair or make them too sweaty' (interview, PE teacher). In some situations activities relating directly to appearance are encouraged with stress on the development of an 'attractive' figure and body shape. This can be through Keep Fit/Aerobic classes or the development of specialist Health and Beauty courses which cover a wide range of issues including care of the hair, nails, diet, make-up, clothes, etc. The difficulty with these last developments in PE is that they reinforce the cultural expectations of femininity. . . .

The message being reinforced in these situations is that young women should not be interested and involved in physical activity in order to develop strength and fitness but should be concerned in enhancing their appearance, in making themselves more 'attractive', particularly to the opposite sex.

The response from young women to the PE lesson can involve resistance to the activities and teaching of PE. . . .

Resistances based on appearance take an intensified form when related to PE. As has been discussed, appearance in relation to 'standards' and 'good practice' is an integral part of the ethos of PE teaching. Young women who use their appearance to challenge their school experiences confront PE by contesting its central ideological tenet. Young women refuse to wear the required PE uniform, they wear make-up and jewellery and will not consent to the 'golden rule' of 'tying your hair back'. These challenges to authority are more obvious in the changing room than elsewhere in the school, and indeed produce a confrontation which can often be avoided by most other school staff. Whereas other teachers can choose to ignore the wearing of a ring or ear-rings which contravenes school regulations, PE teachers not only have their own standards and values around appearance to uphold, but have the added concern of safety during physical activity. Rings, earrings, necklaces, badges and long hair can be in fact, exceedingly dangerous in some physical situations.

The 'sullen stare' takes on particular significance in PE. A sullen, silent 'participant' on the hockey pitch or in the gymnasium is inordinately difficult to manage. . . . In PE, where lively, active behaviour is demanded a silent, sullen participant produces far more conflict and can affect the participation of the whole group. It is a particularly successful resistance to PE for adolescent young women.

**Towards a cultural explanation**

A biological explanation for young women's loss of interest in PE and their resistances within the PE lesson is not sufficient. Whilst acknowledging the physiological changes of puberty I would argue that an understanding of cultural expectations is vital if young women's experiences, attitudes and behaviours are to be fully understood. It is necessary to analyse from a cultural perspective why it is that many young women 'drop out' or lose interest in PE during the period of adolescence. The PE on offer to young women conflicts with their interests and attitudes not simply because they are undergoing biological changes of puberty but because the cultural expectations of gender-specific attitudes, behaviour, role, etc. are at odds with both what is on offer in PE and the values, ideals and ethos underpinning the subject.

PE for girls in most secondary schools remains dominated by team games. Team games are synonymous with sport which in our society is problematic for female participants. The relationship of sport to masculinity is well documented (Young, 1980; Hargreaves, 1982). Sport celebrates a certain kind of masculinity with its sporting heroes dominating the headlines on the sports page. Young women are immersed in a culture of femininity and romance, reinforced through the magazines they read, the television they watch and their everyday experiences. PE appears incompatible with their expected lifestyle. Sport is seen primarily as a male pursuit bound up with masculine values. Young women spectate, support and admire; they do not expect to participate.

Furthermore sport in the form of team games is problematic not only in definition but also in form. Young women's cultures which emphasise the 'best friend' or small groupings do not relate easily to the collective team situation. PE stresses the collective through team sports, gym clubs, dance groups, athletic teams. Young women often reject these situations as incompatible with the expectations of adult femininity (Leaman, 1984). Young, fit, virile men are expected to revel in group camaraderie and team spirit. It is less acceptable for their adolescent sisters.

‘Preparation for leisure’ was stated as a primary aim of PE teaching by every secondary school in my current research. . . . Preparation for leisure creates problems of relevance for all women especially in the realm of physical leisure activities. Deem’s (1984) research confirms this, for in her study of 168 women drawn at random from five areas of a new town, she found ‘scarcely any adult women who continued with any sport or physical activity done at school once they had left, with swimming the only wide-spread exception to this’. Therefore ‘preparation for leisure’ is a dubious objective for young women’s PE. Not only does leisure not exist for many women but where women have opportunities for leisure the most frequently pursued activity is swimming (Deem, 1984). My research suggests that swimming is offered to adolescent young women as an option in schools only where the school has a swimming pool on site. This is restricted further by staffing problems as most departments cannot release a member of staff to cover the numbers opting for swimming. In most schools there is no choice, as access to swimming facilities is not available. The emphasis on leisure as a realistic objective for young women seems particularly illogical given that many PE teachers recognise their own personal limitations in time and opportunities at a private level. Many PE teachers described the problems they had with family and domestic responsibilities which affected their ability to spend more time on extra-curricular activities or personal leisure pursuits. This failure to recognise the problems of using leisure as a relevant and useful concept for women produces a contradictory and, in many ways, an unachievable aim for PE teaching. PE teachers need to look more critically both at the structural limitations and at the reality of everyday experiences for women in physical leisure activities in order to provide a more realistic link between school and future physical participation. The recognition of a sexual division of leisure, as well as a sexual division of labour, by all teachers, should be an important aspect of the teaching of girls in schools. Furthermore, young women themselves often recognise the constraints put on their ‘leisure’ time. Even where they succeed in challenging their lack of access to time, space, etc. (more easily achieved by middle-class young women) they face unequal provision of facilities and opportunities to participate. Their present reality confirms their future ‘leisure’ participation. When they attend youth groups, clubs, etc. they know only too well who dominates the snooker tables, gymnasium, table tennis etc. (Nava and McRobbie, 1984).

The resistance of young women to the discipline and control of PE, described previously as being central to the ideology of PE, is a response similar to the responses of young women to schooling in general. The actual resistance is class- and age-based although within a particularly gendered form (McRobbie, 1978). Although these problems are faced throughout the curriculum, the importance of discipline and control which is so much a part of both the *content* and teaching of PE creates an often intensified conflict between PE teaching staff and students.

Equally resistances to school uniform by adolescent young women are resistances to the style, restriction and enforced uniformity of the dress. As Whylde (1983) states:

> Collar, tie and jacket for boys and skirt and blouse (or twin-set!) for girls imitate the conventional dress of the middle aged and middle class, a group which few pupils will identify with, and against which most will rebel.

Once more the issue of uniform is intensified during PE. PE uniform is one of the major areas of conflict between young women and PE. To many young women the wearing of a standard tee shirt, regulation navy shorts/ skirt plus ankle socks is one of the greatest indignities and embarrassments placed on them. Whilst they react to school uniform for the reasons suggested by Whylde, their reactions to PE kit is enhanced as their developing sexuality, and their desire to achieve adult femininity, meet head on a PE kit which denies not only their individuality but also any hint of a developing sexual person. At a time when fashion, jewellery and make-up are central to their concern with appearance, the uniform, asexual PE kit is an anathema.

Anxiety around PE for adolescent young women is caused also by showering after a lesson and indeed changing in large, group changing rooms. This relates to the fact that girls reach puberty and mature physically at different rates. Again, whilst this is experienced throughout the school, the 'physical' nature of PE intensifies the problems. Measor (1984) found in her research a great reluctance of young women to take showers as a group:

> *Pat:* 'I don't like showers. On the first day we were ever so shy. Everyone has got things different . . . some people have got hairs and some haven't.'
>
> *Carol:* 'There is one big girl in our group . . . she is big chested, and that and she walks through the shower all covered up. It's best to be in between, we all giggle and throw our towels down. She finally went into the shower with her towel. There is one really little girl, who sits there making faces, she looks at everyone, she makes you feel embarrassed.'

The explanations for the problems faced by young women in coping with this situation are clearly grounded in physiology and the physical changes of puberty. However, it is the interaction of physical development and *cultural* expectation that is important. It is not the actual physical changes of the young women's bodies which cause the anxiety but the culturally determined responses to these changes. Those who are 'in-between' or average in their development can cope with the situation. They meet the expectations for desired body shape and development. Those who deviate from the norm face acute embarrassment and often unkind comment. When society emphasises a desired physique for adult femininity, those who become aware of their differences during adolescence are caused anxiety and often retreat or 'hide' from the situation. PE provides the platform where physical differences are unmasked. Adult women are not expected to expose their bodies and are encouraged to dislike their body shape unless it conforms to the 'ideal' feminine stereotype. During adolescence the PE changing room or shower area is an exposed situation where young women's developing bodies are put 'on view'. The problem is not the physical appearance as such, but the desire of young women to achieve the 'acceptable', sexually attractive physique of womanhood. This body shape is culturally determined and strongly informed by ideologies of woman as a sexual object to be admired, viewed and used by men.

## THE WAY FORWARD

School PE fails to provide 'meaningful experiences' for many young adolescent women because it appears at odds with the culture of femininity. Their resistances which are complex and not always consistent, relate to what they perceive as on offer from PE:

(a) the development of muscle
(b) sweat
(c) communal shower/changing facilities
(d) 'childish', asexual PE kit
(e) low status activities.

It is acceptable for the 'tomboy' in junior or lower secondary school to participate in and enjoy these activities but not so acceptable to adult femininity.

As shown, therefore, PE remains trapped within possibilities which will 'appeal' to young women but will consequently reinforce the culture of femininity. This is intensified by the training and ideological constraints of women PE teachers. Even so-called 'progressive' moves, for example, mixed PE, provide only superficial challenges to the ideologies of femininity. Any suggestion of substantive change to give young women positive experiences in PE tends to be met with scepticism because it is assumed that young women are so steeped in the deterministic *Jackie* mentality that they will reject more positive physical values of assertiveness, strength, control, etc. There is not necessarily real substance to this argument. Adult women's experiences are not *totally* determined and the past decade and a half has seen a substantial shift through the development of new directions in the reconstruction of women's sexuality and consciousness. These include the development of self-help groups in medical care/mental health, the emergence of well-women's clinics and other all-women projects geared to giving women more control over their own health, bodies, etc. Women's groups have developed, resisting male violence with rape crisis centres, women's refuges, etc. Education has seen the introduction of 'NOW' courses, 'outreach' projects, women's writing groups, etc., where women are encouraged to gain confidence and assertiveness in intellectual situations. Women's physical control over their own bodies can be seen further in the development of self-defence/assertiveness training and women's fitness programmes which are geared to developing health, strength and physical well-being rather than the traditional construction of 'womanhood' around appearance, body physique, etc. These latter developments indicate a qualitative shift in definitions of 'the physical'. Women in these programmes are reclaiming the right to physical development and appearance on *their own terms* rather than on the terms laid down in the traditions of 'feminine culture' which are learned and reinforced in youth. As Lenskyj (1982) describes from her own experience, after years of upbringing women are:

> alienated from our bodies not knowing the extent of our physical strength and endurance and not daring to find out. Those of us who have dared have found a new avenue for self-realisation as women and as feminists – joyful at the discovery that our bodies are strong and resilient, capable of hard work and hard play.

It is with these developments in adult women's projects that women's PE should be concerned rather than a concentration on equal access to male-based sports, e.g. women into soccer, etc. For these are part of the same institutional relations of patriarchy (i.e. cults of masculinity) which produce young women's sub-cultures and define/constrict young women's opportunities. By contrast, women's PE needs to develop a new programme geared to assertiveness, confidence, health, fitness and the capacity to challenge patriarchal definitions of submissiveness, passivity, dependence, etc. This is by no means an easy task but nonetheless a direction in which we must, at least, begin to move.

The unifying feature of all the adult women's projects mentioned is the emphasis on collective support. PE is in the perfect situation to offer young women opportunities for collective support through co-operative and enjoyable physical activity. Whilst the relationship between teacher and student will retain an age-related power structure, young women can be encouraged to work together through such activities as dance, outdoor pursuits, self-defence, etc. Indeed Willis (1982) suggest:

> A sport could be presented as a form of activity which emphasizes human similarity and not dissimilarity, a form of activity which expresses values which are indeed immeasurable, a form of activity which is concerned with individual well-being and satisfaction rather than with comparison.

Many young men thrive on their collective 'rugby club' experiences. Young women, too, need the space for collective physical experience whilst rejecting and challenging the competitive, 'macho' values of the male sporting ethos. Adolescence is a time to develop group and collective experiences rather than the channelling of young women into individually based activities which deny the opportunities to develop group confidence and identity.

Young women also need the space to develop confidence, interests, etc. This is especially true in mixed schools for the evidence clearly indicates that in all social situations men dominate space – physically, verbally, etc. (See Spender, 1982; Young, 1980.) In co-educational schools the primary female-only space is in the toilets, cloakrooms and changing rooms. These are the areas where young women 'hang out', where they spend time together away from 'the lads' and the teachers (Griffin et al., 1982). It would be a positive contribution if women PE teachers could recognise the need of young women to have their own space in which to chat, plan or simply 'have a laugh'. This is clearly problematic given school organisation and the enforcement of school rules and regulations. However, it would be a positive move to open up changing rooms and facilities during breaks, lunchtime and after school and encourage young women to use the space available for their 'leisure' whether it be netball, table tennis *or* chatting with a friend. Too often young women are allowed into the PE wing only if they are taking part in organised, formal PE activities. It would be an encouraging move to give young women more control over their extra-curricular PE activities and to provide the space for meeting and chatting together.

Just as adult women are beginning to reclaim the right to control and develop their own bodies for intrinsic satisfaction rather than sexual exploitation, so PE must emphasise these values for young adolescent women. They must be encouraged to enjoy physical movement; to develop strength and muscular potential; to work together to discover body awareness and confidence. It will be only when young women collectively become confident and assertive with control both physically and mentally over their own bodies that they will move towards redefining their position. PE has an important contribution to make towards the denial of ideologies of 'femininity'. For this to occur it requires a critical self-appraisal and a more sensitive understanding of young women's position in our schooling system and in wider society.

## ACKNOWLEDGMENTS

Many thanks to Pat Craddock, Rosemary Deem and Phil Scraton for their help, support and critical comments. Also personal thanks to Sally Channon.

## NOTE

This research examines how images of 'femininity' and the construction of gender-appropriate behaviour are reinforced or challenged by the structure, content and teaching of girls' PE in Secondary schools. The qualitative methodology has involved extensive interviews with Heads of Girls' PE Departments in Liverpool Secondary Schools (state), periods of close observation in selected schools and structured interviews with PE advisers, lecturers in the specialist teacher-training college and education committee members involved in reorganization.

## REFERENCES

Deem, R. (1984), 'Paid work, leisure and non-employment: shifting boundaries and gender differences', unpublished paper presented to BSA conference 'Work, Employment, Unemployment', April.

Griffin, C. et al. (1982), 'Women and leisure' in Hargreaves, J. (ed.), *Sport, Culture and Ideology*, Routledge & Kegan Paul, London.

Hargreaves, J. (ed.) (1982), *Sport, Culture and Ideology*, Routledge & Kegan Paul, London.

Leaman, O. (1984), *Sit on the Sidelines and Watch the Boys Play: Sex Differentiation in PE*, Longman (for Schools Council), London.

Lenskyj, J. (1982), 'I am Strong' in *The Women's News Magazine*, University of Toronto, March/April.

McRobbie, A. (1978), 'Working class girls and the culture of femininity' in *Women Take Issue*, Hutchinson, London.

Measor, L. (1984), 'Sex education and adolescent sexuality', unpublished manuscript.

Nava, M. and McRobbie, A. (eds) (1984), *Gender and Generation*, Macmillan, London.

Spender, D. (1982), *Invisible Women: The Schooling Scandal*, Writers and Readers Co-operative, London.

Whylde, J. (ed.) (1983), *Sexism in the Secondary Curriculum*, Harper & Row, New York.

Willis, P. (1982), 'Women in Sport in Ideology', in Hargreaves, J. (ed.) 1982.

Young, I. M. (1980), 'Throwing like a girl: a phenomenology of feminine body comportment, mobility and spatiality', *Human Studies*, Vol. 3, 1980.

Reading taken from J. Horne, D. Jary and A. Tomlinson (eds), *Sport, Leisure and Social Relations*, reissued by Sociology Review, 1993 (first published by Routledge, 1987). Reprinted with permission.

| 12 | Women's leisure today |

Eileen Green, Sandra Hebron and Diane Woodward

## GENDER DIFFERENCES IN LEISURE PATTERNS

What little we know about women's leisure indicates that the activities women enjoy and do most frequently in and around the home are not much different from men's preferred forms of leisure. The 1983 *General Household Survey*, a British government publication based on interviews with a representative national sample of over 10 000 women and nearly 9000 men aged over 16, showed that 98 per cent of both the women and the men had watched television in the month period to the interview; 86 per cent of the women and 87 per cent of the men had listened to the radio; and nearly two-thirds of the respondents – 62 per cent of the women and 65 per cent of the men – had played records or tapes at home (see Table 12.1). Gender differences were more marked for reading, gardening, do-it-yourself, sewing and knitting: more women do reading and crafts, while more men do DIY and gardening. Another national survey of 2000 people aged 15 and over, also carried out in 1983, likewise found that watching television and listening to the radio and music were the three most popular leisure activities, and were done by equal numbers of men and women (NOP, 1983). Again, reading books, knitting and sewing were more popular with women, and gardening and do-it-yourself were for men, with at least 20 per cent more of one gender than the other doing each of these activities.

If we examine patterns of leisure participation away from home, the picture changes to one of much greater gender differentiation. More men than women do out-of-home activities in general, and both the GHS and NOP surveys report men to be much more likely to go out drinking, to gamble and to engage in sporting activities, both indoors and outdoors.

*Sociology of Leisure: A reader*. Edited by C. Critcher, P. Bramham and A. Tomlinson. Published in 1995 by E & FN Spon, London. ISBN 0 419 19420 7.

**Table 12.1** Social activities and hobbies: participation by males and females aged 16 and over

| Percentages participating in the following activities in the four weeks before interview | Males | Females |
|---|---|---|
| *Social activities and hobbies* | | |
| – not on prompt list[1] | | |
| Bingo | 5 | 11 |
| Betting | 5 } 28 | 1 } 12 |
| Football pools | 25 | 11 |
| Other gambling | 1 | 1 |
| Playing games of skill | 16 | 12 |
| Dancing | 10 | 12 |
| Clubs/societies | 11 | 12 |
| Voluntary work | 7 | 9 |
| Hobbies/crafts/arts | 11 | 3 |
| Cooking/wine/preserve making | 1 | 1 |
| Animal keeping | 2 | 1 |
| Leisure classes (excl. sports, dancing) | 1 | 2 |
| Amateur music/drama (excl. classes) | 3 | 3 |
| | | |
| *Total* doing at least one activity[2] excl. leisure classes and amateur music/drama | 60 | 52 |
| | | |
| – on prompt list[3] | | |
| Visiting/entertaining friends/relations | 90 | 93 |
| Going out for a meal | 41 } 73 | 40 } 60 |
| Going out for a drink | 64 | 46 |
| Watching TV | 98 | 98 |
| Listening to radio | 87 | 86 |
| Listening to records/tapes | 65 | 62 |
| Reading books | 50 | 61 |
| Gardening | 50 | 39 |
| DIY | 51 | 24 |
| Dressmaking/needlework/knitting | 2 | 48 |
| | | |
| *Total* doing at least one activity | 100 | 100 |
| | N = 8 744 | N = 10 306 |

[1] These activities were not included on the prompt list and were therefore not asked about specifically. All of them except cooking/wine/preserve making and animal keeping were however included on the aide-memoire card.
[2] Total includes those activities not separately listed (see Table 10.22 of the *General Household Survey*, 1983).
[3] These activities were on the prompt list and were therefore asked about specifically.

*Source*: adapted from the *General Household Survey* (1983) and reproduced by kind permission of the Controller of Her Majesty's Stationery Office.

Youth and social class position cut across gender differences to promote participation in leisure activities away from home.

Women's lower participation rates than men in sporting activities have been recognised for some time. The *General Household Survey* 1983 shows that almost 20 per cent more men than women had taken part in sports, games and physical activities in the month prior to interview, and their patterns of participation in various sports are very different (see Table 12.2). Whereas walking is the most popular single activity for both men and women, yoga or keep fit and swimming were the only other activities done by more than one woman in twenty. For men, in contrast, football, snooker/billiards/pool, darts and swimming all came into this category, with various other activities almost attaining this level of popularity, such as golf, fishing and squash.

The 'big five' most popular leisure activities are, it is asserted, drinking, gambling, watching television, sex and playing football. It does not take a

**Table 12.2** Participation in sports, games and physical activities by males and females aged 16 and over

| *Percentages participating in the following activities in the four weeks before interview* | | |
|---|---|---|
| | *Males* | *Females* |
| *Outdoor* | | |
| Walking 2 miles or more | 20 | 18 |
| Football | 6 | – |
| Golf | 4 | 1 |
| Fishing | 4 | – |
| Swimming | 4 | 4 |
| Athletics | 3 | 1 |
| Cycling | 2 | 2 |
| Bowls | 2 | – |
| Tennis | 1 | 1 |
| | | |
| *Total* doing at least one activity | 39 | 24 |
| | | |
| *Indoor* | | |
| Snooker/billiards/pool | 15 | 2 |
| Darts | 11 | 4 |
| Swimming | 7 | 7 |
| Keep fit/Yoga | – | 5 |
| Squash | 4 | 1 |
| Badminton | 2 | 2 |
| Table Tennis | 2 | 2 |
| Bowls/tenpin bowling | 1 | 1 |
| | | |
| *Total* doing at least one activity | 33 | 18 |
| | N = 8 744 | 10 306 |

*Source*: adapted from the *General Household Survey* (1983), Tables 10.5 and 10.6 and reproduced by kind permission of the Controller of Her Majesty's Stationery Office.

very profound analysis to work out that very few women play football (less than 1 per cent, according to the GHS). Whilst most women, like most men, may watch television, drink alcohol, have sex and gamble, how they do it and what it means to them are likely to be different and hence to provide qualitatively different kinds of leisure experience. Gambling for men mainly takes the form of football pools and horse-race betting: 28 per cent of all men bet in this way, and 5 per cent play bingo. In contrast, only 12 per cent of women engage in these forms of betting, and 11 per cent play bingo. The GHS data and the Dixey and Talbot study (1982) reveal the socio-demographic profile of the typical bingo player to be elderly and working class. . . .

The findings of the major British surveys are borne out by smaller localised studies of the impact of gender on leisure. These include Deem's (1986) study of women's leisure in the new town of Milton Keynes; Dixey and Talbot's (1982) study of women residents of Armley, an established working-class district in the northern industrial city of Leeds; Wimbush's (1986) study of Edinburgh mothers with young children; and our own study of Sheffield women (Green, Hebron and Woodward, 1987). All of these studies confirm the national survey data on the popularity of watching television, reading, and doing home-based crafts for women. Using sources such as these, which provide qualitative data about the place of leisure in women's lives as a whole, it is possible to offer explanations for the patterns of leisure activity noted in these and the large surveys. We cannot only construct a picture of women's leisure activities within and outside the home, but can also indicate how far leisure patterns are a reflection of women's social situation – their age group, their social class, their own and their male partner's employment status, their domestic situation and ethnic identity, as well as their geographical location.

Despite the regional diversity of these studies, a series of common themes clearly emerge concerning the way in which such variations in women's personal circumstances are experienced in relation to leisure. We can begin to identify the social processes that shape the leisure experiences of young women as they grow up, and to show how marriage and motherhood and their position in the labour market structure women's recreational opportunities, by drawing on other studies of the lives led by these groups of women to supplement our limited knowledge of their leisure activities. As yet we have much less qualitative information available about the lives and leisure of older women – which may well reflect the low level of visibility and status of the elderly and their concerns in our society – and of women from ethnic minority groups. These are major gaps in our understanding, and this research urgently needs to be done to inform theory and policy.

## RESEARCHING WOMEN'S LEISURE

Many of the empirical studies of women's lives and leisure ... share a feminist approach to their subject matter. This involves more than just determining what women's patterns of recreation are, and seeking to explain them in terms of the prevailing paradigms in social science. It requires that they should be understood as part and parcel of the women's lives as a whole, and seen through the eyes of the women respondents themselves. This perspective belongs to the tradition of Weber's *Verstehensociologie* in the sense of aiming to understand the meanings and motivations which those being studied attach to their behaviour. It shares the same goal of seeking insight through empathy, even though it derives from different origins, namely the politics of the Women's Movement. Thus the activities (or inactivities!) that women spend time doing need to be analysed within the framework of their lives as a whole. What time do women have available for leisure, after the obligations of paid work and unpaid domestic labour have been met? And what material, cultural and ideological constraints restrict women's access to leisure time and their choices about how it may be spent? How do these constraints operate: are they the result of self-imposed 'policing' attributable to women's desire to earn the community's respect and to avoid its censure, or are they the result of norms being enforced on their behaviour by others? Without this broad contextual setting, research does not take us much beyond the *General Household Survey*'s tables of the percentages of men and women doing various activities. In order to go further than merely documenting and counting women's participation in leisure activities we need to have the theoretical and empirical evidence available to help us explain not just how gender influences leisure, but how gender is constructed, interpreted, perceived and experienced, for all the social groups that comprise this half of the population.

There is now an established body of literature in the social sciences on gender inequalities and differences in relation to various major social institutions, such as the family, employment, education, health, welfare, the media and the law. We are witnessing the beginnings of such a literature in the field of leisure studies. Many constraints on leisure opportunities clearly apply both to men and women, such as the restrictions of paid employment and parenting on leisure time, or the constraining effects of poverty and loneliness. However, there is evidence to show that these factors impinge in different ways, and to a greater or lesser extent on women than on men as a reflection of contemporary definitions of gender roles. Some constraints apply to most women, but to few men, such as the fear of being out alone after dark. The Second British Crime Survey (Hough and Mayhew, 1985) found that half the women interviewed only went out after dark if accompanied, and 40 per cent were 'very worried' about being raped. Over half of the respondents in the Sheffield gender and leisure survey were worried about being out alone after dark and most of these women saw it as a 'big problem' for them (Green, Hebron and Woodward, 1987). Although one might expect that women from affluent households who have access to a private car would be less affected by this anxiety than other women, in fact the similar proportion of women from a diverse range of social backgrounds who share this worry is striking. The Greater London Council's Women's Committee study of women and transport also found high levels of anxiety about using Underground and bus services and walking at night-time (GLC, 1985). Thirty per cent of respondents strongly agreed with the statement 'I don't go out on my own after dark', a proportion rising from about a sixth of the young women to well over half of the over-sixties. Women who know of other women who have been attacked or harassed become more alert to what is going on around them, and may become less willing to go out after dark. The report says: 'It is clear that a very high proportion of elderly and Asian women in particular are severely restricted in their activities at night by fear of attack, and have adjusted their lives to avoid the need to go out alone' (p. 8).

Evidently, then, many women circumscribe their leisure activities outside the home because of worries about their safety, and this constraint affects women's mobility much more than men's. Other constraints apply to both women and men in particular social groups, for example those in the same age group or social class group, but we would argue that even here gender is often a significant source of difference. Elderly men on low incomes who are lonely still have the choice open to them of going to the pub or working men's club, even if one drink may have to last them half the evening, whereas this is not seen as a viable leisure activity for a similarly placed woman. Ninety-three per cent of the Sheffield survey respondents said they would feel uncomfortable going into a working men's club on their own (and in many parts of northern Britain these clubs are the focal point for recreation and sociability in the community), and 84 per cent felt the same way about going into a pub. Women's feelings of being unwelcome in public houses if unaccompanied by men have also been reported from studies done elsewhere in Britain and other Anglo-Saxon cultures (Whitehead, 1976; Dempsey, 1987; Woodward and Green, in Wimbush and Talbot, 1988).

Class position, income level, work situation, age, domestic circumstances and stage in the family life-cycle, as well as ethnicity, all have a major bearing on how women experience leisure, making global generalisations about women's leisure unsafe and probably inaccurate for many women. Some of these variables have a direct impact on access to leisure, and others are mediated through commonsense assumptions about appropriate and respectable behaviour, and how men may treat women.... For example, being a member of a low-income household may of itself limit spending on leisure activities, but even within such household units its members are not seen as equally entitled to personal spending money for leisure outside the home. This point comes out clearly from studies of, for example, the spending patterns of the households of unemployed men. . . . We therefore need to consider how gender influences women's experiences of leisure, not just in terms of the issues that affect most if not all women, such as feeling vulnerable outside the home after dark, but also to examine how gender issues operate differently for women from the various social groups. . . .

As always, the drawing of conclusions is essentially a retrospective process. . . . However, we should also endeavour to identify the likely future directions of leisure in general and for women's leisure in particular. Looking back over our work, what is striking is the enormity of the task we set ourselves. Although we are by no means the first to tackle 'women and leisure', the two areas are so vast that we certainly cannot have told the whole story. This is not false modesty, nor an apologia for our shortcomings, but rather a recognition that there is still much to be done before we fully understand leisure, and women's experiences of it. Leisure is a social process which therefore changes over time. Our concern as feminists continues to be with how to ensure that women are not denied equal access to leisure, whatever its future forms.

The initial premise of our work was to attempt to understand women's experiences of leisure, and to question how far leisure is even a meaningful concept for women. By doing this we also hoped to achieve the important goal of putting women well and truly on the map in the rather narrow field of leisure studies. The apparent male dominance, in terms of approach if not always in terms of the gender of the scholars themselves, had clear implications for the way in which leisure was typically studied. It was separated off as a discrete area of life, predominantly viewed in relation to paid work. Men were the focus of study, by and large. Women, it was assumed, either had the same experiences as men, in which case there was no need to study them, or else they were anomalous and messed up the research findings.

As women and as feminists, we knew that women had to be the focus of our empirical work. We also knew from our own experience, limited as it was, that there was little point in studying leisure as a series of 'activities'. Rather, we wanted to engage with a whole set of social practices which might be incorporated into a broad definition of leisure, set in the context of women's whole lives. Our desire to do this had immediate implications for the way in which we gathered our data. With hindsight, the decision not to question women directly and solely about their 'leisure', but to ask questions about how their time is structured, about their employment and domestic lives, about preferred activities, and so on, proved extremely fruitful. Our attempts to provide feedback to the research subjects as an integral part of the research process was often difficult or expensive in terms of valuable research time, but we would still insist on the importance of breaking down the traditional distance and hierarchy of the researchers *vis-à-vis* the researched. A final conclusion about method relates to the value of being part of a network of researchers – and practitioners – who are concerned with breaking down some of the boundaries of the 'conventional wisdom' (Clarke and Critcher, 1985).

Whilst our own work has necessarily been exploratory rather than hypothesis-testing in nature, we have been convinced that 'leisure' is extraordinarily resistant to being confined to any one, neat definitional category. This might sound like ducking the issue. It would be heartening, at the level of theory, to be able to provide an adequate definition of this amorphous concept. It still frustrates that we have not achieved this. Leisure is a highly personal and subjective mix of experiences. In women's day-to-day lives its definition shifts, is never static, but blurs into and out of other areas of life. Simultaneously, it is also a highly political concept.

This may seem surprising at first sight, given commonsense understandings about leisure and the freedom to choose how one spends leisure time. Looking at the development of leisure as experience and as ideological construction over time is extremely useful in coming to terms with seeing leisure as rather more than individual personal choice. Looking specifically for leisure for women encounters problems, due to the scant documentation of women's leisure *per se*. Fortunately we have been able to make use of some excellent work done by feminist historians on women's experiences more generally. By supplementing these with leisure histories, community studies and so on, we were able to chronicle some of the changes over time and to point to the centrality of some key issues in the development of leisure as we conceptualise and experience it today.

Despite the changing nature of leisure, it has been consistently divided along lines of gender, as well as by class and race. Our work has to a large extent been culturally and geographically specific. However, it seems reasonable to assert that, as in any other fundamentally patriarchal society, British women occupy a socially and economically inferior position. Their material position and prevailing social definitions of masculinity and femininity have a determining effect on the ways in which we understand and live out our lives, including our leisure. For instance, even women who resist prescriptive definitions of femininity, the family and so on, do so in reaction against them. It is impossible simply to ignore them.

The enduring cultural stereotype of women as carers, which for many women is also a reality, has important repercussions. Women's leisure becomes a particularly low priority, both within households and also in society at large. Our own work, in common with that of other researchers in associated fields, has highlighted issues relating to sexuality, respectability and social control as being of the utmost importance *vis-à-vis* women's leisure. We were surprised as we uncovered more and more evidence of the extent to which women's behaviour is constrained, either by ourselves or by others, in response to norms about appropriate female (and male) behaviour. We were also made aware of the variety of strategies that men employ to restrict women's behaviour. Control by men, either individually or collectively, is not only widely practised; it is also widely held to be a normal feature of everyday life.

None of the above are new phenomena; all have strong antecedents. They force us into questioning seriously any definition of leisure as simply freely chosen individual behaviour. So too does taking account of historical shifts in the provision and consumption of leisure. Much of our work has concentrated on individual women's experiences of leisure. However, there is a need to analyse the interplay between leisure and other areas of life, such as education and work, and crucially its role in the economy.

At the level of provision, we have noted the emergence in the nineteenth century of 'rational recreation', a set of beliefs and practices which operate in a paternalistic way to offer the kinds of leisure deemed to 'improve' the lives of those individuals who are less fortunate (read also less educated, less moral, less cultured or civilised) than the provider. Rational recreation as a philosophy has become enshrined in much leisure provision, be it through public subsidy or private patronage. However, women, unlike (working-class) men, were not usually seen as in need of control or direction in their leisure. Given that women have rarely been considered in their own right, they have been far less subject to the kind of leisure provided by the proponents of rational recreation.

Whatever our reservations about such provision, and they are considerable, the important development of the use of public money to finance recreation was a significant feature, and one which might still be used to women's advantage. However, such provision has always been at best marginal, with most people turning to the commercial sector as the major provider of leisure. Not surprisingly, the drive for profit within the commercial sector has seen the public sector lagging behind and often serving to fill in some of the gaps left by the market. Obviously, commercial leisure provision is about the selling of leisure services and goods to consumers who can afford them. For many women, access to money to spend on leisure is limited or non-existent, so the market has not served women particularly well. However, the drive for new markets, increasingly defined in terms of the 'lifestyle' category so beloved of advertisers, has ensured increased and quite imaginative provision for particular groups of women.

Leisure is undergoing a phase of radical restructuring, which has clear implications for the leisure choices that everyone is able to make. State support for the arts, sport and leisure has never had more than a fairly tenuous foothold, but some enlightened work has been achieved, particularly by the more politically progressive local authorities, in terms of broadening access to leisure facilities. At a time when public spending on the most essential provision, namely health, education and housing, is under concerted attack from central government and when the present arts minister, Richard Luce, publicly espouses the notion that 'if it's any good people will pay for it', what is the future for public leisure provision? Local authorities are selling off their leisure facilities to private companies, libraries are having to consider charging users, many galleries, museums and so on have already had to implement charges. Proposals for the deregulation of broadcasting threaten access not only to entertainment but also to essential information. Many women will simply not be able to buy into ever more commodified leisure.

Certainly, the face of leisure provision is changing, and future prospects are not encouraging. But we should remind ourselves that on the whole leisure provision for women has throughout history been extremely partial, and that women's wider social position has made their access to autonomous leisure generally more difficult than for most men. Despite this, and taking for granted that what we want is for women's needs to be met, we did talk to women who are making real inroads into the male bastions of leisure, and to many others who are managing to claim some time, and pleasure, for themselves in the face of very limited resources. This is not to trivialise the very real difficulties and discrimination women face, but simply to ask if we could build on some of these achievements. Perhaps the next stage is to make visible these achievements and to challenge the restricted definitions of leisure that currently hold centre stage.

## REFERENCES

Clarke, J. and Critcher, C. (1985) *The Devil Makes Work: Leisure in Capitalist Britain* (London: Macmillan).

Deem, R. (1986) *All Work and No Play? The Sociology of Women and Leisure* (Milton Keynes: Open University Press).

Dempsey, K. (1987) 'Gender Inequality: The Exclusion and Exploitation of Women by Men in an Australian Rural Community', paper presented at the First International Congress on the Future of Adult Life, Leeuwenhorst, The Netherlands, April 1987.

Dixey, R. and Talbot, M. (1982) *Women, Leisure and Bingo* (Leeds: Trinity and All Saints College).

*General Household Survey 1983* (1985) (London: HMSO).

Greater London Council Women's Committee (1985) *Women On The Move: GLC Survey on Women and Transport*, no. 3, *Survey Results: Safety, Harassment and Violence* (London: Greater London Council).

Green, E., Hebron, S. and Woodward, D. (1987) *Gender and Leisure: A Study of Sheffield Women's Leisure* (London: The Sports Council).

Hough, M. and Mayhew, P. (1985) *Taking Account of Crime: Key Findings from The 1984 British Crime Survey* (London: HMSO).

NOP Market Research Ltd (1983) 'Leisure Activities', in *Political, Social, Economic Review*, no. 43, September, pp. 12–20.

Whitehead, A. (1976) 'Sexual Antagonism in Herefordshire', in Barker, D. L. and Allen, S. (eds) *Dependence and Exploitation in Work and Marriage* (London: Longman).

Wimbush, E. (1986) *Women, Leisure and Well-Being: Final Report* (Edinburgh: Centre for Leisure Research, Dunfermline College of Physical Education).

Wimbush, E. and Talbot, M. (1988) *Relative Freedoms: Women and Leisure* (Milton Keynes: Open University Press).

Reading taken from E. Green, S. Hebron and D. Woodward, *Women's Leisure, What Leisure?*, published by Macmillan Press Ltd, 1990. Reprinted with permission.

# IIIc Ethnicity and Leisure

# 13 | Body talk: images of sport in a multi-racial school

Bruce Carrington and Edward Wood

The success experienced by West Indian pupils in sport often stands in stark contrast to their failure in the classroom. In view of the *perceived* importance of educational credentials in occupational selection and placement and the low status generally accorded to physical education, it is hardly surprising that there continues to be disquiet within the West Indian community about the often extensive commitments of their children in school sport. Indeed, there are indications that many West Indian parents now believe that their children fail to achieve their full academic potential because they are perceived by teachers as possessing physical rather than cognitive-intellectual abilities, and are thus encouraged to concentrate on activities such as sport at school to the detriment of their academic studies (Lashley, 1980; D.E.S., 1981).

These anxieties prompted us to undertake an exploratory investigation which aimed to identify, describe and analyse the social processes accounting for the different rates of participation between white and West Indian pupils in extra-curricular school sport. This study was conducted over a sixteen-month period during 1980/81 at 'Hillsview Comprehensive School' (pseudonyms have been used throughout the case study.) The School, which serves an almost exclusively working class neighbourhood in an urban centre in Yorkshire, has a pupil population of about 1000 boys and girls, of whom 32% are of West Indian descent and 4% of Asian descent, aged between eleven and sixteen. It was selected for investigation because of its ethnic composition. We felt that since the Asian background popu-

*Sociology of Leisure: A reader.* Edited by C. Critcher, P. Bramham and A. Tomlinson. Published in 1995 by E & FN Spon, London. ISBN 0 419 19420 7.

lation of the School was relatively small, it would be easier to make direct comparisons between West Indian background and white pupils.

A variety of research techniques were employed. Questionnaires were administered to the entire teaching staff and to each pupil in the fourth and fifth years. In-depth, semi-structured, follow-up interviews were undertaken with 46 of the 55 teacher respondents and a heterogeneous sample of 50 pupils which comprised girls and boys, blacks and whites, drawn from both the upper and lower bands. Informal group discussions were arranged with both staff and pupils. Data were also gathered from other sources, namely: lesson observation and consultations with local authority advisory staff, careers officers and teachers in adjacent schools.

An analysis covering all of the sports teams fielded by the School, from first to fifth years – soccer, basketball, rugby, netball, hockey and athletics – showed that West Indian background pupils were 3.7 times more likely to participate in extra-curricular sport than white pupils. We found that most of the white male participants (67%) and almost all of the black female participants (92%) came from the upper academic band. This finding, in itself, is not unusual because a number of studies (albeit based upon ethnically undifferentiated samples) have shown that school teams tend to attract more conformist pupils, that is, pupils often with academic inclinations, who are more readily able to identify with the school as an institution (Hendry and Thorpe, 1977). Many of the West Indian background male team members, however, did not fulfil these criteria, for 68% came from the lower band and, of these, there was a substantial proportion of disaffected pupils who seemed to reject most aspects of schooling except for sport.

From the standpoint that black sports success cannot be accounted for in naturalistic terms, the following questions were explored in relation to these findings: (1) Were West Indian background pupils more successful at sport than white pupils because teachers tended to stereotype them as having skills of the body rather than skills of the mind? (2) To what extent did teachers nurture the interests of this ethnic group in sport, especially disaffected black males in the lower band, for purposes of social control? (3) Were West Indian background pupils encouraged by teachers to develop their sporting abilities in the hope that success in one sphere of school activity would compensate for failure in others? (4) Moreover, if West Indian background pupils were channelled into school sport for these, or other, reasons, why were so many apparently willing to cooperate with this channelling? (5) Were West Indian background pupils overrepresented in school sport teams because a significant proportion of the group had internalised the stereotype of black physical prowess and sports superiority? (6) Did sport hold any particular cultural significance for this group? (7) To what extent did West Indian background pupils identify with the achievements of prominent sports personalities, such as Daley Thompson,

Sonia Lannaman, Garth Crooks et al., who as symbols of black success now provide role models for this sector of youth? (8) Were West Indian background pupils more likely than white pupils to hold aspirations of a career in sport? Was there a tendency for the former, rather than the latter, group to perceive sport as providing an avenue of social mobility and an alternative to menial wage-labour or the dole queue? (9) To what extent was the high level of West Indian involvement in extra-curricular sport symptomatic of the growth of 'ethnic-consciousness' among this group? That is, did West Indian background pupils look upon school sport as their own ethnic-territory and seek to exclude other pupils from it?

Our investigations suggested that very few teachers at Hillsview School gave the impression of being overtly hostile to ethnic minorities or 'intentionally racist' in terms of their attitudes or behaviour. Many, in fact, came across as 'liberal-minded' and genuinely concerned with the well-being of pupils irrespective of their colour or ethnic background. Notwithstanding this, however, there were teachers (including some *who regarded themselves as non-racist or even anti-racist*) who behaved in a manner which could be described as 'racist in consequence rather than intent' (Wellman, 1977). Their responses to the question 'Do you vary your approach in the classroom to suit pupils of different ethnic backgrounds?' indicated that they held lower expectations of West Indian background pupils and were prepared to tolerate poorer standards of academic work and behaviour from this ethnic group. The following teachers' comments are typical of this genre:

> I attempt to give West Indians room for manoeuvre when they are not conforming. I give them as much oral work as possible because even the able West Indians become agitated when not writing well.

> West Indian children dislike doing helpful tasks, as they consider one is treating them as slaves. . . . I am prepared to accept louder or noisier behaviour from West Indian pupils than Asians or other groups.

Undoubtedly there were teachers at Hillsview School who operated with a framework of racial stereotypes which influenced both their attitudes and behaviour towards West Indian background pupils as a group. On several occasions in interview teachers described this group as 'lacking in ability', 'unable to concentrate', 'indolent', 'insolent', 'disruptive', 'aggressive', and 'disrespectful of authority'. Although teachers often expressed negative opinions about the behaviour and academic abilities of West Indian pupils, their comments about the abilities of this group in low-status, practical activities were frequently laudatory. West Indian background pupils were variously described as having a 'well developed sense of artistic ability' or 'greater athletic prowess than white pupils', and as being 'ideal for dance and drama' or 'capable of achieving better results physically than academically'. Furthermore, when invited to comment upon the high level of involvement in extra-curricular sport by West Indian background pupils, several teachers made explicit references to what have been characterised as 'the physiological myths surrounding black athletic success' (Gallop and Dolan, 1981). Among this group of teachers there were some who not only perceived West Indian background pupils as having superior physical endowments and skills (and who rationalised the athletic success of this group in stereotypical terms), but who also looked upon sport as providing an appropriate channel for compensating these supposedly 'motor-minded' pupils for their academic failure. We were informed that:

The physique of West Indian children generally, would appear to be in line with getting better results at sport. (Humanities teacher)

West Indians are superior in the power that they can generate compared to white kids. They seem to possess better musculature and don't have the fat you often find on a British kid. (Science and P. E. teacher)

Sport gives them (West Indian pupils) a chance of success. Whereas they're not successful in the classroom they can show their abilities on the sports field. (Humanities teacher)

It became apparent during the course of our investigation that some pupils had internalised these stereotypes of black athletic prowess and physical superiority, or shared their teachers' low expectations of their academic abilities. For example, when asked to account for the distinguished record of the School in sport, one West Indian background pupil remarked:

It's because of the coloured blood. If it wasn't for the coloured blood our school wouldn't be as good as it is.

Another seemed to have some cognisance of the effects of stereotyping and channelling. He explained that

in this School most coloured people *believe* they're better at sport than white people. . . . Also *sports success is encouraged by teachers.* (Emphasis added)

Other pupils, black and white alike, in common with their teachers, suggested that the athletic and academic records of the school were closely interrelated; Hillsview pupils were 'winners' on the sportsfield because they were frequently 'losers' in the classroom! According to Karen, a West Indian background pupil who had participated regularly in extra-curricular netball, hockey, basketball and athletics,

> Many pupils at this school are not very bright. You don't have to
> think about sport – the body does all the work.

Andrew, a white non-participant, expressed similar views. He informed us:

> Hillsview's pupils are not very clever academically, so they concentrate
> on sport where only physical fitness is essential and excel.

There were indications that teachers cultivated the involvement of disaffected, non-conformist pupils in extra-curricular sport for purposes of social control. Furthermore, insofar as West Indian background pupils were often perceived by teachers as having superior physical endowments and skills and singled-out as creating specific disciplinary problems, the chances of a West Indian background pupil being 'sidetracked' into sport were probably greater than those of his/her white peers. Whereas one of the school rules stated unequivocally that non-attenders and disruptive pupils would be barred from school teams, it was apparent that this rule was interpreted with a good deal of flexibility. As one teacher admitted when asked 'Are badly behaved pupils or truants allowed to play in the school teams?'

> Yes – I've let such pupils off detention to play in a team, even though
> there's a formal school rule which says they should not play.

Other teachers also indicated that they felt that the sanctions normally taken out against the non-conformist pupil might be waived in the case of a team member and seemed to advocate an 'unspoken truce' with disaffected pupils, whom they believed ought to be encouraged to play in school teams. Whilst some justified this practice in the belief that success in sport would serve to compensate low-achievers for academic failure, others sponsored the involvement of such pupils in school teams in the hope that it would enable them to identify more closely with the school as an institution.

> Once you reject them it's difficult to get them back. Kids are kept in
> the mainstream through sport at school because, at least for a short
> period of time, they're accepting the rules which the school has laid
> down.

Many pupils appeared to be aware of this 'unspoken truce'. As Alex, a West Indian background rugby player intimated:

> Sometimes you're stopped from playing for legging it – but if you
> come late or muck around in the corridors, you're still allowed to
> play.

Similarly, a member of the soccer team contended:

> Most of the teachers and the headteacher are not bothered about

truanting – but you've got to be in school on Friday if there's a game on Saturday.

In addition to the indirect forms of sponsorship referred to above, some direct pressure was placed upon pupils to participate in school teams. This usually came from the P.E. staff themselves, or from other teachers who assisted with coaching. On most occasions, teachers appeared to rely on their powers of persuasion when recruiting players for teams. However, on others more coercive means were employed!

Female staff, cognisant of the disdain shown by many adolescent girls for team sports – though not necessarily aware of the reasons for this – said that they had made certain concessions to team members to ensure their continued support. Girls, it appeared, were no longer compelled to participate in the time-honoured ritual of communal bathing after the match!

Several pupils, mostly West Indian background, reported that P.E. staff had pressurised them to take part in school teams. One West Indian background girl said a games teacher 'nagged' her incessantly until she finally agreed to play hockey. Another black pupil recounted the following:

That P.E. teachers kept on telling me how good I was at running. They worked on (persuaded) me to get along to athletic practice even though I didn't like the idea.

Sometimes consensual methods were abandoned in favour of force, as Ronald, a West Indian background pupil, with commitments in several sports teams explained:

Teachers kept pushin' me around (when I was) in the first year. They threatened to lower my report if I didn't play.

Some pupils, however, told how they resisted such force. Gary, a white school rejector, recalled an incident where a teacher had 'asked' him to play in the rugby team.

He used to threaten me by saying he'd give me a bad report and by thumping me and twisting my arms. . . .

but added defiantly,

I only turned up for one game.

Let us now consider in more detail the reasons given by pupils for their involvement in, or rejection of, extra-curricular sport. . . .

Both black and white female participants tended to stress the social dimensions of sport and said that playing in a school team gave them an opportunity to be with their friends. A few found the competitive aspect stimulating or indicated that they 'played for fun' or 'to keep fit'. Of those interviewed, Jenny, a white pupil, was alone in perceiving extra-curricular sport as an important channel for the fulfilment of her achievement needs. She told us that she enjoyed representing the school in athletics because:

> If you win, you at least know you're good at one thing.

Many girls said that they participated because they were 'proud to represent the school' or wanted 'to do something to help the school'. The impression gained of the majority of female participants was of conformist pupils firmly ensconced within the consensual fold of the school.

It came as no surprise that boys, from each ethnic group, tended to look upon sport as an appropriate channel through which to express their masculinity, enhance their male identities and maintain contacts with their peers. As one boy responded when asked why he played soccer for the school:

> It's a real man's game, that's all.

The boys tended to stress the cathartic value of sport, claiming that it 'helped them to wind down', 'relax' or 'relieve tensions'. Invariably, with a significant proportion of male participants, especially those of West Indian background, drawn from the lower academic band, the boys were more likely than the girls to look upon sport as providing an alternative to the boredom, frustration and failure which many experienced in the classroom. Predictably the boys gave greater emphasis than the girls to the competitive aspects of sport, saying they 'enjoyed the challenge', 'liked the spirit of competition' or found it 'fun to meet and beat other schools'. Fewer boys expressed mainstream-conformist sentiments when accounting for their involvement in sports teams. According to David, a West Indian background rugby and soccer player:

> There's little winning for the school at heart. You're winning for the team – the school has very little part.

Disaffected white pupils at Hillsview tended to spurn extra-curricular sport, even though many of the boys spent much of their spare time playing soccer or Rugby League. Their rejection of school sport was allied to their rejection of school *per se*. Thus, Paul summed up the feelings of this group, when he said:

> I'm good enough to play in the football team – but I just don't bother to. . . . Sport is just another subject after school.

Unlike Paul and many of his white peers in the lower band, a substantial caucus of disaffected black youth played regularly in school teams, even though their responses to other facets of school and schooling appeared ambivalent or negative. In contrast to their white counterparts, these pupils appeared to regard sport as qualitatively different from other school activities. As Roy, a West Indian background rugby player with an undistinguished academic record who, it seemed, was at war with the school explained:

> I take part because I'm forced to do so. Rugby isn't like lessons. If you're sitting in the back of the class you're picked on . . . but if you're playing rugby it's of your own free will.

How is this differential response to be interpreted? Could it be that disaffected black pupils were less likely to eschew extra-curricular school sport because their rejection of school was not as complete as their white peers (Bird *et al.*, 1981)? Was the high rate of participation among West Indian background pupils due, in part, to the apparent lack of competition from white pupils? Did West Indian background pupils have, in effect, easy access to an almost 'deserted field'?

Furthermore, there was evidence to suggest that the apparent willingness of many black pupils at Hillsview School to participate in extra-curricular physical activities could also be related to the growth of ethnic consciousness among this sector of youth. There were signs that black pupils looked upon sport as providing an opportunity to 'colonise' one major area of school activity and to make it their own. Indeed, there were indications, not only from the school staff but from pupils, black and white alike, that West Indian background pupils had 'colonised' school sport and regarded the sports field as their territory. A variety of strategies were deployed to control this territory. According to one West Indian background team member, Joanne:

> In some teams the coloured girls are right nasty. They shout at the white girls, who drop out because they're frightened that we will make life uncomfortable for them.

Other black pupils, like Alex, informed us that pupils often played a part in team selection and that

> white lads were frequently overlooked unless they were friendly with coloured lads in the team.

There could be little doubt that racial boundaries at the school had become more sharply delineated as a result of the sponsorship of West Indian involvement in sport. Whilst the boycotting of extra-curricular sport by some white pupils could be read as a manifestation of working class resistance to schooling, with others it was more directly related to racial considerations. Moreover it could be argued that racism within this sector of the school population played an important part in determining the ethnic composition of the sports teams. As one white pupil conceded:

There's a lot of prejudice at this school. . . . Some kids won't play for the school because they just don't like West Indians.

Despite their heavy commitments in school teams and although some had internalised black athletes as their personal heroes, none of the West Indian background pupils approached during the course of the research seemed to endorse the chimerical notion of professional sport as a *viable* channel for social advancement. Whereas a few male pupils (7 black and 11 whites), when asked 'if you could have any job in the world what would it be?' indicated that they held fantasies of a career in sport (usually soccer), only one (a white youth) appeared to perceive this as a *real* option.

In conclusion, an attempt has been made to show that the overrepresentation of West Indian background pupils in school sports teams is *in part* the outcome of channelling by teachers who have a tendency to view this ethnic group in stereotypical terms, as having skills of the body rather than skills of the mind and as creating specific disciplinary problems. As we have seen, teachers sponsored the involvement of these allegedly 'motor minded' pupils in sport, and utilised, particularly in the case of non-academic black males, extra-curricular sports involvement as a mechanism of social control. This form of sponsorship may have several undesirable consequences. As Cashmore (1982) has suggested, black pupils may become so immersed in their sport, or sports, that they sometimes neglect their academic work. Indeed sports involvement could be said to detract from academic goals when P.E. teachers and coaches make excessive playing and training demands upon participants. Two of our West Indian background respondents, both from the upper academic band, were cognisant of this problem. Clyde, a participant in several school teams until the fourth year, who was entered for nine 'O' levels, explained:

I dropped out last year because I think my education is more important than school teams.

Similarly, Jenny informed us:

I feel that teachers select the ones who are good at sport and train them to a high standard. But I feel in doing this the child is falling back academically.

Although it is conceivable that some black participants in the upper band may have neglected their studies as a result of their extensive commitments in sport, this was less likely to have occurred with their peers in the lower band. As we have attempted to show, various concessions were made to sidetrack pupils into sport, *who had already been 'cooled-out' of the academic mainstream*. Disaffected black males, in particular, were encouraged to promote their sporting abilities in the belief that sports success by compensating for academic failure, would make them more amenable to the School as an institution. The shortcomings of this coping strategy are self evident: (1) It serves to reinforce both academic failure and unacceptable behaviour. (2) Insofar as the opportunities for success in school sport are restricted, it also denies many non-academic pupils even the consolation of an alternative to academic failure! (3) It can result in an intensification of interracial rivalries and conflict.

At Hillsview School, at least, sport *does not* provide a vehicle for promoting racial harmony and integration. Clearly multi-racial Britain is *not* winning together!

## REFERENCES

Bird, C. *et al. Disaffected Pupils.* Report to D.E.S. by the Education Studies Unit, Brunel University, 1981.

Cashmore, E. *Black Sportsmen*, R.K.P., 1982.

Department of Education and Science. *Interim Report of the Committee of Inquiry into the Education of Children from Ethnic Minority Groups (The Rampton Report)*, London, HMSO, 1981.

Gallop, G. and Dolan, J. 'Perspectives on the Participation in Sporting Recreation amongst Minority Group Youngsters.' *Physical Education Review* 4(1) p. 61–64, 1981.

Hendry, L. and Thorpe, E. 'Pupils' Choice, Extra Curricular Activities: a Critique of Hierarchical Authority.' *Int. Rev. of Sports Soc.* 4(12), p. 39–49, 1977.

Lashley, H. 'The New Black Magic', *British Journal of Physical Education* 2(1), p. 5–6, 1980.

Wellman, D. *Portraits of White Racism*, New York, Cambridge University Press, 1977.

## FURTHER READING

Carrington, B. 'Sport as a Sidetrack' in Barton L. and Walker, S. (eds) *Race, Class and Education*, Croom Helm, 1983.

Reading taken from B. Carrington and E. Wood, *Journal of Multiracial Education*, 2(2), 29–38, published by the Commission for Racial Equality, 1983. Reprinted with permission.

# 14 | Gender, race and power: the challenge to youth work practice

Prathibha Parmar

## INVISIBLE YOUTH

Writings on and about the 'problems' of Black youth have been prolific in the recent past. Much intellectual and practical energy has been spent on analysing the nature of the 'youth crisis' of the 1980s. The debate and its manifestations in various disciplines of sociology and education rotates around the significance or otherwise of youth's challenges to the growth of authoritarian statism.

The riots of 1981 have, in turn, encouraged many local and national state initiatives in the form of *ad hoc* youth projects which make desperate attempts to contain the growing frustrations of unemployed Black young people, yet the experiences of young Black women are predictably absent from these debates and initiatives. . . .

When young Black women are visible it is in a negative and 'pathological' manner. While young women of Afro-Caribbean origin are seen as potentially 'at risk' through a lack of discipline and because of an uncontrollable sexuality which results in unwanted pregnancies, young Asian women are seen as either too meek and mild or as rebelling against their unreasonably backward and tradition-bound parents who insist on such 'barbaric' practices as arranged marriages. . . .

Asian women are identified as failures because of their lack of English, and their refusal to integrate by adopting English eating, dressing and

*Sociology of Leisure: A reader*. Edited by C. Critcher, P. Bramham and A. Tomlinson. Published in 1995 by E & FN Spon, London. ISBN 0 419 19420 7.

speaking habits is seen as the cause of the problems their children experience.

On another level, the Asian family is both condemned for its repressive togetherness and praised for a stability which all would like to emulate. The apparent stability and close-knit nature of the Asian family is often used to deprecate the Afro-Caribbean family – a double standard of representation which is a potential source of disunity amongst the different Black communities. . . .

The danger of such common-sense images of arranged marriage continuing to dominate official perceptions of the Asian family is that this will systematically distort the delivery of public services and resources to a particular group in society, namely, young Asian women.

The following section offers a detailed look at the experiences of Asian girls and young women within educational and recreational institutions. The arguments are based on the findings of a three-year action research project which aimed to identify and meet the needs of young Asian women.

## WORKING WITH ASIAN YOUNG WOMEN

Asian young women have too often been wrongly stereotyped as meek, mild and docile people. This 'common-sense' racist thinking has implications for the way in which many of them are denied access to educational and recreational resources as well as contributing to their experiences of racism in schools. . . .

Such views result in many young Asian women being denied adequate careers counselling, and being prevented from going on school trips and taking part in other school activities. Our work with Asian girls and young women has challenged existing myths and stereotypes about them and our findings indicate the direction in which future work with Asian girls needs to develop.

Our primary role was that of youth workers working specifically with Asian girls and from the outset we both experienced problems with the ways in which professional individuals and agencies perceived us. The majority of the 'caring/helping' agencies and individuals in schools and colleges saw us as social workers/counsellors who would help them to sort out their problems with 'their' Asian girls. . . .

This deep-rooted and pervasive pathologising of Asian cultures and Asian family structures was the biggest obstacle in our attempts to develop youth work activities with Asian girls. The general climate when we began our work was one where many agencies did not recognise the need to develop youth work with Asian girls, while others, whose thoughts were confined within the stereotyped framework of 'culture conflicts' and 'generation gaps', believed that in a couple of decades all 'problems' would be solved as the second generation became assimilated into British society and there was, therefore, little point in doing anything in the present.

The emphasis of our work with Asian girls is, and always has been, to facilitate the positive development of cultural, racial and sexual conscious- ness through activities in a relaxed, non-threatening and non-intimidating atmosphere. In separate Asian girls' groups there is no fear of being sneered at or having to take a secondary role so as not to attract attention because of being 'different'. Despite the fact that girls are often from different cultural backgrounds there are common experiences, perceptions and situations which create a strong, uniting bond amongst them. However, the girls are still subjected to name-calling and jeering taunts from White youth of both sexes because they choose to form an all-Asian girls' group. We, in turn, as workers, have to struggle against the resistance of teachers and youth workers towards separate provision. Even in situations where they are sympathetic we have to take care that we are not being used as an excuse for non-action in this area by White teachers or youth workers and that our work is not used to cover up for their gaps and shortcomings.

We made contact initially with girls and young women through many different channels, such as community and religious organisations, Youth Training Schemes, neighbourhood groups, schools and colleges. While each channel had its own positive and negative features, we could not say that any one channel was the 'correct' one – it was the method of work rather than the channel which determined the success of each group.

## GIRLS' GROUPS IN SCHOOLS

Through descriptions of our experiences of initiating Asian girls' groups in schools we want to highlight the ways in which Asian girls' experiences at school reflect the general racism prevalent in society today. The negative 'common-sense' notions of Asian girls that White society generally has are to be found in some White teachers' attitudes towards them, and in the actions of White students in either ignoring them, or throwing racist abuse, or attempting to beat them up.

Schools were a formal means of gaining access to Asian girls and contact was usually made with the heads of schools which had been identified as having a substantial number of Asian pupils. . . .

The final decisions regarding which schools we should choose to initiate groups in depended on the reception we received from the school authori- ties and on the attitudes of the teachers towards our work. Some schools welcomed our approach not so much because they understood why this was necessary but more out of their need to be seen as practising 'progress- ive multi-cultural policies'. One college only accepted us after they realised that they would be gaining an extra, unpaid member of staff, as a result of timetabling the Asian girls' group as part of a General Studies class.

When the groups met at lunchtime or after school hours, they were affected by the school environment in a negative way. We often had to meet in classrooms, which didn't help to break down the traditional teacher/pupil relationship. We were also sometimes seen as part of a school-initiated project and we had to work hard at creating an informal and non-authoritarian relationship with the girls. Meeting at lunchtimes often meant being disturbed and having racist abuse shouted at us by White students. . . .

Other problems we experienced include the non-acceptance of the groups by some teachers and other school staff such as cleaners, who resented our presence outside school hours. Some of the groups we worked with were not accepted by the school unless teachers were involved, and many of the young Asian women were not able to relax in their presence. One of the major problems we had was from hostile teachers who accused us of being 'racist' because we held separate Asian girls' groups. . . .

We rejected the common approach to work with Asian girls which identified them as a problem group. Most projects set up to look at the special needs of Asian girls have been premised on the fact that this section of the Black community is increasingly becoming a problem for their parents, their schools, and for White society generally.

## GIRLS' WORK IN YOUTH CLUBS

Work with Asian girls is always seen as being 'problem-centred'. We are expected to help girls with their supposedly innumerable problems at home and as long as we don't mention the fact that very often the problems Asian girls have are nothing to do with their families, but more to do with the racism they experience at school from teachers and pupils alike, then peace will reign. Even when we do persist in challenging the idea that the source of the problem is not Asian cultural habits, but the institutional racism of British society, which prevents Asian girls having an equal share of the provisions that exist, our Youth Service colleagues turn a blind eye.

If we link work with Black youth, and Asian girls in particular, to the history of the Youth Service's attitudes *vis-à-vis* work with girls generally, there are many similarities. It is the White male worker who is always seen to be the so-called provider at the club and instigator of activities, that is, the controller. It is he who determines the level, if any, of decision-making that young people are involved in. He encourages the girls to remain 'invisible' or at most peripheral to the activities of the youth club. In fact, 'girls' are seen as an alternative activity for the boys, an activity fostered by the youth workers' attitudes. . . .

Reactions to girls' work initiatives such as girls-only evenings at clubs are seen as a threat to the White male ego, as are initiatives by Black youth. . . .

Both girls and Black youth are demanding equality of opportunity with the majority of people who frequent youth clubs, that is, White boys. As they are seen to be a strong group with a collective consciousness concerning their own situation and status within the wider society, they inevitably threaten the status of existing structures.

Youth work with Asian girls is seen by the Youth Service as supplementary social education for youth at risk, and therefore not necessarily the responsibility of the Youth Service. . . .

So, if our work doesn't fit in with the standard evening youth club times, and instead we want groups to meet in the early evening, that is, after school or during the lunch break at school, then we are not doing youth work but social work or counselling and, therefore, the Youth Service wants no responsibility for it. However, having a disco on three nights a week seems to constitute youth work in some Youth Service clubs. It seems that while all agencies working with Black youth, especially in the Youth Service, make youth fit into existing provision, their real needs will not be met. It is only when more young people themselves make their demands heard that many feel their needs will finally be met: national and local government call these cries 'riots'.

For Asian girls and young women, being a section of the Black community and being female has a double disadvantage. The Youth Service must begin to change not only its ethnocentric approach but also its gender bias if it is to adequately meet the needs of Asian girls.

## WHY SEPARATE PROVISION IS NEEDED FOR ASIAN GIRLS

Having explored the concept and practices of the youth service and its provision, it is quite clear that the existing structure and functioning of the Youth Service is not suited to meeting the needs of Asian girls. There are a number of reasons, therefore, why it is necessary to direct and organise youth work activities with and for Asian girls and young women separately from White girls and boys.

First, separate provision is required because of the 'special' needs that Asian girls have: needs which are different from those of male Asian youth and White male and female youth. These needs arise primarily from their position as determined by their race, age, class and gender. It is the way in which their identities and experiences are influenced by these structural factors that determine their access to various resources and facilities not only within the Youth Service but also more widely in society. So the specific needs of Asian girls are primarily not about whether they have facilities to play table tennis or football, or to go canoeing, but it must be assured that facilities suitable to their needs *are* made available outside the conventional youth clubs environment in which the activities are dominated by White boys and girls. There is also a need for a more fundamental concern about how the Youth Service and other institutions can ensure that they, the Asian girls, have an equal share of the youth work provision. To do this the Youth Service needs to encourage and recognise more innovative types of youth work such as, for example, girls meeting at each other's homes to do group activities. One way of legitimising this style of detached youth work would be to channel resources for workers and activities to develop work in this area. This shows how an institution should change, and not how a specific client group should change, in order to fit in with existing structures and provisions. Separate groups and clubs for Asian girls can provide, in the short term at least, a redressing and more equal distribution of resources and facilities for the recreational and social educational needs of Asian girls.

General leisure and recreational facilities are geared towards meeting the needs of White male youth, thus excluding other sections of youth in society. Because the Youth Service is not free from the racism of other institutions in society, it is clear that racist attitudes and structures which are prevalent in such areas as education and social services are also present in the Youth Service. Asian girls-only groups provide an atmosphere free from threat and intimidation from White youth, making it possible to facilitate the development of a positive cultural, racial and sexual identity. Such groups provide the space and opportunity for the girls to meet in a comfortable and tension-free environment, giving girls and young women the opportunity of acquiring skills necessary to cope with the consequences of the racism they face daily, skills they are not taught or given a chance to develop by the institutions they pass through, such as schools, colleges and employment schemes. By virtue of being together, with a shared heritage, there is no fear on their part that they will be looked down upon or that their conversations about their favourite Indian film star, the latest Asian film or song, and so on will have to be carried out surreptitiously in case the English girls and/or boys mock them. So, although the activities, the programme and the content of our face-to-face work may or may not be that different from work with White girls, it is the methods of work with which these activities are carried out that is crucial.

The term 'youth club' occasionally has unacceptable connotations for Asian parents. Clubs are seen to be places where there is smoking, drinking, gambling and dancing and also places where girls and boys mix freely with each other. Although it was found through our contact with parents that sometimes this was the reason for their reluctance to send their daughters to youth clubs, there was another crucial reason which is not acknowledged and this was their fear that their daughters may be victims of attacks on the streets – not only sexual attacks but also racial ones. There has been a rise in the number of street attacks on Asian people and there is a legitimate fear amongst the Asian communities that they are a target for these acts of racist violence. Therefore, the precautions the Asian parents take in not allowing their daughters to venture too far away from their homes in the evenings are necessary precautions determined by real fears. In a situation where Asian parents see hostile forces attempting to alienate their children from them and their cultural traditions it is important to allay their fears. Our findings show that it is essential for parents to be consulted and their trust to be gained. If Asian parents feel that their authority is being questioned and their cultural values are being challenged by unsympathetic outsiders, they are justified in being suspicious of anyone who wants to involve their daughters in activities outside the home. Legitimate activities on premises approved of by parents and organised by women they have come to know and trust have been proved to be acceptable.

## WHO SHOULD DO THE WORK?

We believe that there is a fundamental necessity for Asian women to do youth work with Asian girls and young women. There are several reasons for this: initially it is because we share similar linguistic, cultural, religious and social backgrounds; and we are also affected by the racism prevalent in our daily encounters and therefore understand exactly what these experiences feel like.

It is because of this dual experience of belonging to minority groups and the resulting racism that we are better able to understand the girls' experiences. We, too, are caught in the evolutionary processes of political, social and cultural changes taking place within the Black communities and therefore have a much better grasp of 'conflict' as individuals. More importantly, communication between us and the parents is not patronising; we do not, like most White workers, make judgements concerning the norms and values upheld by the girls and their families. This, of course, determines the quality of the relationship that the worker and the family can build up. Being Asian, we see the lifestyles of the girls as valid and we do not hold the typical Western view of Asian family life as being oppressive to girls and young women.

In conclusion, we would emphasise that work with Asian girls and young women requires a different approach, method and conceptualisation of youth work practice. There needs to be acceptance, without having to continuously justify the validity of youth work with young Asian women which is not necessarily club-based. Funding for work with Asian girls must not depend on the extent to which it is problem-centred and crisis-orientated. A variety of different projects such as organising festivals, residential courses, adventure weekends, holiday schemes, day trips, and so on, should be encouraged by provision of adequate funds by the Youth Service. Too often, Asian girls, like other young Black women are totally ignored while funding for work with girls goes to White girls and funding for work with Black youth goes to Black young men. There needs to be greater awareness by the educational and recreational institutions of the need for separate provisions for work with young Asian women. This is the only way forward for Asian young women to develop a confidence and consciousness as young Black women in British society.

## CONCLUSION

The findings outlined above seriously and systematically undermine the theoretical and politically established forms and practices in this field. A serious implication of these findings is the need to re-evaluate existing forms of training for youth work practitioners.

The challenge of anti-racist and anti-sexist youth work practices cannot be ignored. Feminist youth workers' interventions in the field have sharply focused on the experiences of groups of young women hitherto ignored: work with young Black women, young lesbians, and disabled young women are areas where many of the 'norms' in youth work practice and training have been questioned.

A consideration of the multiple oppressions operating in society not only challenges the assumptions upon which much of the available Youth Service is based but also necessitates a look at the 'crisis' conditions under which the Youth Service is attempting to survive.

Youth work practice cannot be carried out in a vacuum and what is being demanded is the recognition that the oppressive power systems that operate in wider society also operate within the Youth Service itself. Training is an essential part of the service and the reluctance to integrate issues of race, gender and sexuality into the overall framework of youth workers' training courses has serious consequences not only for youth workers but also for the youth they are supposed to be reaching.

In the long run, if these issues are not taken up and serious attempts made to change the fundamental premise and ethos of youth work theory and practice, the youth service will remain irrelevant to the changing needs of young people in society. Ultimately, its inflexibility and inability to change can only be interpreted as its unwillingness to make the space for radical interventions, thus aligning itself with the state's attempts to control and manipulate young people's anger and resistance.

## NOTE

The research project was carried out jointly with Nadira Mirza and . . . first published in *GEN*, Women and Education Group, no. 1, July 1983.

See Parmar, (P.) (1981) 'Young Asian Women: A Critique of the Pathological Approach', *Multi-Racial Education*, vol. 9, no. 3.

Reading taken from P. Cohen and H. S. Bains (eds), *Multi-racist Britain*, published by Macmillan Press Ltd, 1989. Reprinted with permission.

# Activities

**INTERPRETATIVE EXERCISES**

1. Choose one activity from each of the following leisure forms: sport, arts, gambling, tourism, shopping, media consumption. Discuss the ways in which class divisions and distinctions express themselves.
2. How do the concepts of 'masculinity' and 'femininity' enhance your understanding of the following:
   (a) sport and sporting performance
   (b) friendships and sexuality
   (c) body image
   (d) film and music styles
   (e) health and fitness
   (f) alcohol and drug use/abuse.
3. Construct a model to illustrate the main factors which make people 'drop in' and 'drop out' of sports and physical activities.
4. Contact your local authority leisure services and ask them about their policies towards the following groups: ethnic minorities, women and the unemployed.
5. List the ways in which alcohol consumption is related to people's leisure.


**ESSAYS**

1. Critically evaluate the explanations suggested for **either** the prominence of Afro-Caribbean males in competitive sport **or** the apparent failure of the youth service to cater adequately for the leisure needs of Asian girls.
2. How convinced are you that white middle-class males are the most privileged group in leisure?
3. 'Sociologists have overemphasized the importance of social class in understanding leisure in the UK.' Discuss.

4. What contribution has feminist analysis made to your understanding of leisure?
5. 'Racism is a central feature of the leisure experience of black people in the UK.' Discuss.
6. 'The concept of youth must be interrogated by the processes of class, race and gender. Nothing illustrates this more clearly than youth leisure life-styles'. Discuss.
7. What evidence is there to suggest there is 'a harried leisure class' in the UK?

# PART FOUR

# Types of Leisure Provision

# Introduction

It has become customary to talk of three main types of leisure provision: commercial, voluntary and public. Debates about leisure policy have often prioritized public forms of provision by central and local government, aimed at the appropriate community focus. Many leisure centres, for instance, have been developed by the local governmental machine, for the good of the community, and often with the grant-aided assistance of the national or regional Sports Council. But commercial provision has continued to offer leisure possibilities to individual, discrete and mass markets, and to compete successfully for the leisure consumer. Bingo, pubs, home video, the cinema, new shopping experiences, theme parks – all of these, albeit aided and facilitated by planning processes and sometimes new forms of partnership in the public sector, have been provided predominantly by commercial providers. Millions of people form their own leisure in clubs and voluntary groups, too, exerting an informed and potentially autonomous form of control over their own leisure experiences and culture.

It is too crude and simplistic to talk of these sources of provision as separate sectors. The mathematical or military metaphor is too sharp, implying too rigid a distinction. For in actuality the types of provision can overlap – clubs play badminton in municipal facilities or meet for committee meetings in public-house function rooms. Voluntary groupings of specialist leisure consumers can create particular markets for the specialist output of, say, the CB radio enthusiast, or for the public exhibition of anything from the cabbage to the household cat. The forms of organization within leisure might therefore be quite varied and complex. But the process of production of the leisure experience, facility or organization will usually be anchored in a particular type of provision. The readings in this section are organized on this basis.

In the Thompson piece the production end of the package holiday

*Sociology of Leisure: A reader.* Edited by C. Critcher, P. Bramham and A. Tomlinson. Published in 1995 by E & FN Spon, London. ISBN 0 419 19420 7.

phenomenon is the main focus. Smith's material looks at the consumption end of the leisure process, examining the various ways in which pubs have emerged, and focusing in more detail upon one particular type of pub.

Bishop and Hoggett reveal the range of forms of what they call organized enthusiasms, and Finnegan describes in evocative ethnographic detail one form of music-making in an English town.

The Wilson piece overviews the politics of leisure provision, and Whannel's chapter evaluates the role of public sector agencies and the state in the development of leisure policy, using the focused example of sport.

# IVa Commercial Provision

# 15 If you can't stand the heat get off the beach: the UK holiday business

Grahame F. Thompson

In the autumn of 1985 a fierce battle emerged between United Kingdom holiday firms in an effort to enhance their share of the 1986 summer holiday market. This involved in particular two 'market leaders', Thomson Holidays and Intasun Holidays. Each began to cut prices, implicitly challenging the others to follow in a tit-for-tat sequence. Anything between 30 per cent and 60 per cent was being cut from the price of holidays. Some of Thomson's holidays to Spain sold for only £25 a week or £35 for two weeks, and 500 Intasun Holidays were offered for £39 each. Partly as a protest at these 'irresponsible' price reductions NAT Travel, a smaller holiday firm, introduced a ten-day coach/camping holiday for £5 at one stage. People were seen queuing overnight outside travel agents to be able to cash in on a £20 holiday for four! The holiday sale season (some would argue 'silly season') was on. But behind these bravado tactics lay some intriguing and important features of the development of both United Kingdom holiday firms and of the United Kingdom economy itself. It is these features that are explored in this chapter. While the 1985/6 period forms the focus of my analysis this particular episode should not be seen as unique in the context of the United Kingdom holiday industry. In the early 1970s something of a similar competitive battle emerged in which a series of well known holiday firms at the time either collapsed or got into severe financial difficulties (Clarksons, Horizon Midland, Court Line amongst others). It was confidently predicted that some firms, particularly

*Sociology of Leisure: A reader.* Edited by C. Critcher, P. Bramham and A. Tomlinson. Published in 1995 by E & FN Spon, London. ISBN 0 419 19420 7.

the smaller ones, would also go out of business as a consequence of the 1985 round of price cutting. (This was trumpeted under the holiday industry's unofficial motto 'if you can't stand the heat, get off the beach'.) Indeed, in 1984 some eighteen smallish tour operators failed and in late 1984 an important firm, Budget Travel (the tenth largest at the time) also suddenly went out of business. Pundits of the travel scene were heard suggesting (and exaggerating) that as many as 200 to 300 travel firms could go bankrupt if things went badly. In the following sections the components, structure, and tendencies involved with the firms making up the holiday industry are analysed; and recent competitive battles are reviewed.

## THE STRUCTURE OF THE INDUSTRY

The United Kingdom tourist industry was worth £11 billion in 1986, half of which was spent on the 10.5 million overseas inclusive tour holidays taken and 7 million independently organized overseas visits. There were approximately 700 firms offering holidays of some kind to consumers in the United Kingdom in 1986. However, most of these were very small organizations only arranging a few hundred or perhaps a few thousand holidays a year. The twelve largest companies in mid-1984 are shown in Table 15.1. The two main rivals that began to emerge in the early 1980s were Thomson, the traditional market leader, and Intasun, a fast growing holiday and leisure group of companies. The growth of the top eight firms in terms of the number of air tours authorized by the Civil Aviation Authority (CAA) is shown in Table 15.2. Whilst the total number of holidays authorized increased by nearly 50 per cent over the period shown both Thomson and Intasun expanded by a greater proportion but with Intasun far outstripping Thomson's growth. In fact, 1985 was a rather bad year for the overseas travel trade despite a surge of late bookings in the autumn as the indifferent summer took hold. Two previous years of good domestic summer weather had depressed the anticipated number of overseas holidays and this is probably reflected in the low 1985 figures shown for a number of operators. The 1986 and 1987 figures show a rapid pickup for the larger firms in particular.

These figures include the number of authorized (or anticipated) holidays. They are not the same as the actual numbers arranged by each operator, but they do indicate the broad magnitudes involved. The shares of the market in terms of actual holidays taken (*ex-post* market shares) of four of the main operating groups are shown in Table 15.3.

This demonstrates clearly the importance of the two leading companies in their fight for market share. But the general implications of the table are also important since it demonstrates the relative concentration of supply. Four firms are responsible for 50 per cent of the market. Under

**Table 15.1** The United Kingdom's top twelve tour companies: operating and financial details

| Tour operator | Number of holidays authorized by the CAA (Summer 1984) | Associated airline | Parent company | Turnover £'000 | Pre-tax profits £'000 | Profit margin[b] % | Return on capital[c] % |
|---|---|---|---|---|---|---|---|
| Thomson | 954 500 | Britannia | International Thomson Organization | 478 528 (end 1984) | 23 046 | 4.8 | 14.8 |
| Intasun | 550 000 | Air Europe | Intasun Leisure Group | 240 733 (1984/5) | 24 844 | 10.3 | 57.9 |
| Horizon | 544 000 | Orion | Horizon Travel | 151 944 (1984/5) | 12 518 | 8.2 | 13.8 |
| British Airways Holidays | 533 600 | British Air Tours | British Airways | 97 500 (1984/85) | 3 200 | 3.3 | na[e] |
| Rank Travel | 365 000 | British Cal.[d] Charter | The Rank Organization | | | | |
| Cosmos | 300 000 | Monarch | Cosmos Motoring Anslatt (Leichensteine) | 97 604 (end 1983) | 1 764 | 1.8 | 3.8 |
| Blue Sky | 219 610 | British Caledonian Charter | British Caledonian Airways | 45 604 | 223 | 0.5 | 20.0 |
| Thomas Cook | 203 800 | | Midland Bank | 261 940 (end 1984) | 16 738 | 6.4 | 25.3 |
| Global | 174 000 | | Great Universal Stores | | | | |

| | | | | | |
|---|---|---|---|---|---|
| Sunny Tours (Budget Travel) | | 130 000[a] | | | |
| Portland | Britannia | 128 400 | 32 050 (end 1983) | −217 | −0.7 | −9.13 |
| Holiday Club International | International Thomson Organization Bass | 126 000 | 16 496 (end 1983) | −1 743 | −10.6 | −9.5 |

[a] Sunny Tours (Budget Travel) ceased trading on 24 October 1984.

[b] Profit margin = $\dfrac{\text{Pre-tax profits}}{\text{Turnover}} \times 100$.

[c] Return on capital = $\dfrac{\text{Pre-tax profits}}{\text{Net capital employed}} \times 100$.

[d] Rank Travel owns 50% of British Caledonian Airways (Charter) Ltd.

[e] Not extractable from consolidated account.

*Source*: ICC Keynote Report, *Travel Agents/Overseas Tour Operators* (1985), Appendix Table 2 and Company Reports (various years).

**Table 15.2** Number of air tours authorized by CAA ('000) 1981–7

|  | 1981 | 1982 | 1983 | 1984 | 1985 | 1986 | 1987 | % change 81–7 |
|---|---|---|---|---|---|---|---|---|
| All operators | 6 662 | 7 000 | 7 900 | 8 623 | 6 847 | 9 840 | na | 47[a] |
| Thomson | 856 | 899 | 966 | 954 | 1 313 | 2 100 | 2 700 | 215 |
| Intasun | 359 | 353 | 509 | 550 | 880 | 1 200 | 1 800 | 401 |
| Horizon | 361 | 428 | 481 | 544 | 409 | 590 | 884 | 146 |
| Rank | 345 | 354 | 316 | 366 | 323 | 405 | 477 | 38 |
| British Air Tours | 444 | na | na | 534 | 269 | 391 | 478 | 8 |
| Portland | 76 | na | na | 128 | 233 | 176 | 223 | 103 |
| Cosmos | 276 | 350 | 300 | 300 | 225 | 250 | 250 | –9 |
| Blue Sky | 148 | 261 | na | 219 | 219 | 150 | ?  –[b] | 1[a] |

na = not available.
[a] To 1986 only.
[b] Blue Sky sold to Rank, consolidated under Wings title at end of 1986, sold to Horizon, which was subsequently taken over by Bass in 1987.

*Source*: ICC Keynote Report, *Travel Agents/Overseas Tour Operators* (1985, 1987), and *The Observer*, 19 July 1987.

many circumstances this would be looked upon with some suspicion – giving rise to accusations of severe oligopoly or even near monopoly. However, the industry is highly competitive, as suggested above. This is because of two main reasons which are closely linked and which will be considered in more detail later.

One of these involves the ease of entry into the industry. It is not difficult to set up a holiday firm and expand rapidly. The other is ease of exit from the industry, not just by a company if it gets into financial difficulties and is forced to leave, but also by any particular customer. There are many alternative types of holiday on offer and even within the package sector the provision of a financial bond by firms and other guarantees give particular holiday-makers a relatively firm assurance that they will get the holiday they want or one very nearly like it. However, this being said, the trend towards concentration of capital is very rapid in the industry and this is likely to increase in the near future. In addition, if widespread liquidations emerge as a result of recent intensified competitive pressure there could be more severe disruption of holiday plans. The

**Table 15.3** Tour operators market share (% volume by air)

|  | 1981 | 1982 | 1983 | 1984 | 1985 | 1986 (est). |
|---|---|---|---|---|---|---|
| Thomson | 18 | 18 | 19 | 20 | 21 | 25 |
| Intasun | 10.5 | 11 | 12 | 14 | 16 | 23 |
| Horizon | 7.5 | 9 | 8 | 9 | 5 | 8 |
| Cosmos | 9 | 8 | 6 | 7 | 5 | 6 (British Air Tours) |
| Others | 55 | 54 | 55 | 50 | 53 | 38 |

*Source*: ICC Keynote Report, *Travel Agents/Overseas Tour Operators* (1987), Table 13, p. 19.

collapse of Budget Travel, for instance, left some 20 000 holiday-makers without adequate holiday cover in 1984 (Table 15.1) and important companies continued to collapse – in 1987, for instance, Biggles and Jetwing collapsed.

Let us now return to Table 15.1 and look at the operational details and financial situation of the companies mentioned there in greater detail. As far as operational details are concerned perhaps the most interesting feature is the way tour operators are usually part of larger, more diversified, groups. Inclusive tour operation is thus just one, and sometimes a very small, part of the parent company's business. This was particularly so in the case of Thomson, British Airways Holidays, Rank Travel, Blue Sky, Thomas Cook, Global, and Holiday Club International, these all being travel firms operated by large leisure-based parent companies or diversified conglomerates. Even the tour companies themselves include a range of different brand names under their umbrellas. Thomson Travel, for instance, includes the Thomson label proper, plus Portland Holidays, Britannia Airways and Lunn Poly, the travel agent chain. Intasun includes the Intasun label, plus Club 18–30, Golden Days, Ski Scene, Lancaster Holidays as well as its own airline, Air Europe. In 1985 Intasun acquired Global Tours from Great Universal Stores in a further step in its diversification and concentration moves. In addition, Global itself included such names as Golden Circle and Overland Holidays, as well as its own name. Rank Travel was made up of Wings and OSL in 1985, while British Airways Tours included the Enterprise, Sovereign, Flair, Alta (Speed Bird), and Martin Rook holiday names as well as its own airline company, British Air Tours. The more independent companies shown in Table 15.1 were Cosmos and Horizon. Cosmos has been losing market share and falls out of the top four companies in 1986 as British Air Tours takes over (Table 15.3).

The Horizon Company itself has an interesting history, being a firm that got into financial difficulties as Horizon Midland in the mid-1970s. When it collapsed, two 'public' bodies stepped in to effect a rescue, namely, The Greater Manchester Passenger Transport Executive (GMPTE), and Nottinghamshire County Council. These two bodies took a major stake in the company since Horizon, with its associated airline Orion, was one of the main users of Manchester Airport and East Midlands Airport. Its collapse could have had serious roll-on effects on the finances of these airports, and the relevant local authorities stepped in. This rescue operation proved reasonably successful, as shown by Table 15.4.

But with a declining profit margin and declining return on capital (particularly in 1985–6), and with the sale by the GMPTE of its shareholding at a considerable profit, Horizon needed a new injection of resources. To keep up with the competitive pressure put on it from Thomson and Intasun, Horizon was itself diversifying in this period. Apart from its

**Table 15.4** Horizon Travel Ltd: financial results 1978–86 (£'000)

|  | 1978–9 | 79–80 | 80–1 | 81–2 |
|---|---|---|---|---|
| Turnover | 31 269 | 50 179 | 72 577 | 96 833 |
| Pre-tax profits | 2 951 | 3 815 | 7 381 | 13 402 |
| Profit margin[a] | 9.4% | 7.6% | 10.2% | 13.8% |
| Return on capital[a] | 44.9% | 40.0% | 45.3% | 36.4% |
|  | 82–3 | 83–4 | 84–5 | 85–6 |
| Turnover | 118 487 | 124 206 | 151 944 | 198 330 |
| Pre-tax profits | 14 368 | 12 564 | 12 518 | 4 590 |
| Profit margin[a] | 12.1% | 10.1% | 8.2% | 2.3% |
| Return on capital[a] | 28.8% | 20.4% | 13.8% | 5.8% |

[a] Calculated as in Table 15.1.

*Source*: Company reports.

original holiday retailing company, it has set up a chain of travel agencies, developed a flight training centre in connection with its Orion airline subsidiary, moved into holiday hotel development and even into selling holiday properties abroad. These later developments were aided by the Bass brewery group taking a 27 per cent stake in the company in 1985 – after it had been sought by Grand Metropolitan, another leisure grouping. This brought with it Bass's own Holiday Club International and Pontins Holidays. In addition, Rank Travel was consolidating its holiday interest by buying Blue Sky from British Caledonian (Table 15.1) along with the Arrowsmith company, and organizing these under its Wings Holiday label. Wings was subsequently sold by Rank to Horizon at about the same time as Horizon was itself purchased more or less outright by Bass for £90 million in May 1987.

Thus there has been some significant organizational development in the industry even since 1985 when Table 15.1 was drawn up. All this goes to show, however, the great uncertainty associated with the holiday industry. It exists on relatively thin and unstable margins, requiring the heavyweight financial resources of a larger group if it is to survive for long.

The other main operational feature that Table 15.1 highlights is the way most of the big firms are associated with an airline. This became an emergent feature of British (and other European) inclusive tour companies in the late 1960s as the expansion of charter non-scheduled activity gained momentum. It was pioneered by now defunct companies such as Eagle Airways, Court Line, and more recently, Laker Airways. It represents another arm of holiday firm diversification. Not all of each airline capacity is restricted to the holidays of its associated holiday company, however. The airlines also sell their capacity to those firms not operating an airline. Table 15.5 shows the main operators and their seat capacity in 1985.

Clearly the airlines' authorized capacity does not match up to the company market shares as shown in either Table 15.2 or Table 15.3. In addition

**Table 15.5** General Air Tours: major operators 1985

| Holiday firm | Charter airline | % of charter seats |
|---|---|---|
| Thomson | Britannia | 28 |
| – | Dan Air | 22 |
| Intasun | Air Europe | 9 |
| Enterprise, Sovereign etc. | British Air Tours | 12 |
| Horizon | Orion | 8 |
| Cosmos | Monarch | 9 |

*Source*: ICC Sector Report (1985), Table 6, p. 10 plus text.

there is a major charter airline shown in Table 15.5 which has not appeared before. Dan Air offered 22 per cent of capacity in 1985 but is not organizationally linked to any single tour operator and functions as a totally separate company.

The final four columns of Table 15.1 give details of the financial position of the companies as far as this could be discerned from published data. The first point to make here is that holiday firms are big business. Thomson Travel, for instance, had a turnover of nearly £500 million in 1984. Profit margins vary between the firms but are low relative even to the indifferent performance of British firms more generally. It would be useful to chart these trends over a number of years for each of these firms, rather like the analysis offered for Horizon in Table 15.4. Overall industry data of this kind are collected in Table 15.6, giving an indication of profitability for the industry as a whole. This goes to confirm that the figures shown in Table 15.1 are fairly representative of the industry more generally.

This table also confirms the seeming decline in overall profitability during the 1980s and particularly in 1986. Eight of the top thirty companies in 1986 recorded losses, amounting to £19 million (in 1987 six companies recorded losses totalling £14 million). While the top three or four companies now seem to be in reasonable financial shape it is the medium-sized firms in the top thirty that are feeling the pressure. It is from this group that more collapses are likely or in which reorganizations and consolidations will occur. . . .

**Table 15.6** Profitability of top thirty operators[a] (£ million)

| | 1980 | 1981 | 1982 | 1983 | 1984 | 1985 | 1986 |
|---|---|---|---|---|---|---|---|
| Turnover | 906.9 | 1019.7 | 1299.5 | 1407 | 1799 | 1840 | 2130 |
| Net profit | 43.8 | 52.2 | 27.7 | 55.3 | 53.3 | 60.7 | 35.6 |
| Profit margin[b] | 4.8% | 5.1% | 2.1% | 3.9% | 3.0% | 3.3% | 1.7% |

[a] Top thirty are those with over 50 000 holiday sales per year.
[b] Calculated as in Table 15.1.

*Source*: ICC Keynote Report, *Travel Agents/Overseas Tour Operators* (1987), *Financial Times*, 28 May 1987.

## DOMESTIC HOLIDAY SUPPLY FIRMS

So far, overseas holidays have formed the focus of my attention. But very large numbers of domestic holidays are also taken – about 30 million in 1986. Clearly in looking at the travel agent sector we have already been analysing something of the domestic arm of the industry since these agents also arrange domestic holidays or parts of them. However, the domestic holiday situation is much more fragmented than overseas tourism. The 'inclusive tour' is less well developed, for instance, and most holidays are independently arranged and are for much shorter periods. This makes for a radically differentiated supply structure, one not easily captured in a manageable set of statistics. Perhaps the most suitable starting point is to look at the major domestically based leisure groups, the activities of which are summed up in Table 15.7. This gives a breakdown of their main holiday-based activities and similar financial details are given for the holiday firms discussed in Table 15.1. Points to make in the context of this table are, again, the very large turnover involved and the fact that profit margins are healthier and more stable than in the tour operator case. Two of the organizations mentioned in the table are also prominently involved as parents in the tour operator case, namely Bass and, until recently, Rank. Most of the organizations involved are themselves again parts of large conglomerate groups with diversified interests, not necessarily just in the leisure services area. Grand Metropolitan and Rank, for instance, have wide-ranging manufacturing and property interests, though the others tend to be associated with at least the provision of leisure-based products in their diversified activities. Trust House Forte is probably the group most closely centred upon leisure and holiday-based activities, being mainly a hotel and catering operation.

One other point to note from Table 15.7 is the ownership of 'holiday camps' by the companies listed. In fact holiday camps is a misnomer as these have recently been renamed 'holiday centres' or 'villages' in an effort to up-grade their market image. Large investments in this area also have been made in recent years, as indicated in Table 15.8. They have capitalized on the move towards self-catering by heavily introducing this element into their operations and have also benefited from the 1983 and 1984 slight trend back towards domestic holiday taking. In addition, these holiday centres are increasingly catering for second holidays – a few nights or a week or so spent off-season – taken in addition to the main holiday abroad. Thus the image of a Billy Butlin, Fred Pontin or Harry Warner (or Joe Maplin even!) coaxing their 'campers' into early morning collective exercises is long gone and unlikely to return, except on television.

As mentioned, domestic short-break holidays of three or four nights away from home are the fastest growing segment of the market. The Mecca Leisure Group has already set up its own travel company to cater

**Table 15.7** Major United Kingdom hotels, catering and leisure groups: operating and financial details (1983/4)

| Group | Activity | Chains/brands | Turnover £'000 | Pre-tax profits £'000 | Profit margin[c] % | Return on capital[d] % |
|---|---|---|---|---|---|---|
| Trust House Forte | Hotels | THF, Post Houses, Little Chef, Happy Eater | 1 148 600 (10–'84) | 105 200 | 9.2 | 9.4 |
| | Catering | Motorway Services, Airline Catering Industrial Catering (Gardner Merchant) | | | | |
| Grand Metropolitan | Hotels | Intercontinental, Others | 1 510 700[a] (3–'84) | 99 300 | 6.6 | 9.6 |
| | Catering | Berni Inns, Clifton Inns, Chef and Brewer, Industrial Catering | | | | |
| | Holiday centres | Warner[c] | | | | |
| | Other tourism | Travelscene,[c] Mecca Entertainments | | | | |
| Bass | Hotels | Crest | 571 300[a] (3–'84) | 36 000 | 6.3 | [b] |
| | Catering | Toby Inns, Old Kentucky | | | | |
| | Holiday centres | Pontins, Coral Bookmaking and Bingo | | | | |
| Rank | Hotels | Rank (London) | 334 000[a] (3–'84) | 19 300 | 5.8 | [b] |
| | Catering | Motorway Services | | | | |
| | Holiday centres | Butlins, Leisure Caravans | | | | |
| | Other tourism | Wings[c] | | | | |
| Ladbroke | Hotels | Ladbroke, Comfort | 738 500 (3–'83) | 35 100 | 4.8 | [b] |
| | Holiday centres | Ladbroke | | | | |
| | Other tourism | Casinos | | | | |

[a] Leisure services divisions only.
[b] Capital employed in leisure services division not given in accounts.
[c] Profit margin = $\dfrac{\text{Profits}}{\text{Turnover}} \times 100$.
[d] Return on capital = $\dfrac{\text{Profits}}{\text{Net capital employed}} \times 100$.
[e] Subsequently sold in 1986/7.

*Sources*: ICC Keynote Report, *Tourism in the UK* (1986) and company reports (various years).

**Table 15.8** Leading British holiday centres 1984

| Centres | Ownership | No. of centres | Estimated visitors | Nights spent | Investment |
|---|---|---|---|---|---|
| Pontins | Bass | 30 | 850 000 | 5.2m | £30m (since 1981) |
| Butlins | Rank | 6 | 815 000 | 5.0m | £9.5m (since 1982/3) |
| Ladbroke's | Ladbroke Group | 16 | 500 000 | na | £6m (since 1984/5) |
| Haven Holidays | English China Clays[a] | 18 | 350 000 | na | na |
| Warners | Grand Met.[b] | 10 | 150 000 | 1.4m | £7m (since 1984/5) |
| Total | | | 2 665 000 | | |

[a] Sold to Rank in February 1986.
[b] Sold in 1986.

*Source:* J. C. Holloway, *The Business of Tourism*, London: MacDonald & Evans, 1985, Table 4, p. 140, and newspaper reports.

for and organize this kind of holiday, and others are likely to follow suit. The 'holiday village' idea is being heavily marketed in the United Kingdom. A major development here was the Dutch company's Sporthuis Centrum Recreatie investment in a complete holiday village in Sherwood Forest, opened in 1987. This attracted the English Tourist Board's largest ever single development grant of £1.5 million.

Blackpool's Pleasure Beach still boasts the single most popular tourist attraction in the United Kingdom with an estimated 6.5 million visits in 1986. This was followed by the main London museums, headed by the British Museum at 3.6 million visits (*The Economist*, 1 August 1987). Of these attractions for which an entrance fee is charged, Madam Tussauds in London headed the list with 2.4 million visitors, closely followed by Alton Towers in Staffordshire with 2.2 million. The fastest growing attraction in recent years has been the 'Jorvik Viking Centre' in York (0.9 million visits in 1986) owned by Heritage Projects Limited. This company is planning more such ventures, notably 'The Pilgrim's Way' in a Canterbury church and 'The Oxford Story' in Oxford. It is the recognized market leader in this field.

Finally, we can look a little more closely at the main hotel groups operating in the United Kingdom. These are listed in Table 15.9 according to the number of rooms they operate.

In the case of United Kingdom hotels it is again the large diversified conglomerates that are heavily involved plus brewery groups (Scottish and Newcastle, Vaux, Greenhall Whitley, Allied Lyons, Bass). Surprisingly, perhaps, North American hotel chains are not strongly represented in Britain, Holiday Inns being the only one to appear in the table. But groups like Hilton and Sheraton were just hovering outside of the list, both with over 1000 rooms in the United Kingdom. All this was poised to change rather rapidly by the late 1980s as these groups, plus the third largest American hotel chain Ramada, made a determined effort to increase their stake in London in particular, on the backs of the upsurge in American tourists coming to the United Kingdom largely because of exchange rate changes. It has already been pointed out above how Intasun had joined with Ramada to manage its new London hotel interests. In fact the world-wide Hilton chain was taken over by the Ladbroke Group in a £645 million deal completed in September 1987 (Ladbroke also owns the Texas Homecare d-i-y store chain). In addition, Intasun has pulled back from its initial moves into the hotel market. The company was returned to private ownership in mid-1987 in what was seen as a retrenchment and change in direction of its development. Things are thus still very unsettled in this area.

**Table 15.9** Hotel ownership (1985)[a]

| Chain | Parent | No. of UK hotels | UK rooms |
|---|---|---|---|
| Trusthouse Forte Hotels | THF | 208 | 21 000 |
| Ladbroke/Comfort | Ladbroke Group[b] | 50 | 6 200 |
| Crest Hotels | Bass | 60 | 5 700[c] |
| Thistle Hotels | Scottish & Newcastle | 39 | 5 100 |
| Mount Charlot Hotels | Mount Charlot Invest. | 42 | 4 600 |
| Queens Moat Houses | Queens Moat Hs. | 57 | 4 500 |
| Holiday Inns of America (UK) | Holiday Inns of Canada | 17 | 4 100 |
| Embassy Hotels | Allied Lyons | 42 | 3 000 |
| Swallow Hotels | Vaux Breweries | 32 | 3 000 |
| Grand Metropolitan Hotels (Intercontinental & Forum Hotels) | Grand Metropolitan | 8 | 3 000 |
| Viriani | Viriani Group | 19 | 2 200 |
| Rank Hotels | Rank | 5 | 2 100 |
| Reo Stakis Hotels | Stakis | 24 | 2 000 |
| De Vere Hotels | Greenhall Whitley | 14 | 1 500 |

[a] Does not include private consortium hotels: e.g. Inter, Best Western and Prestige.
[b] Ladbroke purchased Hilton Hotels in September 1987.
[c] Beds.

*Source*: Derived from ICC Keynote Report, *UK Tourism* (1985), Appendix Table 11, and *Accountancy*, January 1985.

## CONCLUSION

The United Kingdom holiday industry was in a period of rapid change and flux in late 1985 and this is likely to continue for some years to come. Indeed it could be argued that ever since the 1960s when inclusive charter holidays began to 'take-off' the United Kingdom industry has been in a continued state of flux. It is recognized to be one of the most 'dynamic' in the country. Failures, mergers, acquisitions, and diversification are the day-to-day diet of firms involved with the industry. Competitive pressures are intense and economic fluctuations are highly significant to the fortunes of companies. Add into this vagaries of the weather and a veritable hubbub of movement and change emerges. But this is itself dependent upon a number of rather more enduring features, perhaps the most import-ant of which has been the continual growth in demand for overseas holidays despite the deep recession in the economy. It is the number of first-time overseas holidaymakers, 'new' consumers for this particular market, that has remained surprisingly stable through the late 1970s and early 1980s, increasing by about 1 per cent per year. In effect this has meant approximately 400 000 new and inexperienced customers coming on to the overseas market each year, and it is this that has kept the traditional inclusive tour package alive. In this context there is always room for some sharp operator to move up the industry hierarchy of market share, although this is probably becoming more difficult as large groups become consolidated and the industry generally matures. It has been estimated that the real cost of an average package holiday was 16 per cent less in 1987 than 1980, and this value for money is likely to keep the large groups well placed at the top of the market share listings.

However, competitive pressures can still be generated by another feature of the industry mentioned before – the relative ease of entry into and exit out of the big league. Amongst the hundreds of small firms expertise is continually generated and a taste for the big time engendered. It was the small firms who first spotted specialized market segments and exploited them, and they are encouraged in this by the ability to sub-contract most of the holiday provision to other operators. In particular, aeroplane seats can be contracted relatively easily and hotel beds booked cheaply. It is not even that difficult to set up an associated airline company given the leasing arrangements organized by financial institutions and the aircraft producers, and the developed secondhand market in airliners. A further advantage for holiday operators is the traditional nature of consumer booking arrangements whereby many millions of pounds are deposited with them several months in advance of the holiday being taken. This enables the operator to keep its own financial resources low and in effect secure commitments on the basis of the cash flow advanced to it by customers. These 'loans' (which is in effect what they amount to) can also be invested over the winter and spring period at considerable gain to the operator.

To some extent this latter advantage has been eroded in recent years by the tendency to go for late bookings, at least by the 'experienced' holiday-maker. Clearly, from the operator's point of view, one of the favourable elements to emerge from the competitive price battle of late 1985 was the reversal of this tendency, at least temporarily. One of the reasons that 'loss leaders' of £25 holidays could be easily tolerated, and even a more general price reduction installed, was the advanced booking this drew in. Thomson, for instance, was reported to have sold 400 000 1986 holidays in two weeks in November 1985 at the height of the price war, and other main operators probably did equally well. This was likely to produce an income of £16 million on the deposits advanced by customers.

The price war of autumn 1985 then was little more than an advertising exercise, though it did reduce the general price of holidays for 1986. However, tendencies in the economy and in the internal organization of firms were likely to have allowed this without too great an increase in risk to longer term financial viability for the larger operators. Inflation had slowed down in the United Kingdom to 5 per cent per year which produced a greater sense of economic security in terms of planning expenditures ahead. Added to this was the increase in real incomes of those still in work partly as a consequence of reduced inflation but also because of private sector wage rises running well ahead of inflation levels. Another contributory factor was the expected favourable exchange rate payments and downward pressures on hotel bed prices, particularly in Spain. As far as internal operations were concerned costs had been reduced by the extensive installation of computer technology, particularly with respect to booking and internal control procedures. Thus, all in all, a fall in the price of holidays would probably have emerged in 1986 largely because of these changes in underlying economic conditions, and need not have been accompanied by the razzmatazz of a full-blooded price war. However, this did serve to advertise the industry, create excitement, and generate a lot of early bookings that might not otherwise have come forward. A similar situation is very likely to be repeated in years to come.

## ACKNOWLEDGEMENTS

I would like to acknowledge the support of the Open University Faculty of Social Science Research Fund for financial assistance, and Leon Martin for research assistance, in completing the analysis for this chapter.

Reading taken from A. Tomlinson (ed.), *Consumption, Identity and Style*, published by Comedia, 1990. Reprinted with permission.

# A participant observer study of a 'rough' working-class pub

## 16

Michael Smith

The article describes a three-month participant as observer study of a 'rough' working-class pub – a type different from the 'respectable' working-class and 'posh' middle-class pubs. Patterns of usage and users are explored and the role style and social-control strategies of the publican arc reported. Finally some general issues are posed for further research in relation to the pub as a context of work and leisure.

## INTRODUCTION

The category of 'rough pub' is one that evokes the image of a beer-sodden culture, perpendicular drinking, criminality and a 'tough masculine' complex of values. The attempt to research such a pub was made with some indecision: there would be no claim to generate 'results' which might be applicable to more than a few pubs and a small number of participants and publicans. What could be learned by the study of a rough pub?

Firstly, it became clear from conversations with pub regulars, mainly working class, that some pubs and some publicans did have a reputation such that 'no respectable person would go into that particular pub' – places frequented by 'mad buggers and head bangers'. The comfortable picture of Roger and Mary sipping their drinks in the oak-beamed Rose and Crown – sharing in the conviviality of a controlled situation – is hardly

*Sociology of Leisure: A reader.* Edited by C. Critcher, P. Bramham and A. Tomlinson. Published in 1995 by E & FN Spon, London. ISBN 0 419 19420 7.

congruent with the 'sawdust on the floor' image conjured up by a rough pub. Was such a pub a type and thus conceptually located at one end of a spectrum in terms of usage and users? Universal knowledge was not the aim of the research but, having identified such a context, it would have been sociologically unimaginative not to attempt a participant as observer study.

Secondly, it was very clear that there had been in the UK a licensing and brewing industry policy of imposing a 'Civilising morality' in the ethos of rational recreation, upon the public house and alcohol consumption, of creating 'wholesome behaviour' in wholesome environments (Smith, 1982). The success of such policy strategies could be evaluated to a certain extent by examining a 'rough pub'.

Thirdly, a casual visit to the pub to see if it could offer insights into pub usage in relation to sociability, types of users, the masculinity of the culture generated, and role style of the publican, led to its inclusion in the research. It was felt to constitute an important strand in the objective of sociological knowledge building. It also offered an opportunity of probing further the elements of a conceptual framework for understanding the public house as a social context (Smith, 1983). The study was also evoked by the knowledge gained on the first casual visit to the pub. The publican himself was said to have a police record 'as long as your arm', and circulating at the bar – emanating from Dennis the 'binman' – was a range of well-thumbed pornographic literature, which posed in a stark and revealing way the maleness of the sexual stereotyping of women and the dominantly masculine culture of the public house concerned. 'The Hole in the Wall', the appropriately titled pub concerned, was thus approached with more than vague academic interest.

## THE HOLE IN THE WALL

The location of the public house was in a run-down inner city area. The affluence of once-busy small manufacturing concerns and clean front door-steps of quite smart terraced houses had given way within the last 15 years to planning blight – areas of bulldozed housing and others awaiting slum clearance. It was a depressing grey area reminiscent of the kind of description of 'Luke Street' in Liverpool and the rough pub 'Casey's' studied as part of an explanation by Gill (1977) of the growth of delinquent subcultures.

> Luke Street accommodation is poor and crowded. Casey's offers a refuge from the stresses of families living in such conditions. When the men go into Casey's they take it easy and family responsibilities will not intrude on their enjoyment. They can drink, play darts and

talk ... In its time it would have been a respectable pub sharing in a modest way in the prosperity of the town ... As a result of its age, the decline of the town and recent housing and industrial development in its immediate surroundings, the pub has changed into a depressing corner pub in a physically depressing area.

The 'Hole in the Wall' had much of the locational feel of Luke Street and shared some characteristics of a previous working-class pub studied and reported upon elsewhere (Smith, 1981) – small, tenanted, with the 'home' above the pub. The pub was divided into three areas, a bar–lounge area, a small second lounge and a games room. It was a garishly tatty pub, with low copper-topped tables, creamy-going-brown paintwork and, although once carpeted, the carpet was well trodden and wearing thin. Wallpaper was torn from the wall in places and there were two clocks, one permanently stopped at 12 o'clock and the other often a quarter of an hour fast. The pub boasted two space invader machines, a juke box, a gaming machine and a television; it felt distinctly crowded even when there were few people present.

It is important to highlight several initial aspects of the participation process. Going into the pub, ordering a drink and standing at the bar was viewed as a mildly provocative act by the 'regulars'. A bar group was much in evidence in the 5–7 p.m. period (the pub opened at 5 p.m.) and the researcher was quickly told that he 'could not stand there' because it was Tommy's spot – 'he'll shift ya when he's in'. Tommy was 'in' fairly soon after the researcher, and as he was about twice the size of the researcher, it was decided that situational tact was the better part of sociological valour – the researcher shifted. The clear designation of bar positions as 'reserved' was the first indication of exactly how regular were the members who constituted the bar group, and how closed the group was to outsiders. The second indication was in relation to whose 'right' it was to sit on the only bar stool. It was reserved for the 'king', as the regulars called him, the man who could 'take out' or overpower any other in the pub. The third interesting aspect of the entry into the pub, which subsequently became clear, was the researcher's reaction to the pornographic literature circulated, a bar-group virility test for the new participant. The offer by the researcher to have it 'reprinted' meant he was regarded as a 'f ... ing good 'un' and 'accepted', although his rough clothes did not quite match his less rough voice.

The publican, Terry, was behind the bar less often than in front of it. The regulars complained that he was 'never there' (i.e. behind the bar) and Dennis the binman poured the newcomer his first pint. Terry was usually found playing pool (at lunchtimes and early evenings) or running a gambling card group (late evening in mid-week) with the young male regulars – with one or two young women attached to the group. The card group was very much a situation of inter-personal male interaction with the publican being central to the group itself. Terry shared quite freely with the bar group his marriage conflicts. His wife was not talking to him during the first week of the participant observation process and it became increasingly obvious that she was subject to considerable conflict between the demands of running the pub and looking after the house 'upstairs', with one child of eight.

The strategy of the researcher as participant observer was threefold: firstly to become a member of the bar group, visiting the pub for the 5–7 p.m. session during the week; secondly to visit the pub from 8.30 p.m. through to closing time, both on weekdays and at weekends; and thirdly to visit at lunchtimes, usually from 12.30 to 2.00 p.m. but occasionally earlier and staying later. The period of participant observation was three months.

## SOCIAL USAGES OF PUBLIC HOUSE SPACE

The first question posed in the research was what kinds of relationships existed between the designated physical space and the actual social usage of the space, in terms of open, negotiable and closed social space. In the rough pub the social usage patterns did vary somewhat with when people came: the time of day, the day of the week and the proportion of regulars in the pub. However, something like 98% of pub participants were regulars and were manual workers, and that included the women who visited the pub 'on the look out', including Irish Mary who several of the regulars regarded as 'the biggest slag in the place'. When people came and what they did, however, seemed very little related to the physical structure of the pub, in terms of designated usage. To a large extent the users divided into two distinct categories: young 'tough' regulars, almost exclusively males by themselves and older (35–60) males, also by themselves.

The younger males tended to play machines and pool, and were the main participants of the regular card gambling sessions. The older males tended to form a distinct bar group, always standing at the bar, and were generally 'large drinkers'. In the time it took the researcher to drink half a pint, most were well through their second and managed between five and six pints in a two-hour session. About 60% of the regulars walked to their local, the others arriving by car and bus, or 'wagon'. The king, Sid, was twice the size of Tommy, and Tommy was twice the size of the researcher! They were both builders' labourers and there appeared to be a fairly strict masculine ranking order around the bar; Sid sat at the end of the bar 'presiding', Tommy took up a midway position whilst the researcher joined an unemployed 'engineer' (a lathe turner) at the end of the bar, the researcher being of unknown and unproven qualities.

The two groups, the middle-aged bar group and the group of tough young regulars, were the predominant users of the pub, along with an itinerant group of women, often coming in by themselves, standing at the bar 'dressed to kill', buying one drink, very conspicuously doing nothing but standing at the bar. Irish Mary was a 'regular', usually coming on Thursdays and Fridays about 7 p.m., some other 'regular' women coming in after 9 p.m. by themselves or in twos, sometimes leaving by themselves, sometimes not. Very occasionally a middle-class couple, to judge by dress and speech, strayed into the pub and usually survived one drink, even on one occasion deciding not to have a drink, but standing, looking and leaving rapidly. It was social worlds away from middle-class suburbia.

To assert that there was little relationship between designated social usage of physical space in the pub, and actual social usage, requires further elucidation. What seems most characteristic of the pub was the almost complete absence of different social space usage where distinct 'things' happened. It was not so much that social space was 'portable' as that there was little differentiation in usage patterns. There was almost a complete absence of closed or private social space, although there were tables to act as social shields to interaction, they were at knee height in the area opposite the bar. The second possible area of private social space was the second lounge area, but this was used almost exclusively for the evening card game. The second area was 'invaded' by two machines, the juke box and a space machine. The absence of closed or 'private' social space appeared both as a result of the physical structure *and* the patterns of usage of participants, *but* also importantly, was a result of how the publican played his role. The bar area was very much less an arena for encounters than a place where regulars usually met each other, stood, often facing outwards towards the rest of the pub, and talking to the publican – who could be chatted to almost wherever he was.

The apparent lack of social space differentiation was at first sight slightly puzzling. After some consideration, however, it was realised by the researcher that the 'social' situation which was almost exclusively male and rough working class, with only a small proportion of women as appendages (sitting watching 'their men' play cards or waiting to be 'picked up' or, rarely, involved in sexual interaction in a corner) was in reality a 'private' situation of homogeneous group interaction, albeit age stratified in terms of focal interests. It was as though the bar-group maleness extended to the entire pub. The sociability dynamics were along the same sociability dimension: 'men as men' drinking a great deal, meeting regulars whom they regarded as mates, but with younger men forming the card gambling group, playing pool, the gaming and fun machines and the juke box; and the older men just standing (except Sid) and drinking and exchanging both jokes and information about work, gambling, cars, and deals.

The paradox of both 'open' and yet 'closed' usage of the social space was not because 'couples' wanted to be with each other, or because there were distinct sex and class groupings, but because it was more or less a 'one class' public house, part of the undermass in the terrain of differentiated working class culture. The 'private social space' typical of middle-class individualized, segmented and inter-personal interaction was operative, but the whole pub area constituted private social space usage for the whole group of regulars. Social space in the rough pub was not differentiated sufficiently to be 'portable' and seemed to result from a combination of three elements in the situation: the relative lack of physically differentiated areas where things were 'supposed to happen'; the usage patterns of participants which clearly demonstrated that the group of regulars could be 'anywhere' in the pub; and the role style of the publican, one of participation and integration with the regulars. All three elements fostered the more or less permanent experience of private interaction and, along with such experience, the potential deregulation of social norms. The mixture of immediacy, hedonism, masculine core values and social closure was a recipe which required little sociological ignition. The best – and perhaps the only viable – research strategy was to buy a round, be prepared to change sides or beat a rapid retreat.

## SOCIAL RELATIONSHIPS AND SEXUAL STEREOTYPES

The researcher as a participant observer was concerned to disentangle and understand the patterning of social relationships that existed – who met whom, why and what they did, and the links of participants to non-public house relational networks. At best what could be substantiated was situationally contingent, partial, and only gradually unfolded during the period of research.

There was firstly a very clear masculine hierarchy in the relationships which were evident in the particular public house. Such a hierarchy was age-differentiated, in that whilst *physical prowess* – potential and actual – and interestingly *drinking capacity*, were the two distinct elements in the relational matrix, they appeared to operate differently for the two main age groups of users. For the young males, often skinheads and denim or leather jacketed, the form which masculine competitiveness assumed was very much focused around the games, the pool, cards and the space invader machines rather than drinking itself. Many were, or appeared to be, under the legal age of drinking and would tend not to be found at the bar. Many were unemployed and looked it. They played punk-rock style music on the juke box, and on occasions took over the pool area as their distinct territory for affirming an all-male subcultural identity. Most of the 'lads' were locals, had been academic rejects at school, and gave the appearance in the pub of 'doing nothing', rarely talking much – except to 'f...' everything and play for pints – often a pint for the best of three games. The pub appeared to offer some relief to the boredom of living, an affirmation of incorporation into the tough maleness of the emanating bar group world of male power, status and drinking – with its accompanying dichotomized experience of women who are not part of the maleness of such a world. The transition from the young group of regulars to the bar-group was fairly ritualized via the card game – usually five-card stud or poker. The stakes were quite high – a 50p per person 'pot' for the best of three games. The invitation to join the group was at the discretion of the publican himself and often he would incorporate one or two of the younger regulars into the group. The card group included one or two older regulars, rarely the hard drinkers, and becoming a member of the group appeared to signify a step in the hierarchy of masculine values and membership acceptance.

The second major group of pub users were the older males, almost without exception by themselves, although they knew each other. Some were employed in the same firm or in the same kind of work – they were predominantly labourers, some Irish, some from around Newcastle. Three or four were laid off from the building trade, as well as a number of others from a range of manual occupations, including Fred the caretaker, John who was a tailor's cutter, a railway porter and Stan, who was on the 'sick' and looked it. Relationships between the older male regulars appeared to be very much occupationally based and they seemed to use the pub as 'home from work', to talk about work problems – compensation, insurance, redundancy, 'making money on the side' – as well as about gambling, horse-racing, and cars in particular, and very little about women. Although there was bar pornography it was not bolstered by a range of casual comment and witty jokes about women in terms of sexual stereotyping. There was no telephone in the pub area and thus no wives phoned and the nearest equivalent was children coming to the pub door, as happened on several occasions, around 6.30 p.m., asking for 'Dad', to tell him that 'tea was ready'.

There was little ambiguity about how women were defined – 'women – f... ing cows' – and there was little discussion at the bar about wives, marriages or sexual adventures. It was almost as though the bar group 'did things' rather than talked about them. There was a very clear self image of 'men as men' and work as 'labour', and much focus on survival in a situation of poverty, hardship and economic–social inequality. But there was also a sense of collectivity and this may well explain why Stan, on the sick, was readily accepted in the hierarchy of the bar group relationships; he would not be sent to the 'infirmary', the regulars assured him, and they freely lent him money without any expectation of being repaid.

The collectivity extended to the family and the 'women folk' who came in on Friday and Saturday nights. Although the usage of the pub was predominantly male, after 8 p.m. on Fridays and Saturdays (especially Saturdays) the older women came in pairs, joining their husbands, mostly not in the sense of standing or sitting with them, but in the sense of separately being there together. And the language changed for the night and the situation had made much of the experience of the conjoining of separate worlds, with older children being allowed in as part of the family sharing process, sometimes sitting around with their 'Mums', usually in the back room. The men were dressed differently on Saturdays; Sid the king was smart and shaved, Dennis the binman with his blue woolly hat and always slightly smelly was not to be seen; even Stan looked different and the situation had all the hallmarks of festivity and a special occasion.

Not all the women on Saturdays were older and married. Acolytes of the young male neophytes were to be found, usually in twosomes, but without a regular boyfriend and forming a parallel grouping. The situation was reminiscent of the findings of the Worktown (mass) study except it was as though the pub was transformed into a lounge, even to the extent of some of the older women standing at the bar, expecting and receiving compliments about their hairstyles and jokes about their lack of drinking capacity. There seemed to be a distinctly protectionist orientation adopted by the publican's wife to women who came into the pub. It was she who put the male regulars 'in their place' in terms of language and behaviour, on Saturdays and on other occasions, but usually out of the earshot of Terry. It was also Freda who ran the bar for most of the time and although Terry was certainly around the pub on Fridays and Saturdays, it was then 'extra help', Terry's sister, came in.

Thus far there has been reported some unfolding of the social situation and patterning of social relationships in the 'rough' pub. The decor was rough and there was a sense in which the social usage was that of a 'private-collective world'. The proportion of regulars was very high, and the maleness of the pub very much more than solely restricted to the bar group. The focal interests of participants, and the degree to which regulars knew each other, seemed to result in a very integrated sociability-drinking-activity public house subculture. That subculture was predicated upon the maleness of a group of users with a focus on drinking for the older males and activity for the younger males. Of particular interest was the masculinity of the pub subculture and orientations towards women. Women were not a particularly predominant focal interest in terms of conversation and interaction in the pub. This tended to suggest not only a separateness of female and male social worlds (perhaps deriving from the sharp segregation of work from women and family) but acceptance of traditional role-playing and gender stereotypes of appropriate behaviour. Such a segmentation was made all the more interesting by the presence of 'not very nice girls', as the licensee's wife described them, prostitutes who came in on a client-touting pub-tripping routine. They did the 'round' of the pubs, often starting with the 'Hole in the Wall' or finishing there.

A description of who met whom and what they did does yield some explanation of why. Relationships between the behaviour of participants and the focal interests of the pub's regulars suggest a fairly narrow range of values and interests. The pub provided a refuge from the uncertainty of life experiences; the hardness and harshness of work as labour, of insecure employment, the male toughness of 'making a living'. The gathering was one of 'ragged' men (and most during the week were wearing their working clothes which were an odd collection of woolly jumpers, worn jeans, anoraks or short duffle coats, and frequently sporting woolly hats reputably made from the worn out jumpers) which portrayed a visual roughness. The experience of communality and sociability appeared to derive from the immediacy of sharing together the maleness of a man's world, and the blurring of the edges of social reality in the levity and forgetfulness induced by drink.

It was a world in which women could share, on male terms – the wives on Friday and Saturday evenings and the 'not very nice girls' as part of the availability of sex for money. The participants were hard drinkers but it was rarely a situation in which deregulated behaviour actually occurred. Part of being a man was to be able to 'hold your drink', to 'take women if you wanted to', and to exploit *in the outside world* the economic arrangements which were themselves exploitative and representative. The ethic seemed *not* to use the pub to assert male virility – it required little demonstration. The most deregulated behaviour was in the language, which was certainly disinhibited. What seemed above all to characterize participants was the contrast between the pub, as a world of certainty, mates, fuddled joy, accepted male values, and the uncertainty of the world outside. The 'Hole in the Wall' was an oasis of certainty for the participants, an ordered world of understood communality in a hostile and uncertain external world.

## THE PUBLICAN'S ROLE – CUSTOMER AND FAMILY DIMENSIONS

The erstwhile sociologist in the reputedly rough pub was concerned to explore the dimensions of the work role of the publican, a tenant not a manager. How did the publican relate to the customers, and what impact did running the pub have on the family in terms of the *pervasiveness* of the demands of the role? The publican, Terry, was highly involved with some aspects of the role; however, there was a marked ambivalence in his orientation towards the *formal demands* of the role – 'he was never there'. The publican had been tenant of the pub for four years and left much of the running of the pub to his wife. At lunchtimes he was rarely to be seen and seemed to have a very variable schedule in relation to the teatime trade and even Friday and Saturday evenings. . . .

He was within five or six paces of the bar wherever he was. *He* was the role of the publican, and rather than separating himself from the regulars, was a fully fledged member of the group constituting the public in the public house. Some attempt was made to uncover why Terry was so variable in his pub appearances and the researcher surmised that he was 'doing deals'. It transpired that Terry dealt in second-hand cars and it was this which explained his somewhat variable appearances. However when he was there he certainly evidenced all the indications of a role style pervaded by an active participation.

But the regulars in Terry's pub seemed to have little to offer in terms of cheap goods and bargains. Most were just managing to survive. Thus Terry, according to his wife, spent a lot of time in several other pubs making contacts and dealing. From observation it seemed as though he accepted the precariousness and maleness of the social world of his pub, but selectively fostered its big spenders, the card group members and the hard drinkers.

In terms of *time* pervasiveness, the publican 'managed' the extent to which he was in the pub itself. He often came in mid-way through the teatime session, about 6.30 p.m. or between 8.30 and 10 p.m., flushed with success or otherwise. . . .

The publican's separation of himself from the time pervasiveness of 'running a pub' appeared to equate with his separation of himself from his wife and family. His orientation to the pub, with a marked sense of ambivalence, did seem to derive from the basic incompatibility of two role demands, being a member of the pub regulars *and* being exposed to his wife and family at the same time. He welcomed the former but not the latter. . . .

The family lived over the pub and access to the living area was via the games room. There was one child aged eight. Stephen spent a lot of time in the pub during the evening, even staying up until closing time during the week, effectively he was allowed the run of the pub (in his pyjamas) and often sat in on the card game or played the space invader machine. It was almost as though there was little division between pub life and family life. The rather haphazard division of labour between the publican and his wife was clearly a major source of tension in the public house work situation, and this appeared to be exacerbated by her disillusion with pub life, often expressed to the pub regulars, and the collapse of any separateness between being and not being in the pub for her and her son.

Terry and Freda rarely indulged in open disagreement in the public house situation but the bruise on Freda's face on one occasion was unlikely to be the result of an accident.

## NORMATIVE DEREGULATION AND SOCIAL CONTROL

Thus far very little has been reported on the unruly 'image' of the 'rough' pub and the publican's role in the social control process in the particular public house. Very little 'trouble' occurred in the particular pub during the period of observation and participation. Certainly the effect of high alcohol consumption was to create a rowdy scene – loud voices, colourful language, some regulars 'falling about' or gradually physically subsiding as they propped up the bar. None of the behaviour, however, fitted the categories of 'head bangers' or 'mad buggers', although there was rich mythology of what had happened on some celebrated occasions in the past; how the 'king' had 'taken out challengers to his supremacy'. . . .

In one sense the rough pub was certainly a normatively deregulated context, in that there were a range of expectations and permitted behaviours which would have been 'out of place' in any other 'public' context. However, in terms of the maleness of expectations, hard drinking and the hierarchical values of the regulars in the rough pub, what was permitted and accepted was less 'deregulated' than structured by the different values and interests of the pub users. What was permitted and accepted was fostered by the ways in which the publican's role style itself fitted with the usages, values and focal interests of the pub regulars. As reported earlier, the publican played his role *vis-à-vis* the pub users in an almost totally informal style, being himself one of the regulars, displaying a high activity profile in the group. He himself drank little in his own pub, always carried his pint around with him, usually closed the pub on time, but equally did not seem too concerned about the amount of alcohol consumed, about the clear sexual usages of the pub by the 'not very nice girls', and was quite prepared to 'propel regulars towards the door' if they began to be too 'uppish'.

The publican's role in the normative regulation of the social context of the public house had two other important elements which require some comment. Firstly, as already indicated, there seemed to be little differentiation between the pub and the home. While Terry showed a resistance to the time pervasiveness of the work role, and was discriminating in terms of which regulars he fostered, there was a distinct normative deregulation in the way children, especially his own son, were allowed in the pub. There was nothing particularly remarkable about children coming into the pub at certain times, but to have the publican's eight-year-old child around the pub, taking sips of his dad's beer, sitting among the colourful language of the card group, symbolized the social symbiosis of pub life and family in the publican's role style. It was symptomatic of the informal control strategies which characterized the publican's approach to running the pub.

Secondly, it was interesting that the police kept a fairly close watch on the pub, as well as using it for gaining information about people they wanted to 'talk to'. 'Hey up, the fuzz', was the reaction of one of the regulars as two square-shouldered plain-clothes men came in looking for someone. It was not a pub which the police themselves frequented casually or socially – they went to the 'Nelson' up the road (a pub which sold real ale and which was a mixed-class pub) or to a 'respectable' working-class pub. The police, in uniform, descended on the pub one Friday evening just after 11 p.m., after closing time but in the drinking-up period. The pub's reputation seemed to warrant such regular visits – about once every two months. Nothing particularly remarkable happened on the visit but it was clear that it was a very visible reminder to the regulars, and the publican, of the fact that the police were keeping a watch on the pub. There was none of the tolerance of after-hours drinking by the police which appeared to characterize the respectable working-class pub reported elsewhere (Smith, 1981).

## CONCLUSIONS – A ROUGH PUB?

. . . This preliminary study suggests certain important sociological issues.

Are there, in relation to usage of different pubs, different modes of sociability and participation both between pubs as well as within them, and are such differences related to class, sex and age characteristics of users? Also, different public houses offer varying physical–spatial features (such as the shape of the bar, the arrangement of the seating, plushness of the decor), as well as different games–activity facilities. While these features may not determine the patterns of sociability and interaction of pub participants, how do they relate to the focal interests of participants who are 'regulars'? The relationship between the physical-spatial structure of public houses and the focal interests of dominant users may well be mediated by, and reflected in, the structure of social space, the extent of openness to interaction of users in a situation of voluntaristic participation. Thus, the categories of open, negotiable and closed social space as part of an evolved conceptual framework may be important components of usage both within pubs and between them, fostered by the physical–spatial elements of a pub when combined with the focal interests of particular groups of users. How far is the dominant male bar-group subculture, its sexual stereotyping and hard drinking, elements of the rough pub, not characteristic of 'respectable' working-class pubs and 'posh' middle-class pubs? How far are there important differences between the role styles of publicans? The publican in the 'rough' pub evidenced a high separateness from the family in terms of running the pub. Perhaps particular role styles are not unrelated to 'types' of pubs and sociability styles of the users. Equally perhaps the publican's role style fosters particular kinds of 'regulars' and derives from the conception of occupational identity held by the publican.

The series of studies of which this paper forms a part suggests some clues to these issues. Given that there are over 75 000 pubs in the UK and 67% of the UK adult population visit a pub at least once a month, perhaps sociologists ought to try to understand more fully the patterning of social usages, and the role of the public house in class-culture patterning. Such understanding should be predicated upon a generous view of human nature, an acceptance of the importance of the class and gender values, and a more systematic explanation of the relationship between alcohol, leisure and social contexts.

## REFERENCES

Gill, O. (1977) *Luke Street*, Macmillan, London.
Smith, M. A. (1981) *The Pub and the Publican*, Centre for Leisure Studies, University of Salford.
Smith, M. A. (1982) *Leisure, the Public House and Social Control*, Centre for Leisure Studies, University of Salford.
Smith, M. A. (1983) Social usages of the public drinking house, *British Journal of Sociology*, September.

Reading taken from M. Smith, *Leisure Studies*, 4, 293–306, published by Chapman & Hall, 1985.

# IVb Voluntary Provision

# Mutual aid in leisure

17

Jeff Bishop and Paul Hoggett

It is an interesting fact that people will join together to form groups around anything which provides the slightest opportunity for organization. Of all the activities we encountered, there are perhaps just two – cookery and do-it-yourself – around which clubs or associations do not appear to have been built (perhaps because both of these are home-centred activities). Virtually every other leisure activity we have so far encountered that appears to be an essentially individual pursuit – for example, collecting things, gardening, wine-making, drawing – also generates a self-organized, collective form. Here we would like to make a distinction between collective forms of leisure activity which occur in the context of self-run groups and those occurring in day or evening classes; only the former can be properly considered as forms of self-organization. However, as we shall see later, the boundary between such groups and classes may often be a very nebulous one. There are also 'fraternities'.[1] The best-known example of these is probably train-spotters, but their 'collectivity' is clearly of a different order to that of a group with a bounded and relatively stable membership. They are, however, strongly self-organized. Nevertheless, the distinctions are useful and our essential focus will generally be upon groups, not classes or fraternities.

The sheer range and scale of leisure activities in which people engage during their spare time is a remarkable but little understood phenomenon. Consider the following activities around which, to our certain knowledge, local clubs, societies and associations have been formed:

| | |
|---|---|
| Basketball | Table tennis |
| Old-time dancing | Skittles |

[1] We have been unable to find any suitable non-sexist term to replace 'fraternity'.

*Sociology of Leisure: A reader*. Edited by C. Critcher, P. Bramham and A. Tomlinson. Published in 1995 by E & FN Spon, London. ISBN 0 419 19420 7.

Chess
Cats
Aerobics
Orchestras
Football
Lapidary
Fishing
Morris dancing
Tennis
Flower arranging
Bridge
Gardening
Fuchsias
Windsurfing
Railway preservation
Allotments
War games
Cricket
Wine
Philately
Photography
Horse riding
Canoeing
Women's Institutes
Microlights
Harmoniums
Netball
Ballroom dancing
Guitars
Whist
Keep fit
Judo
Wrestling
Athletics
Brass bands
Caving
Handball
Darts
Metal detectors
Volleyball
Parascending
Orienteering
Rat fancying
Computer games

Beekeeping
Meditation
Antiques
Hockey
Toy dogs
Aquarism
Hang-gliding
Numismatism
Naturalism
Snooker
Mums and toddlers groups
Clocks
Practical conservation
Vintage motor cycles
Military modelling
Modern sequence dance
Computers
Rowing
Film and video
Folk dance
Wives' groups
Squash
Sub-aqua
Sailing
Weight-lifting
Motor scooters
Handicrafts
Bird watching
Choirs
Slimming
Boxing
Aikido
Drama
Light opera
Lace making
Softball
Macramé
Yoga
Bowls
Gymnastics
Shove-ha'penny
Upholstery
Silk-screen printing
Oil painting

Point-to-point
Family histories
Lacrosse
Climbing
Local history
Industrial archaeology
Skating
Mouse fancying
Leek growing
Caged birds

Rifle and pistol shooting
Model railways
Cycling
Whippets
Dress-making
Swimming
Aero modelling
Pigeon racing
Canal preservation
Model boats

It is difficult, if not impossible, to classify much of this activity – is ice-dancing, for example, a sport or an art-form? Is photography an art or a hobby? Nevertheless we can try to allocate particular activities to one of four categories: sports, arts, crafts, hobbies. Obviously some groups cannot be placed in these categories; for example, youth groups, mothers and toddlers clubs or Women's Institutes.

## SPORTS

This is probably the easiest category to grasp, covering many well-known activities from football to archery, handball to pistol shooting. However, a plethora of new sports – hang-gliding and softball, for example – have emerged only recently in Britain and many new developments have occurred within existing sports, such as swimming, where 'swim-jogging', synchronized swimming, etc., have all appeared during the last few years. Within all sports, however, major differences can be observed in terms of their organization (teams are essential in football but unimportant in pistol shooting), size of club (400–600 for swimming, twenty-four for badminton) and form of training (whereas the 'coach' is essential to swimming, gymnastics or judo instruction, training is pursued informally among peers in shooting, angling or snooker).

## ARTS

This covers painting, drama, music, dance and so forth. Within each of these a host of different activities take place. 'Dance', for example, covers everything from Scottish country, Northumbrian, morris and square-dancing, through to modern ballroom, old-time, ballet, 'break' and disco dancing.

## CRAFTS

This term includes a variety of pursuits from lapidary to weaving. Almost without exception the products from craft groups are individual, although members may work together to prepare a set display or exhibition. The boundary between craft and hobby can become hazy, as with aquarism or military modelling, and some activities – especially photography – can be thought of as equally art, craft or hobby.

## HOBBIES

This includes a vast range of activities such as rearing and breeding (insects, plants and animals); collecting (clocks, stamps); accounting (train-spotting, bird-watching); modelling, gaming, preserving, restoring, etc. The range here is considerable and one hobby group would probably never imagine themselves to have anything in common with another. It also becomes less easy to distinguish anything resembling training (which might occur in a class) because it is assumed by participants that the whole process of taking part is in itself educational.

Hobby activity also appears to rely more on peer-group support than on external display, so its products are more likely to be generated for fellow enthusiasts than the general public.

## WHY DO ENTHUSIASTS JOIN GROUPS?

First of all, there are a large number of activities which are by their very nature collective, for example, team games, drama, folk dance, bands and orchestras. Secondly, free association would appear to be necessary for certain leisure activities where the required facilities can only be collectively provided. Thus, for most individuals, the cost of establishing a personal shooting range would be prohibitive. Similarly, a number of anglers join fishing clubs because, in many areas nowadays, access to adequate stretches of water is extremely difficult. One joins a club to gain access to a particular gravel pit or part of a river. For similar reasons, many inland yachtsmen join yachting clubs, snooker players join snooker clubs and so forth. Of course, such facilities can be provided by other forms of organization, public or commercial. Thirdly, competition is another factor leading to interaction and forms of social organization. Very often competition may lead to the organization of an activity, even though competitors may never meet each other. This is the case, for example, with inter-club rifle shooting competitions or some photographic competitions.

Clearly, free association is a necessary condition for the performance of many leisure activities, but there are others for which it appears to be an entirely discretionary strategy. Why, for example, do aquarists or gardeners form themselves into clubs, when major aspects of their hobby can be pursued quite satisfactorily alone at home? Again, we would suggest three reasons. First, leisure groups provide a vehicle through which social exchange can take place; people with common enthusiasms can exchange information, provide each other with informal guidance and training, trade anecdotes, etc. This is linked closely to the immersion of enthusiasts within their own particular sub-cultures. Secondly, groups provide opportunities for creating collective rather than individual products – for instance, most of the best model railways to be seen at exhibitions throughout the country are club layouts, often the product of thousands of person-hours' activity. Thirdly, groups provide opportunities for making friends and meeting people, suggesting that the substantive activity itself may be of secondary importance. Even the most competitive of sports clubs will tend to have a highly developed social side to the club's activity. As we shall see, for many organizations this purely social dimension to their existence may not be quite legitimate to discuss openly but may shape their final identity far more than the nature and rules of their ostensible leisure activity. If this is true, it provides a serious challenge to the traditional, 'functional' model of leisure planning. . . .

## THE SCALE OF SELF-ORGANIZED ACTIVITY

We have considered the range of activities. What about the scale? In Kingswood we located around 300 groups. Our search was by no means comprehensive but, assuming an average membership of around ninety, this produced 28 500 people active in the area. This would seem a very high percentage of a total population of around 85 000 (although it should be remembered that some were members of two or three groups, and that some group members came from outside this area). Only 37 per cent involved sporting activities. There were, for example, five photography societies, eight drama societies, four chess clubs and five gardening clubs. The total includes just over 100 'multi-function' groups, many of which contained additional single-purpose clubs (for example, youth football teams, pensioner choral groups) which were not counted separately in our estimates. Furthermore, many single-purpose sports club fielded several teams – some soccer clubs, for example, contained up to four separate teams, each competing in different divisions of the same league.

Our research also suggests that over half of the groups in Kingswood had been running for more than fifteen years, many for much longer. Downend Cricket Club, for example, started in 1893, Frampton Cotterell

Badminton Club in 1945, North Bristol Cribbage League in 1946, Severn Road Club (Cycling) in 1932 and so on.

We have quoted this example because it is typical of what one might call 'middle England'. In our other sampled area of north-west Leicester activity was not so widespread and mostly fairly recent. Here a preliminary survey located 228 groups (the population of this wedge of north-east Leicester was approximately 68 000) with an average membership of about fifty-five. Many of the same activities occurred as in Kingswood, but sport tended to be more of the indoor variety, probably reflecting the lack of outdoor facilities common to most city environments, and martial arts appeared to be more popular, specifically within the large Asian community. Although north-east Leicester possessed some very old clubs (Belgrave Amateur Boxing Club, 1947, West Humberstone Allotment Society, 1918) there was a much greater preponderance of newly formed (post-1970) clubs here than in Kingswood (about 66 per cent as opposed to 40 per cent). To illustrate scale further, we could consider one community college in north-east Leicester. A by no means comprehensive tally of the groups in existence at this one centre would reveal two adult and one youth football clubs, one largely Asian cricket club, a gardening club, a lapidary society, an Irish society, a community orchestra, a photography club, an audio-visual club, a junior gym club and two yoga clubs.

## WHO PARTICIPATES?

In illustrating both range and scale of activity, there is a danger of implying that men and women, old people and children, the disabled, ethnic groups and all social classes participate in these activities to the same degree and in the same ways. It should be obvious that this is not true but our own experience during the research would also lead us to reject the opposite argument – that there are always major, and often worrying divergencies. Perhaps the most significant variations occur along lines of gender, race and class, so we shall deal first with these before some brief comment on age and disability.

In relation to gender, some simple facts are useful. Of those groups replying to our questionnaire, forty-five were exclusively for, or likely to be dominated by, men, and thirty-one for women. However, fifty-five were mixed and these results show little variation between Kingswood and Leicester. Recent campaigns have focused on leisure participation by women, but the assumption of lower levels of female involvement has emerged primarily from information about sports. Our numbers are too small to allow more detailed analysis but we would suspect that, while it is probably true that women participate less in sport, they are very well represented in arts, crafts and hobbies. Such propositions about participation also begin to seem less clear cut if one considers our purely anecdotal knowledge of the type of leisure organization which women join.

Our brief coverage of multi-function groups shows the number and variety of these specifically for women and it did appear to us that women often prefer not merely a woman-only group but also one not tied to a specific activity. Perhaps this is a reflection of a lesser concern for competitiveness and substantive activity, more a concern for social support. Such arguments may also apply to another phenomenon noticed only briefly in our work. It appeared to us that many women also prefer involvement in classes rather than formal groups, yet such involvement was not always as passive recipients; rather, many classes for women became 'proto-groups' in which there was less emphasis on the 'teacher' and more on reciprocation and sharing (for example, keep fit). One further reason for women's involvement with classes is almost certainly that such classes are far less continuously demanding than involvement in groups. Classes start and finish at set times and on set dates; no (or little) member organization is required and to miss one week is almost expected rather than a surprise – all far more appropriate to a woman occupying a traditional role at home.

The interplay between ethnicity and leisure participation was more elusive. Most crafts and hobbies appear to remain largely within the culture which first generated them; we know of no black railway modellers or white Asian volleyball players. (Asian volleyball is quite different from its European namesake.) It is not surprising to find most environmental groups being white, Anglo-Saxon dominated because of the roots of such concerns in long-term history rather than the most recent multi-cultural dimension. Within sports, however, the interlinking is far more fluid, although we noticed a general trend for ethnic groups to 'club together', even in activities dominated by no single group. Some variations are, however, clear and informative. In Leicester (our only source in the absence of a mixed community in Kingswood) cricket appeared to be a highly integrated activity, the majority of clubs containing players from the black and Asian communities as well as local whites. Football, however, was very highly segregated with many teams comprised solely of one ethnic group. We also came across a number of multi-function groups specifically for a single ethnic group and usually also for men and women only. Such examples are, of course, to be expected within, for example, Muslim communities. In summary, however, it did seem to us that ethnic minority groups are less likely to become involved in or form the type of group we are describing here. This cannot be taken to mean that they do not find outlets elsewhere or even that alternative forms of organization are culturally preferred. We certainly experienced no direct exclusion on ethnic grounds, but it no doubt exists, hence limiting choice. There are clearly some important issues here for further work.

In considering class, some of the above issues reappear, with the same provisos about our coverage. First, as with gender and ethnic variations, one expects to find class variation in choice of activity – croquet and whippets are two everyday stereotypes. This we found, though to a much less dramatic degree than we expected. There was a tennis club in Kingswood; none emerged in Leicester. There was a boxing club in Leicester; none emerged in Kingswood. There were folk dance groups, flower arranging and gymnastics in each. Secondly, in terms of simple quantity of participation, while the crude numbers in both areas were surprising, it is probably also true that the participation in Leicester was lower. This would have been seen even more dramatically a few years ago in Leicester, before the intervention of the Urban Programme, because a large number of current groups were formed as a direct result of that initiative. Thirdly we could find nothing in the varying patterns between Leicester and Kingswood to indicate less involvement by working-class people in formal, structured, organized groups in preference for more open and less ordered settings. Fourthly, we did, however, find purely anecdotal evidence that problems of unemployment and poverty can affect participation inasmuch as less disposable income is available for equipment, kit, materials and so forth.

In terms of age, there was little to report that is not self-evident. Few pensioners play football and no young women attend luncheon clubs. Yet many clubs have members who are ex-players or were at one time major participants, but who now involve themselves either just socially or in organization – and are often indispensable for that. At the same time many multi-function groups for the elderly contain extremely passive members who have never been involved in self-organization before. If age does not appear to act as an inhibitor, neither does youth; we came across many groups which either had no lower age limits or which had them but did not invoke them. As mentioned before, there were also a large number of groups run quite specifically for children – gymnastics, karate and so forth – and most of these tended to be run by someone equivalent to an evening class teacher.

For disabled people the picture is very varied. Naturally many hobby, art and craft clubs can and do welcome disabled people, while others no doubt make it clear that they are not welcome. Participation in sport is more problematic, although we found people involved in archery and snooker. We located only one sports club specifically for the disabled (an angling club in Kingswood), perhaps because most provision takes the form of sessions and clubs run by local authorities or interest groups. In both Kingswood and Leicester we spoke to people involved in running groups for the disabled, and those to whom we spoke – themselves disabled – offered strong views on charitable provision, even on the Physically Handicapped/Able-Bodied Clubs which were established specifically to break down barriers. The impression was that they would prefer either true integration in everyday groups or to have their own groups run entirely by themselves.

In summary, then, although the picture is probably not as lopsided as many would suggest, it does seem that women, blacks, Asians (and other ethnic groups), the elderly, the disabled and working-class people do participate less, in different types of group and in somewhat different activities. Partly because of our sample numbers, and partly because we do not consider such variations dramatic enough in relation to our prime focus, we do not deal distinctly with such variations. . . .

## TERMS

We have tried here to convey some idea of the myriad groups involved in leisure activity, of the range and depth of activity which they cover, and of the leagues, federations, etc. which build from this bedrock. What concepts can we employ to bring some order and meaning to this vast and superficially random area of activity? The conventional academic or professional answer to this question would be to invoke the title we used ourselves at the outset of our research work. One could suggest (as did our research clients at the outset) that we are focusing on the 'Voluntary Sector in Leisure and Recreation'. Without getting embroiled in a tedious semantic argument, we wish to claim that this title is actually very inappropriate, even dangerous in its bearing on the territory we are beginning to describe.

Consider the word *voluntary*. In our conversations with group members, we met very few people who would accept that their involvement in their group constitutes any form of *volunteering*. Indeed, some would vehemently deny that they are volunteers because, even if they are virtually full-time organizers of large groups, their motivation is primarily that of personal pleasure in their activity rather than one of offering philanthropic effort and service to others. (We are aware that we may be dealing here with stereotypical notions of 'voluntary', etc.)

Next consider the word *sector*. This implies some coherence, shared sense of identity and common aims. Our conversations with members lead us to think that it is inconceivable to imagine bringing together a drama group with a rifle club, a folk dance society and a military modelling club. Indeed, we found that even a local Sports Council had difficulty sustaining corporate interest amongst its members. One can consider the general position of this 'sector' in leisure as compared to the voluntary sector in welfare. For the latter (as Wolfenden stated) one part of their role is to fill the gaps left by the public sector, and hence they can create little action-space of their own, independent of formal provision. In the world of leisure, the relationship is the opposite: it is the public sector which has to try to fill the gaps and provide the 'enabling' which permits the many distinct clubs and societies to continue. If we were to be slightly cynical, we would suggest that the use of the construct 'voluntary sector in leisure' is a process generated by those in power (who generally have a simple functional model of leisure) with the intention of bringing a diverse territory into some form of order to make it manageable. Without a sense of the cultural richness of the varied groups, and of their independence from certain socio-economic forces, one is bound to reduce complexity to a 'sector'. We are clearly hinting here that – perhaps not deliberately – the actions of some agencies involved with the world of leisure are in danger of reducing this cultural richness, of 'colonialising' a diverse territory. We return to this issue in our final chapter.

Finally, let us look at the word *leisure*. Many have struggled with definitions of this odd term. A crude Marxist analysis would place leisure as a superstructural element, residual to underlying socio-economic forces and an indicator of the alienation of the populace from work and from constructive political action. For those from the liberal tradition, leisure may not have such rigid links to other areas of social and economic life, nor is it a territory manipulated deliberately by those in power to pacify the proletariat. It is, however, a spare-time, individualist activity rather than a locus for social cohesion and change. Underlying both definitions, there is also that strong functionalist tradition which sees any group activity as merely a means to an end and denies that involvement with a group can offer significant personal and social benefits in its own right. Neither perspective construes leisure as the site for relatively autonomous forms of collective activity which play a significant role in the overall cultural life of a society.

We feel that the issue of the language we use is crucial. The phrase 'the voluntary sector in leisure and recreation' is a misleading one. While we can offer no ideal alternative, the term we use – despite its own limitations – is 'communal leisure'. We must now describe those aspects of the groups constituting communal leisure which serve to demonstrate our object – if it is not a voluntary sector. We would argue that the majority of these groups are mutual-aid organizations whose ostensible prime purpose is a leisure or recreation activity. *They are collectivities which are self-organized, productive and which, by and large, consume their own products.* This is why they may be more than merely 'leisure groups' – because there is probably no other setting in our society where people can freely come together to produce something outside the market economy, primarily for consumption by themselves or their friends and neighbours. ...

The basis of mutual aid is reciprocity, to the extent that relationships – essentially the exchange of effort and involvement – are governed by a very loose concept of 'give and take'. A small hockey club may be watched by only a handful of people, but these are almost certain to be committee members or ex-players. While the club may be the organizational product of these 'spectators', such effort only has real value when reciprocated (in a different form) by the players on the pitch. (One can even add that the outcomes are equally dependent upon the visiting team!) It is this aspect of the quality of the exchange relationship which leads us to use the apparently odd terms 'production' and 'consumption'. Clearly many groups *produce* something. For gardeners this is obvious, similarly model-lers, artists and photographers. If one views a play or an exhibition as a 'production', it becomes possible to construe a netball game or a badmin-ton match as a production also. In other words, in communal leisure people come together to engage in a specific type of productive activity, whether it be individual (to produce a necklace), corporate (some scenery), tightly specified (a football cup match) or rather open-ended (a gardening show). Furthermore, there is a sense in which group members see the overall identity and character of their group as a product also. Almost any group we encountered was able to locate itself in terms of its character in relation to others and each was quite proud of its balance between substantive (for example, competitive) aspects and the more diffuse social factors. If we look now at *consumption*, a fuller meaning becomes available to the idea of reciprocity, because the essential distinguishing factor is that the products we have described are, in mutual aid groups, consumed by the producers themselves. The consumption does not have to be direct and immediate; thus after much preparation a drama group will present its production to an audience. We have, however, noticed that the majority of small drama societies generate audiences comprised almost entirely of friends, relatives and local residents – another form of 'us' rather than 'them'. There are certainly some extremes in which all the products of a group are exclusively for consumption by group members – perhaps a small flower-arranging group with no teacher as such, no exhibitions and no contact with wider flower-arranging circles. There are, however, many groups, probably the majority, in which the products are ostensibly avail-able for public consumption (on a park playing field or at a military modelling exhibition, for example), but where the only 'consumers' are the participants and their peers (military modellers from other clubs) or ex-participants (as in the hockey club). It is probably even true that the absence of the general public, far from demeaning the value of what is presented, actually enhances its value because comment or criticism is a reaction by recognized peers. It is this important dimension of self-con-sumption which utterly transforms the meaning of the activity from that experienced in commercialized or professionalized forms of leisure.

In describing what we consider to be the key elements which serve to distinguish communal leisure from other areas of activity – collectivity, self-organization, production for self-consumption, mutual aid – we are aware that we are offering 'ingredients'. They do not, however, of themselves adequately characterize or explain the remarkable resilience and often assertive independence of the world of communal leisure which we experienced in our work. We will find ourselves returning frequently to this elusive aspect which we shall call 'identity' and which is far more than just a mere addition of ingredients. It is ultimately this aspect of the many groups which is both precious and yet at the same time most threatened.

Reading taken from J. Bishop and P. Hoggett, *Organizing Around Enthusiasms*, published by Comedia, 1986. Reprinted with permission.

# The hidden musicians

**18**

## Ruth Finnegan

The world of jazz was more fragmented than those discussed so far, in its musical styles, social groupings, training, and the model drawn on by participants. Jazz was regarded as distinctive, but at the same time as shading on one side into rock or folk, on the other into brass band or classical music. Within 'jazz' too there were several differing traditions each with its own devotees, making up networks of individuals and groups rather than the more explicitly articulated worlds of, say, brass band or fold music. But, as will become clear in this chapter, jazz was certainly played and appreciated in Milton Keynes. To the outsider it was less visible than classical, operatic and brass band music on the one hand or the plentiful rock bands on the other, but for the enthusiast 'in the know' there were many opportunities for both playing and hearing jazz.

Take first the various playing groups. In the early 1980s there were about a dozen jazz bands in or around the Milton Keynes area. Some were local only in the sense of having one member living in the locality and making regular appearances there, but for many most of their members were locally based. A few were short lived, but some had been going for years (often with some change of personnel or developing from an earlier group) and in many cases put on regular performances with a healthy local following. Three of the bands playing in Milton Keynes in the early 1980s – the Original Grand Union Syncopators, the Fenny Stompers and the T-Bone Boogie Band – can illustrate some of the accepted patterns as well as differences in the local jazz scene.

The first two had much in common. They shared the same basic jazz format of six players: clarinet or saxophone, trumpet or cornet, and trombone (the 'front line' where the solo spots were concentrated) with a rhythm section of banjo, percussion and (string) bass, some players

*Sociology of Leisure: A reader.* Edited by C. Critcher, P. Bramham and A. Tomlinson. Published in 1995 by E & FN Spon, London. ISBN 0 419 19420 7.

doubling on occasion as vocalists. Both bands put on regular performances both locally and (less often) further afield to enthusiastic audiences. . . .

The T-Bone Boogie Band was different yet again. As they themselves publicised it, they went in for 'rhythm and blues with an element of self ridicule', for 'blues and mad jazz' and, as one of their admirers expressed it, 'boogie, ragtime, bop and riddum 'n' blooze'. They presented themselves as a zany 'fun band', but their act followed many traditional jazz and blues sequences, with beautiful traditional playing interspersed with their own wilder enactments of blues. They spoke of these as 'improvised out of nowhere, on the spur of the moment', but they were in practice based on long hours of jamming together as a group.

These three bands were not the only jazz groups functioning in Milton Keynes and the picture must be completed by briefly mentioning some of the others. These included the five-piece Momentum, putting on about twenty performances a year, mainly early fifties bebop, on a combination of flugelhorn/trumpet, reeds/saxophone, bass, keyboards and drums; the Mahogany Hall Jazzmen playing Dixieland early jazz and ragtime regularly once a fortnight or so in local pubs; and the long-lasting Wayfarers Jazz Band performing 'mainstream' and Dixieland jazz in pubs, wine bars, social clubs, colleges and fêtes in both the Milton Keynes and the Luton–Dunstable area – not quite a 'local' jazz band, though one very active member lived locally. Among the other local or near-local jazz bands (several of them overlapping in personnel with those already mentioned) were the Alan Fraser Band, the twosome blues and early jazz Bootleg Band, the Concorde Jazz Band, the Holt Jazz Quintet, the zany 1920s New Titanic Band with its stage pyrotechnics, the very fluid Stuart Green Band, the Colin James Trio, Oxide Brass and the John Dankworth Quartet (this last based on WAP and giving occasional performances there); there were also the short-lived Delta New Orleans Jazz, the New City Jazz Band, the Pat Archer Jazz Trio and (for a few struggling months) the MK Big Band.

All these bands put on public performances, sometimes singly, sometimes on a regular basis at particular pubs and clubs in the area. In addition there were probably several other groups who met more for the pleasure of jamming together or playing on private occasions than for taking on public engagements. The Saints group of six 11-year olds on clarinet, flute, trumpet, percussion and piano, for example, played jazz or pop together and performed in school assemblies and the end-of-term concert, while the highly educated all-female Slack Elastic Band played 'big band' and popular jazz of the thirties on trumpet, saxophone and string bass as a rehearsal rather than performing band, and the newer Jack and the Lads with trumpet, saxophone, guitar, bass guitar and drums were initially performing just for enjoyment on the Open University campus. There were doubtless other groups playing privately – an opportunity more open to them than to the larger and louder brass bands, operatic groups or amplified rock bands.

The administration of jazz bands differed from classical, operatic and brass band groups in that they seldom adopted the formal voluntary organization framework. The numbers were smaller, for one thing: with a couple of exceptions like the short-lived MK Big Band, there were usually five or six players so that jazz groups were run on personal, not bureaucratic lines, geared to individual achievement rather than the hierarchical musical direction characteristic of larger groups. This also fitted their open-ended form, for though there were certain common groupings of instruments, the actual instrumental compositions of jazz groups was more variable than in most other musical worlds.

The fluidity was also evident in the music-making itself. Jazz musicians were tied neither to written forms nor to exact memorisation, but rather engaged in a form of composition-in-performance following accepted stylistic and thematic patterns. This, of course, is a well known characteristic of jazz more generally – not that anyone has ever managed to define 'jazz' too precisely – so it was no surprise to find it at the local level in the views and behaviour of those classifying themselves as jazz players. Local musicians often commented on the freedom they felt in jazz as compared to either classical music or rock. One commented that with rock 'it's all happened already' (i.e., already developed in prior rehearsals), whereas in jazz the performance itself was creative; another player explained his enthusiasm for jazz through the fact that 'it allows a lot of expression for the individual'. Similarly a local jazz drummer talked about how in classical playing, unlike jazz, he had had 'no real chance to create in a number, no choice about what to do' and so ultimately preferred playing jazz to classical music.

This aspect was also very apparent in the performance of local jazz players. Far more than other musicians they would break into smiles of recognition or admiration as one after another player took up the solo spot, and looked at each other in pleasure after the end of a number, as if having experienced something newly created as well as familiar. As one local jazz player put it, 'we improvise, with the tunes used as vehicles, so everything the group does is original'. Local jazz musicians often belonged to *several* jazz bands, moving easily between different groups. A musician who played both jazz and rock explained this in the following terms: with a rock band you are dependent on joint practicing since the whole performance is very tight, whereas with jazz, providing you have learnt the basic conventions, 'I can play traditional jazz with a line-up I've not met before.' Jazz groups were thus less likely to have regular rehearsals than the other small bands: when they did play together it was often based on their general jazz skills rather than specific rehearsals of particular pieces. This open nature in performance also explained the high proportion of jazz 'residencies' by which the same band was booked to appear at the same venue once every fortnight or so. Audiences were likely to get tired of the same music time after time (a problem for rock and country and western bands), but were not bored by the more fluid jazz performances: 'numbers are practically made up on the spot'. . . .

Jazz in Milton Keynes, then, was more a fluid and impermanent series of bands and venues than an integrated and self-conscious musical world. There were not strong historical precursors in the area, and the local players never managed to set up a permanent venue where they could be sure of regularly hearing jazz by local and regional players over a matter of years. In addition, apart from the (general purpose) Musicians' Union, to which few local players belonged, there was no national association to which local groups could affiliate (unlike the classical, folk, operatic and brass band worlds) – or, if there was, it was apparently of little interest to Milton Keynes players. In all, there seemed to be a less distinctive view of what 'jazz' was and should be than with some of the other forms of music in Milton Keynes, and the experiences of jazz players and enthusiasts were defined more by the actual activities and interactions of local bands that labelled themselves as 'jazz' than by any clearly articulated ideal model.

Despite this, there *were* shared perceptions and experiences – unformulated though these were – of what it was to be a jazz player and to play jazz. This was shown most vividly in the way jazz players, far more strikingly than rock musicians, went in for membership of more than one jazz group and moved readily between bands; it was easy to ask guests to come and jam, from named stars from outside or ex-members who happened to be around to a ten-year-old boogie-woogie pianist from the audience. For though both the form of music-making and the constitution of the groups were in a sense fluid, there were definite shared expectations about the jazz style of playing, the traditional formulae, and the modes of improvising within recognised conventions: 'all jazz lovers know the tunes already', as one player expressed it. Players in other groups were recognised as fellow experts – more, or less, accomplished – in the same general tradition of music-making, and bands engaged in friendly rivalry with each other, going to each other's performances 'to smell out the opposition' or – on occasion – to look for a new player themselves. Similarly they were prepared to help out other bands, filling in at short notice if they were in difficulties.

Even though for practically all the players discussed here jazz was only a part-time leisure pursuit and not widely acclaimed throughout the city, both the musical activity itself, and the shared skills, pride and conventions that constituted jazz playing seemed to be a continuing element in their own identity and their perceptions of others. Once involved, 'as a musician, you need to play . . . something you've got to do'; for, as another player put it, 'it's a blood thing, it's in your veins'. . . .

The multiplicity of pathways matches the heterogeneity often seen as characteristic of urban life, the overlap of many relatively distinct paths reflecting the many-sided, situational, often changing lives that people lead in towns today. But they bring, too, a sense of belonging and reality: travelling not in an alien environment but along familiar paths in time and space, in family continuity and habitual action. The pathways have their continuities too. They depend on regular sets of largely predictable and purposeful activities that it is easy to overlook if attention is focused primarily on networks of individuals or the interaction of multiple special-interest groups. Not *everyone* follows these particular pathways, of course. But those who do are scarcely likely to agree either with the anonymous letter-writer complaining of the lack of 'community spirit' in Milton Keynes or with social theorists positing impersonality, alienation or calculation as the basis of urban life. For they are themselves forging and keeping open the routes which to them bring not just value and meaning but one framework for living space and time. The *specific* conditions within Milton Keynes (or any locality) are likely to be unique, but I have no doubt that other towns too have their pathways which represent neither tight-knit 'community' nor alien anonymity but one established and habitual way in which people find their meaning in urban living.

These pathways, then, are one of the ways in which people within an urban environment organise their lives so as to manage, on the one hand, the heterogeneity and multiplicity of relationships characteristic of many aspects of modern society, and, on the other, that sense of both predictable familiarity and personally controlled meaning that is also part of human life. In our culture there are many pathways that people do, and must, follow – within employment, schooling, households, sport, church, child-rearing. Within these many paths, who is to say that the pathways to do with music are the least important, either for their participants or in the infinite mix of crossways that make up an urban locality and, ultimately, our culture?

There is one final point to re-emphasise. This is that the continuance of these pathways – so often either ignored or taken for granted as 'just there' – depends not on the existence in some abstract sphere of particular musical 'works', but on people's collective and active practice on the ground. The structure and extent of this work by the local grass-roots musicians and their supporters often goes unrecognised. . . . These pathways of music-making are not 'natural' ones that cut their own way through the bush, but were opened up and kept trodden by those who worked them. This is very clear with innovative forms of music-making, where people are creating new pathways; but exactly the same point applies to keeping up the older established paths where even 'tradition' means active fosterage if it is to be maintained. Some people can drop out from time to time, but enough must continue to keep the paths clear so that when one group dissolves or one individual passes on their work is replaced or complemented by that of others. The old picture of blind tradition passing mechanically down the generations, as if irrespective of human act, is easily rejected once made explicit, but it still often influences us into assuming that our accepted cultural forms – classical music performances, church choirs, brass bands, rock groups in pubs, carol singing at Christmas – somehow carry on automatically. On the contrary. These paths may be trodden deep, but they only continue because thousands of people up and down the country put thousands of hours and an unmeasurable quantity of personal commitment into keeping them open. As Peter Burke put it of the classical culture of earlier centuries:

> The classical tradition ... has often been described in terms of metaphors like 'survival' or 'inheritance' or 'legacy'; one needs to make an effort to remember that this inheritance was not automatic, that it depended on beating some knowledge of certain classical authors into generation after generation of schoolboys (1980, p. 4).

Exactly the same point could be made of the traditions of local music-making in modern towns and the manner in which they – among other pathways – constitute the structure and rituals through which people live out their lives. Some paths go out of use, others are kept trodden only with a struggle, some seem for a time effortlessly open. But all depend on the constant hidden cultivation by active participants of the musical practices that, with all their real (not imaginary) wealths and meanings, keep in being the old and new cultural traditions within our society.

**REFERENCE**

Burke, Peter (1980) *Popular Culture in Early Modern Europe*, London: Temple Smith.

Reading taken from R. Finnegan, *The Hidden Musicians*, published by Cambridge University Press, 1989. Reprinted with permission.

# IVc Public Provision

| 19 | # Leisure in the welfare state |
| --- | --- |

John Wilson

Social democratic states like the United Kingdom have 'mixed economies' in which some aspects of production and distribution have been national-ized. In such regimes, support is given to the notion of the 'public house-hold' which exists alongside the private household and the market; it is the agency for the satisfaction of public needs and public wants, as against private wants (Bell, 1973, p. 220). As 'head' of the public household, government is essentially involved in the direction of the national economy through tax and monetary policies, transfer payments to redistribute income, social security schemes and various forms of subsidy. The govern-ment commits itself to redressing the impact of economic and social inequalities and in so doing creates a welfare state. Inevitably, the welfare state becomes an arena for the fulfillment not only of clearly public needs but also of private and group wants. Claims on the community take the form of 'entitlements' – to decent housing, affordable health care, old age security, unemployment compensation and the like. 'Entitlements' is another word for what T. H. Marshall (1950, p. 11) called social rights, 'the whole range from the right to a modicum of economic welfare and security to the right to share to the full in the social heritage and to live the life of a civilized being according to the standards prevailing in society.' Social rights thus include an equal claim to a 'style of life' as well as money income. The recognition that everyone has a right to a certain style of life interferes with the market principle of capitalism – just as an increase in the naked function of the market interferes with the enjoyment of egali-tarian social rights.

In the welfare state, leisure also comes to be looked upon as an entitle-ment, a service to be delivered by the state, much like health care. The enjoyment of leisure is considered a basic individual right. The public

*Sociology of Leisure: A reader.* Edited by C. Critcher, P. Bramham and A. Tomlinson. Published in 1995 by E & FN Spon, London. ISBN 0 419 19420 7.

expects state intervention in leisure and sees leisure provision as an important social service, even if people do not make full use of the amenities available. The leisure citizen, to whom benefits accrue as of right, stands in contrast to the leisure consumer, who must earn them in the marketplace. However, in such 'mixed economies' there is rarely any coherent leisure policy or program at the national level, many 'taste publics' exist, and private commercial organizations still dominate the provision of leisure services, while the state plays a secondary role. The state is torn between improving the cultural level of the public on the one hand (a kind of paternalism to which welfare statism is subject) and allowing the public to find its own level on the other. The result is a kind of cultural democracy providing 'entertainment' rather than culture. . . .

## THE GOVERNMENT AND LEISURE POLICY

Just how active the national government has been in the formation and execution of leisure policy has depended somewhat on the party in power, although the long-term trend has been toward more centralization and toward statutory powers and away from voluntarism. By the late 1960s both political parties had begun to appeal to a newly affluent working class and to college-educated professionals on the basis of their policies toward leisure. Conservative governments preferred to minimize government control over, or subsidy of, leisure, espousing a form of cultural democracy of the dollar in which the market regulates supply and demand. Labour governments have been more concerned to achieve equality of leisure opportunities through collective action. However, even the Labour government has not pursued the goal of leisure equality directly through the administration of leisure but rather through equalizing conditions of work.

There can be little doubt that public bodies like the Sports Council and the Countryside Commission have underrepresented working-class people and reflected mainly middle-class leisure interests. However, the impact of this bias on leisure behaviour is far from clear. It has been limited by the fact that the marketplace has been the major determinant of leisure activities in Britain. Public providers of leisure have no captive audience. The public picks and chooses, and if the government seeks to compete with private enterprise in the bid to be the chosen provider, it must do so on terms dictated by the market and by consumer choice.

Battling both commercial interests and working-class apathy, the members of the sports and leisure establishment have sought to win approval of a leisure policy that would combine the goal of equality of access with the preservation of individual freedom. The Minister for Sport wrote in 1972 that 'the provision of sport and recreational opportunities is indeed a social service that in its own way is almost as important to the well-being of the community as good housing, hospitals and schools' (McIntosh and Charlton, 1985, p. 13). The House of Lords Select Committee on Sport and Leisure (1973, p. xxiv) declared that 'Providing for leisure is a service which public authorities now have a duty to undertake.' It was claimed that properly planned and supervised leisure would reduce the incidence of heart disease, reduce boredom and 'urban frustration,' combat 'hooliganism and delinquency among young people' and, through international competition, raise national morale. Committee members believed recreation to be one of the community's everyday needs, and declared that provision for it should be 'part of the general fabric of the social services.'

The Committee sought to justify government intervention in leisure on the usual grounds. The government must seek distributive justice ('leisure services should be available to all, whether they can afford to pay for them or not, and whether their neighbourhood is rich or poor': p. xxix); the government will always be needed to fill in the gaps left by the market (private enterprise is 'not concerned to see that an adequate range and location of facilities are available': p. xxix); government is necessary to protect public amenities and collective goods (to 'prevent the increased pressure for countryside recreation from damaging both agriculture and the countryside': p. xxix); government must come to the aid of voluntary work (which will usually be underfunded when it comes to major projects); the welfare state idea has established a sense of entitlement among the citizenry: 'The public in this country are not accustomed to paying the full economic rate for their facilities, and the American example of commercial sports halls will not be followed in the near future' (p. xxxi).

The Committee thus adopted an integrative approach to leisure policy, seeking to absorb all social groups in the life of the nation, 'to make us all participating citizens' (Clarke and Critcher, 1985, p. 139). In pursuit of a European-wide 'Sport for all' policy, the Sports Council likewise sought to make recreational facilities available to as many groups as possible. Special groups, referred to as 'sports illiterates,' were targeted for special attention. These included the elderly, women, the disabled and those who had never been exposed to sport educationally (McIntosh and Charlton, 1985, p. 16). 'Sport for all' was justified not only for its own sake, but also as a means of spreading health and social benefits and promoting social solidarity in inner-city areas.

Government priorities are usually reflected in budgets. The importance attached to leisure by postwar United Kingdom governments is difficult to gauge from budget figures because of the diffusion of responsibility for this provision across many government departments and because some departments, such as Education, do not list leisure expenditures separately. Expenditures on sport are recorded by the Sports Council and show a steady growth in support for sport until 1980. The amount of money the central government spends directly on sport is minuscule, but spending on sport by all government authorities is nearly twice that spent on the prison service or passenger subsidies to rail, bus, underground and ferry services in any given year (McIntosh and Charlton, 1985, p. 41). Dissatisfaction with the amount of expenditure by central government on sport has from time to time been expressed; but in principle and in financial terms, the aim of treating sport as a social service like housing, health and education has been achieved. Funding for sport at the state and local level has kept up with inflation as well as has funding for housing, health, or education.

Political differences in the approach to leisure are not hard to discern. Most Conservatives favor a kind of cultural democracy, allowing people to express their leisure wants through the operation of the free market. They believe in the essential autonomy of leisure and are angered by attempts to use leisure for other purposes. They find the encouragement of leisure as disturbing as its censorship or suppression. Socialists, on the other hand, see leisure as being inevitably political and seek to make it serve the right political ends short of imposing a homogeneous leisure culture on what they see as an essentially pluralistic system. In this respect they differ from Conservatives, who believe in the essential homogeneity of culture.

Despite these philosophical differences – representative, perhaps, of the more extreme viewpoints – Labour and Conservative governments have been strikingly alike in their willingness to invest money in leisure opportunities (Bramham and Henry, 1985, p. 16). Conservatives tend to approach leisure from the standpoint of economic efficiency and 'wastage of talent,' whereas Labour is more concerned with the amelioration of social inequality and an increase in social mobility. With enabling legislation and financial assistance under the Countryside Act of 1968, local councils and other agencies have embarked on major programs of developing rural land for recreation and protecting existing facilities from urban sprawl (Groome, 1985, p. 97). However, the economic stagnation of the 1970s and 1980s and the attendant government spending cuts have resulted in fewer new facilities being planned or built, the closure of old buildings and reduced opening hours for existing ones, and have exacerbated the problems caused to lower income groups by the absence of mass transportation.

In the 1980s leisure policy in the United Kingdom came under the influence of a 'new Right' politics in which leisure is seen pre-eminently as an area of sovereignty of the individual best left untouched by the state. The Thatcher government's policy toward leisure was an integral part of its drive to reprivatize the economy and minimize the role of central governments. The Sports Council, which had already assumed the role of a clearing house through which potential commercial sponsors could be put in touch with sports bodies requiring funding, was restaffed to be more sympathetic to the government's 'new right' economic philosophy; the

BBC came under increasing pressure to tolerate the use of commercial sponsorship in the sports events it covered; joint public–private ventures were encouraged; 'user fees' were instituted and other means explored (e.g. vending machines) to make leisure facilities self-supporting. Attempts to make local government more rational and cost effective also seriously affected the leisure component. Under a new system in which the central government requires local authorities to draw up 'structure plans' justifying broad land-use policies – a reform which in principle could serve to better protect recreational opportunities – local governments are expected to emphasize a number of 'key issues' (e.g. housing). Leisure, however, is not one of the issues thus identified; it is treated as a residual concern in this new land-use planning procedure, best catered to by private industry.

## CAN LEISURE BE ADMINISTERED?

The political management of leisure services in a mixed economy will almost inevitably run the gamut from a policy in which the state is seen as stimulating and smoothing the working of the market for leisure to one where the state is intended to compete with and perhaps eliminate the market for leisure services. The first position is exemplified by the English Tourist Board (a government agency), which sees itself as enhancing people's leisure lives by stimulating private sector economic growth and employment. A spokesman for the Board approaches tourism and leisure as a marketing issue: 'We want to provide a product people want to buy' (Thorburn, 1984, p. 14). The second position is exemplified by a spokesman for the socialist-run Greater London Council (abolished in 1986). He points to the vast sums of money being earned by the 'culture industries,' money spent on gambling, home entertainment equipment, sports and sports equipment, books, toys and the like, and sees in this demand something for which the state could cater as well as private industry. Furthermore, public catering to these needs would avoid the kind of neglect of disadvantaged groups for which private enterprise is criticized (Tomkins, 1984). Mixed economies such as that of the United Kingdom therefore show no consistent or integrated policy toward leisure. In some respects this policy is closer to that found in the United States; in other respects it comes closer to the total elimination of the private market for leisure services in the interests of the state, a policy found in the kind of regime to be discussed elsewhere. . . .

While we can expect the welfare states to become more and more involved in leisure, and particularly in sport, it is unlikely that any will endorse the view that the state itself should provide leisure services on any significant scale. Leisure cannot be equated with education, medicine and shelter as a state function because there is an inherent contradiction in the planning on which the welfare state must depend on the one hand and the freedom necessarily entailed in true leisure on the other. Leisure is, by definition and general consent, set apart from work, a kind of 'idleness' to which people claim the right; and yet the state must encourage productivity and reinforce the work ethic. Leisure means people doing what they want, without constraint or supervision; and yet the state must ensure a measure of conformity and order. Free choice of leisure opportunities means open access, but the government must look after the long run and protect the people themselves against the social costs of excess demands on leisure amenities. These are contradictions inherent in the social democratic state. Without full nationalization, and without the kind of colonization of leisure attempted in totalitarian regimes, these contradictions will continue to generate political conflicts over the use of leisure.

## REFERENCES

Bell, D. (1973), *The Cultural Contradictions of Capitalism* (New York: Basic Books).

Bramham, P., and Henry, I. (1985), 'Political ideology and leisure policy in the United Kingdom,' *Leisure Studies*, vol. 4, pp. 1–19.

Clarke, J., and Critcher, C. (1985), *The Devil Makes Work: Leisure in Capitalist Britain* (Urbana: University of Illinois Press).

Groome, D. (1985), 'Increasing opportunities for enjoyment of rural recreation in Britain,' *Society and Leisure*, vol. 8, pp. 95–108.

House of Lords, Select Committee on Sport and Leisure (1973), *Second Report* (London: HMSO).

Marshall, T. H. (1950), *Citizenship and Social Class* (Oxford University Press).

McIntosh, P., and Charlton, V. (1985), *The Impact of Sport for All Policy* (London: Sports Council).

Thorburn, A. (1984), 'Planning – the people business,' in A. Tomlinson (ed.), *Leisure: Politics, Planning and People* (Eastbourne: Leisure Studies Association), pp. 14–19.

Tomkins, A. (1984), 'Cultural policy, the market and the local state,' in A. Tomlinson (ed.), *Leisure: Politics, Planning and People* (Eastbourne: Leisure Studies Association), pp. 140–4.

Reading taken from J. Wilson, *Politics and Leisure*, published by Allen & Unwin, 1988. Reprinted with permission.

# 20 Sport and the state

Garry Whannel

In many countries the state has developed a systematic policy towards sport and put it into practice. Cuba is an excellent example. This has not happened in Britain. The recurrent pattern has been one of *ad hoc* improvisations, carried out by a variety of separate, largely voluntary organisations, with unco-ordinated plans and persistent financial problems. This chapter will examine the Sports Council and the problems of a state policy towards sport.

I earlier outlined the development of sport in England in terms of shifting patterns of dominance. The aristocratic patronage of the eighteenth century was replaced in importance by the rise of sport institutions dominated by sections of the upper–middle class of the late nineteenth century. These predominantly amateur–paternal sport organisations dominated English sport until the post-war era. From the early 1950s the growing internationalisation of sport, its penetration by capitalist commerce, the effect of television and the associated growth of sponsorship gave birth to a new form of patronage – the economic patronage of sponsorship. Only in the last 20 years has the state played much of a role.

The state intervenes in the field of sport and leisure in three main ways. First, it tries to ban certain activities, such as attempts to outlaw bowls and football in the sixteenth and seventeenth centuries. There was the wave of anti-cruel-sport legislation in the nineteenth century. Bare-knuckle boxing remains illegal and a new lobby is under way to ban boxing altogether.

Second, the state regulates and licenses activities. The most notable example is the control of betting and gaming. The whole social practice of gambling, and hence horse-racing and greyhound-racing in their current forms, is in no small part determined by state legislation. The 1960 Betting

*Sociology of Leisure: A reader.* Edited by C. Critcher, P. Bramham and A. Tomlinson. Published in 1995 by E & FN Spon, London. ISBN 0 419 19420 7.

and Gaming Act brought the off-course betting shop into being. In 1953 there had been 4000 arrests for street betting in London, but by 1967 there were a mere three. A vastly profitable and legal industry had been created.

Third, the state provides facilities. The long fight by the labour movement gradually forced the reductions in working hours and increase in public holidays that made leisure time a possibility for urban workers. Conservative concern with social control and liberal pressure for social reform led to a growth in municipal provision of parks, wash-houses and swimming pools. But the scale should not be exaggerated. In 1909 there were more public hard courts for tennis in Hamburg than in the whole of England.

## THE RISE OF THE SPORTS COUNCIL

State involvement in leisure was largely *ad hoc* and local from the mid-nineteenth century until the 1930s. The first impetus towards a central coherent organization grew out of concern over national fitness. The international capitalist crisis of the 1930s had caused severe cuts in public spending and unemployment for between two and three million people. Children left school at 14 but could obtain unemployment benefit after 16 only by attending the compulsory Junior Instruction Centres.

The rise of fascism in Europe prompted British establishment figures to compare the nationalistic fervour of fascist youth movements with the supposed listless, apathetic state of Britain's youth. Within the ruling classes, both those who admired and those who feared the rise of fascism felt some need for action. These half-formed feelings combined with the growth of a consciousness about physical culture stemming from the medical and physical education professions. The many existing voluntary bodies also felt the need for a forum to co-ordinate activities.

The Central Council for Recreation and Training (as it was then called) was formed in 1935, through the initiative of Phyllis Colson, a physical education organiser. It had royal patronage and the support of the Board of Education. It brought together organisations of sport and physical education, along with a large medical presence. The declared aim was 'to help improve the physical and mental health of the community through physical recreation by developing existing facilities for recreative physical activities of all kinds and also by making provision for the thousands not yet associated with any organisation'.

The government was also prompted to act by concern with fitness. It formed a National Fitness Council, which had a brief and unhappy life. The outbreak of war eventually defused the paranoia over national fitness. After the war the CCPR was to turn its attention to the provision of facilities and, in particular, to the development of National Recreation Centres.

The CCPR was an independent body, but most of its income came from statutory grants. So in the late 1940s and 1950s it featured in post-war reconstruction, along with the growth of the welfare state and the expansion of state intervention in the mixed economy.

Its most significant achievement at this time was the establishment of seven National Recreation Centres. These provided residential facilities for a variety of sports. The centres mainly served more committed sports people and part of their role was to raise standards at the highest levels to boost British chances in international competition.

The physical education world was becoming increasingly concerned with preparing for international competition. English assumptions of sporting dominance were shaken when Hungary's footballers beat England 6–3 at Wembley in 1953. English sporting administrators felt threatened by the growing power of both America and the communist countries in international sport. There was a reaction against the traditional amateur–paternal ethos.

The CCPR set up the Wolfenden Committee in 1957 to recommend ways in which statutory bodies could help promote the general welfare of the community in sport and leisure. Confusion between developing an elite and serving the general interest is a typical feature of English debates over sport policy.

The Wolfenden report, *Sport and the Community* (1960), found that there was an overwhelming case for statutory financing of sport. It expressed concern that sport, which then came under the Minister for Education, was a low priority. The report recommended the establishment of a sports council of six to ten people to control expenditure of around £5 million per year.

A distinct political consensus was developing. In the 1959 election campaign both major parties were against a minister for sport but in favour of a sports council along the lines of the Arts Council. But the victorious Conservatives then did little. Lord Hailsham, given special responsibility for sport, increased government expenditure, but dragged his feet over the proposed sports council.

Labour came to power in 1964 committed to a sports council but, as a statutory body required legislation, they initially set up an advisory council. Seven years of uncomfortable negotiation followed as the relationship between this advisory council and the CCPR was worked out. The problems were a reflection of a typical desire on the part of the British state to prevent institutions appearing to be state controlled. A Minister for Sport would be answerable to parliament, whereas a quasi-independent council, even if appointed by the government, would be outside the parliamentary political process.

By 1968 a compromise had been arrived at. In 1969 Denis Howell, the Minister with responsibility for sport, was moved from the Department of Education and Science to the Ministry of Housing and Local Government. Sport funding was no longer a part of the education budget. It acquired greater status as a result.

The 1970 Conservative government resolved to establish a statutory and executive sports council which would disburse funding. This would effectively take over many of the functions of the CCPR, which was offered the option of self-destruction. There was strong feeling in the CCPR against this and in the event the Sports Council took over the full-time staff and resources of the CCPR, which then re-structured itself into an independent forum of sport organisations.

The character of the two organisations has been very different. The Board of the Sports Council is appointed by the Minister and so is a quasi-autonomous part of the state. The CCPR is somewhat more democratic, being composed of representatives of the various governing bodies of sport.

## THE SPORTS COUNCIL AND SPORT IN THE 1970S

The new executive Sports Council was established in 1971 by Royal Charter. Its brief again reflected the conflict between the needs of the elite and the grassroots. It was supposed to develop knowledge of sport and physical recreation in the interests of social welfare and to encourage the attainment of high standards in conjunction with the relevant governing bodies.

The prevailing wisdom in the early 1970s was that leisure time would increase, participation would rise and that there was serious under-provision for sport and recreation. Given a legacy of chronic under-provision, and an uphill struggle for adequate funding, the most significant advance has been the expansion of sport centres. In 1964 there was just one purpose-built sport centre in the whole of England and Wales. By 1972 there were still only 30. By 1978 there were 350.

The prediction of rising rates of participation has proved to be true. So, in a sense, with over three million people on the dole, has that of increased leisure time. As funding has become progressively tighter, the emphasis has switched from the provision of new facilities to the maximum exploitation of existing ones. In recent years the Sports Council has begun to identify low-participation groups – the disabled, the over-50s, and women, especially those with young children. . . .

Since the mid-1970s, the inner cities have increasingly been seen as areas of special concern. The drive to develop sport facilities in these areas stems partly from a progressive liberal reformism. But it is also clear that many policy makers see inner-city sport as a way of defusing social tension, as a form of social control. Since the riots of 1981 it has suddenly become much easier to obtain funding for inner-city projects. Nothing loosens the purse strings like panic.

## STATE POLICY AND SOCIAL REALITY

No political party in Britain has a clear policy for sport. The Liberals have just produced an extensive document on the arts but nothing equivalent on sport. Conservative Central Office told me that 'we don't generate policy when we're in office'. The Labour Party support the right of access to common land, oppose apartheid in South African sport and oppose the sale of sports grounds into private hands. The SDP are still working on it. Other parties of the left and right have little to say on the subject.

So policy is formed by a combination of Sports Council action, ministerial whim and – crucially – local authority policy and spending patterns. Up until around 1976 the expansion proposed by the Sports Council was in relative harmony with the aims (as opposed to the actual practice) of government policy. But commitment to expanded provision has come under increasing pressure. Restrictions on state spending threaten public provision. At the same time the rise of sponsorship is re-shaping sport in ways that bypass the Sports Council. Privatisation increasingly threatens public sport facilities. The Sports Council's response is totally inadequate.

Its current strategy advocates a budget rising from the current £22 million to £46 million in 1987. Realising that this prospect is fairly remote, it outlines the effects of limited growth and standstill budgets over the same period. Yet the strategy fails to highlight the crisis in public provision, does nothing to pinpoint the causes and is of no help in fighting cutbacks. At a time when the gulf between rich and poor in sport is widening, the Sports Council not only has no effective strategy but fails to recognise that there is a problem.

Public spending cuts affect sport provision in many ways. Few new facilities are planned. Old ones are threatened with closure. Staff cuts reduce opening hours. Lower spending on maintenance leads to collapse of facilities. Poorly maintained tennis courts drive people away, reducing revenue and encouraging further staff cuts. In some places cuts in ground staff have encouraged vandalism. Mobile security services have then been called in – a depressing manifestation of the growth of a law and order society. Higher fees reduce use. In Wandsworth swimming pool and weekday tennis fees have doubled in the last year. The CCPR estimated that in 1980 £20 million was lost in spending on sport and recreation. In the same year the Thatcher government offered a £50 million bribe to move the Olympics from Moscow.

In sport, as in the health service, an impoverished public sector sits side by side with a booming, and expensive, private sector. Major spectator sports already cast their eyes mainly at the affluent end of the market. Football has thrown resources into the provision of elaborate executive boxes. For £120 Keith Prowse offered a top-price seat at Wembley. The price included a champagne reception and a four-course meal. But the highlight was a buffet party with Jimmy Tarbuck afterwards. For an outlay of £6000 Abbey Executive Services will provide 20 Wimbledon Final Day tickets, along with a luxury lunch, limitless wine and strawberries and cream. But it is not just spectator sports that are being transformed. Private clubs thrive on the boom in physical leisure. At the Cannon Sports Centre in the City of London city executives' subscriptions of £350 per year are often paid by their bosses, who can claim part of the cost against corporation tax.

Of course a large proportion of sport and recreation provision has always been in private hands. Our two major spectator sports, football and cricket, have always jealously guarded their facilities against encroachment by the public. The premier tennis facilities are maintained for the year-round benefit of a tiny elite, on the huge profits of Wimbledon fortnight. In the mid-1950s, when only 47 of Britain's 130 athletic tracks were in public hands, Finland had 500, and Sweden 800 for a population of 7 million. At a time when open land is being gobbled up by property developers, school recreation grounds, seen as surplus to requirements, are also being sold for development.

Privatisation poses a greater threat to public provision. Local authorities are increasingly prepared to offload their traditional responsibilities for short-term gain. Privatisation is a new form of asset-stripping in which assets belonging to us all are sold to private capitalists at knock-down prices. The much touted increase in efficiency that privatisation is supposed to bring is largely a myth, as those unfortunate enough to live under the Wandsworth Tories are currently discovering.

Privatisation results in either a worse or a more expensive service, or in greater exploitation of workers. Often it means all three. Any hope of public accountability is also lost.

Already some boroughs, such as Hillingdon in London, are experimenting with a form of halfway house on the road to privatisations, whimsically referred to as an entrepreneurial partnership. The Manor Leisure Centre near Peterborough, complete with sports hall, cricket and football pitches, swimming pool and tennis courts, has been put up for sale. After closing tennis courts in Carshalton Park at weekends to save overtime, the London borough of Sutton then made three out of five available for exclusive private use. Richmond Park golf course currently breaks even and thus pays for itself, providing a high popular public service. But the government are determined to privatise it.

Private enterprise has its eyes on the potential profits in this field.

Commercial Union, Dunlop, Debenhams, MacAlpine and Watneys have formed a consortium, Cavendish Leisure, to promote the privatisation of swimming pools. Their strategy is to blame restrictive practices by NALGO and their claim that admissions at pools cover only 18 per cent of the costs suggests that they would charge a lot more.

They will probably get ministerial support. A campaign last year to get public swimming baths to open early in the morning failed to gain Minister of Sport Neil MacFarlane's backing. MacFarlane does, however, appreciate the value of early-morning swimming. He swims 20 lengths every morning – in a private pool.

Unfortunately the Sports Council shows little awareness that these developments constitute a problem. Its current strategy seems to involve active encouragement of entrepreneurial partnerships.

The Sports Council has consistently failed to give any encouragement to progressive forces. On the two most public aspects of sports policy, apartheid and tobacco sponsorship, the Council has tried desperately to avoid taking a clear position. On apartheid, the report of its recent fact-finding tour does little to convince readers that the Council is in the forefront of the battle to maintain the spirit of the Gleneagles agreement. On tobacco, it is reluctant to take a stand against such a major source of money. Its discussions have no doubt been aided by the presence on the Council up till 1982 of Sir James Wilson, chairperson of the Tobacco Advisory Council.

The Sports Council is a profoundly undemocratic body. It is run by a board appointed by the Minister and accountable only to him. It is also heavily male-dominated and until very recently has done little to acknowledge, let alone alleviate, the factors inhibiting women's involvement in sport. Its recent prestigious international conference, Sport and People, had not a single woman speaker, apart from the closing address by the organiser. It has lost touch with the grassroots of sport. It has evolved a strategy incompatible with the current economic situation and has failed to acknowledge fully the threat to past achievements.

Reading taken from G. Whannel, *Blowing the Whistle*, published by Pluto Press, 1983.

# Activities

## INTERPRETATIVE EXERCISES

1. Select and visit one significant commercial form of leisure provision, such as a restaurant, pub, sports or health club. Find out what you can about who uses it, what they do and how they behave, and how the facility is presented and laid out. Prepare a two-page report on your observations and findings.
2. Note down the clubs of which you have been a member. Then list all the people with whom you share membership of that club. Are there any patterns which then emerge in terms of the type of person who is a member of a particular type of club? Consider, in this, the importance of age, gender, class and ethnicity in the respective make-ups of clubs.
3. Garry Whannel asserted, in the early 1980s, that the Sports Council had 'lost touch with the grassroots of sport'. Look at recent strategy statements from the Sports Council (London), and consider whether the same criticism could still be made.
4. Select one person from each of the following age categories – youth, young adult, middle-age, and elderly – and conduct a 15-minute interview with them on their main weekly out-of-home leisure activities. Then classify these according to whether the activity is provided mainly by the private/commercial, voluntary or public/state provider. What patterns can you identify from this exercise?
5. List the main holidays that you have taken in both your home country and abroad – what market trends can you glean from such a list? If there are none, what kind of holidaymaker would you describe yourself as?

**ESSAYS**

1. With reference to a detailed case-study of a club or a voluntary activity from either your own experience or available literature, discuss Bishop and Hoggett's observations on 'the key elements which serve to distinguish communal leisure from other areas of activity'.
2. 'There can be little doubt that public bodies like the Sports Council and the Countryside Commission have underrepresented working-class people and reflected mainly middle-class leisure interests' (Wilson). With reference to current data on participation as well as provision, assess the validity of this judgement.
3. Describe the conditions which allow, in the holiday industry, 'relative ease of entry into and exit out of the big league' (Thompson), and consider whether such conditions prevail in the sports industry.
4. 'No political party in Britain has a clear policy for sport' (Whannel). Discuss the current validity of such an assertion, with reference to the present day.
5. Using Finnegan's concept of 'pathways', consider how leisure can be seen as a source of meaning in a confusing modern world.

# PART FIVE

# Theories and Prognostications

# Introduction

We have deliberately chosen to organize this reader around a series of topics, clustered around themes, which we take to be the most accessible and common way of introducing students to the key issues in the sociology of leisure. It will by now have become apparent that quite often debates about particular topics or themes reflect wider theoretical debates about the nature of leisure as a whole and indeed of society itself. As the sociology of leisure has burgeoned in recent years, theoretical arguments have become more refined and complex. We have been guided on our selection of extracts, here as elsewhere, by the need to give students a way into debates which they may subsequently pursue at a more advanced level. We have therefore simplified current debates in the sociology of leisure into three schools: those of pluralism, Marxism and feminism. We have chosen clear statements of positions which can usefully be juxtaposed and compared.

Kenneth Roberts, robust as ever, puts the case for a pluralistic view. It is mistaken, he argues, to look for one overriding explanation or dimension of leisure behaviour. He particularly argues against attempts to stress the importance of class and commercial interests as determinants of leisure. He prefers a position which recognizes the complexity, variation and genuine choice involved in leisure behaviour which he identifies as typical of a pluralistic view. Clarke and Critcher, by contrast, argue that leisure is turned into a commodity to be consumed like any other. Moreover, patterns of consumption reflect the inequalities of class, age and gender built into society as a whole. Thus leisure can never be free of the constraints of a capitalist society.

An extract from an article by Rosemary Deem represents the viewpoint of feminism, which takes both pluralism and Marxism to task for ignoring the leisure experiences of women. This is no accidental insight, since it is typical of male-dominated sociology. The result is that women are rendered

*Sociology of Leisure: A reader*. Edited by C. Critcher, P. Bramham and A. Tomlinson. Published in 1995 by E & FN Spon, London. ISBN 0 419 19420 7.

invisible in both studies and theories of leisure. She argues strongly for a feminist perspective on leisure which places gender experience and inequality at the heart of leisure studies and the theories of society which ought to inform it.

Theories about present society often involve ideas about how society is developing. To explore the topics of the future of leisure, we have chosen a lengthy extract from what has become the definitive text on the subject by Tony Veal. We have selected Veal's comprehensive discussion of nine methods of forecasting. Variations on these methods can be found in many strategic plans in both the private and public sectors and many examples can be found of attempts to forecast the future which have gone awry. We have some way to go in understanding the present of leisure, so should not be too surprised to find that predicting its future remains an elusive goal.

# Va Sociological Theory

## Kenneth Roberts

Like the mass society analysis, the class domination theory spotlights genuine tendencies. Few would dispute that the theory also serves a purpose in sketching and alerting us to a scenario that *could* become a reality. But to exactly *what extent* does the theory explain leisure behaviour and provision in present-day society? While class domination theorists are mainly of left-wing persuasion, their theory is most readily reconciled with reality in the socialist world. In Western societies there are convincing grounds for insisting that the tendencies upon which the theory rivets attention remain, as yet, subservient to other processes. Furthermore, as we shall see, much of the evidence that the theory marshals is susceptible to alternative and, on balance, more convincing interpretation.

It is hardly realistic to treat the class domination theory as a set of hypotheses to be rigorously tested through a strategically designed research project, since this level of theory rarely proves wholly right or entirely wrong. Many writers have already proved that modern societies are sufficiently complex to offer numerous illustrations both in support and opposition. . . .

### THE FUNCTIONS OF LEISURE

Some correspondence between uses of leisure and the wider social order is inevitable. Leisure may help to consolidate the social system, offering gratifications which act as safety valves reconciling men to an otherwise unacceptable society. Leisure may also carry the imprint of values consistent with existing economic and political practices, thereby legitimising the social order. But does it necessarily follow that these functions of leisure

*Sociology of Leisure: A reader*. Edited by C. Critcher, P. Bramham and A. Tomlinson. Published in 1995 by E & FN Spon, London. ISBN 0 419 19420 7.

are manifestations of an oppressive capitalist infrastructure together with its state apparatuses of social control? The truth is that leisure, or the alternative forms in which play can be institutionalised, performs comparable functions in all societies. . . .

In opposition to interpretations derived from conflict theory, functionalist sociologists have brought leisure within their own perspective. Whereas class analysts see leisure as reflecting and reinforcing broader patterns of conflict and domination, functionalists stress the contribution of leisure to the well-being of society as a whole. They draw attention to leisure as an arena in which individuals can develop and practise generally useful skills such as sociability, and how consorting with people who 'understand' enables life's tensions to be borne.[1] These are exactly the kinds of evidence to which the class domination theory draws attention, and the inescapable conclusion must be that this evidence is susceptible to alternative interpretation. Contemporary sport may display the imprint of the capitalist infrastructure. But so what? In a capitalist society enterprises are inevitably going to profit from leisure. Likewise the technology and styles of organisation in wider use are inevitably going to be incorporated into leisure industries. These extensions from the rest of life into leisure occur in all cultures. It is difficult to conceive of a society in which people will not use opportunities for play to release tensions, and to develop skills and personal attributes which are more generally rewarded. If such features of leisure can be discerned in our own society we should not be surprised, and neither should we rush to the conclusion that our leisure is particularly unfree. Gardner has illustrated the numerous ways in which American sport reflects the surrounding culture.[2] The commercialism and competitiveness that are valued in economic life spill over into sports, which are then prized for nurturing and rewarding these American values. To gain acceptance in America, it helps if sports can manifestly demonstrate their consistency with American values and character. Indeed, Gardner argues that the popularity of baseball can only be fully understood when account is taken of its advantage in being a peculiarly American game. These linkages between sport and the wider social order are not in dispute. But what do they prove? Do they reveal American sport as an apparatus of social control and domination? Or are we merely confronting interrelationships between leisure and other institutions that are inevitable in any society?

## THE ROLE OF THE STATE

Without denying all credibility to the class domination theory we must recognise additional grounds for state involvement in recreation. It is possible to account for a great deal of state involvement in leisure without attributing any sinister motives. To begin with, it is difficult to imagine any society in which the state could adopt a completely *laissez-faire* approach to recreational tastes and behaviour. . . .

If we want to live in a society as opposed to anarchy, leisure activities must be contained within a framework of law. Until we have a totally consensual society, there will always be arguments about whether the public needs protecting from influences that some consider harmless. At the moment the availability of alcoholic drink, opportunities to gamble, and the right to witness sexual acts on screen and stage are cases in point. Government controls in these areas cannot be realistically interpreted as signs of a repressive state in action. That these issues are at all controversial simply reflects the fact that different sections of the public possess different tastes and values.

Second, if they attempt to plan the use of land, governments must inevitably become involved in planning for leisure activities that involve using large spaces in either urban or rural areas. If national parks and other places of 'natural beauty' are to be preserved as recreational resources and managed so as to cater for the visiting public with car parks, toilets and other facilities, is there any alternative to supervision by some public body? Similarly if land in urban areas and on the fringes of cities is to be kept available for sport and recreation, it is difficult to see how this can be guaranteed except by the state. Two-fifths of all the land in England and Wales is currently subject to some type of active conservation,[3] and it is impossible to believe that the public's scope for recreational choice would be enhanced by removing this control. Likewise with other resources where the supply is finite, including broadcasting wavelengths, it is difficult to imagine the public being adequately served by anything other than a system of government regulation.

Third, a great deal of local and central government involvement in the leisure field is the inevitable by-product of quite different concerns. Rightly or wrongly, depending upon the political philosophy, since the nineteenth-century governments in Britain and other industrial societies have been assuming a widening responsibility for public welfare by promoting, for example, health and education. These concerns unavoidably spread into leisure. Although today they are increasingly recognised as recreational services, the libraries, parks and swimming baths administered by local authorities in Britain were not originally developed merely to allow people to enjoy themselves, and they retain important non-recreational purposes. Similarly in America, before the First World War, what can now be recognised as recreation provision normally had other principal objectives, particularly conservation, health, and preservation of historic landmarks.

Finally, if recreation opportunities are to be made available to economically disadvantaged groups, public provision is a logical if not the only method. If the state did not subsidise sport and other forms of recreation that involve the use of land, the majority of children would be unable to participate. The state does promote sport, particularly through education, but it is surely naive to see this as a subtle plot to implant acquiescent values into the minds of the young, or as a strategy to stimulate a profitable demand for sports equipment. Local government departments responsible for recreation are increasingly paying attention to the needs of other disadvantaged groups including the disabled and the ageing. Some of the services provided remain little known. For example, it is not widely broadcast that in 1974–75 local authorities helped to provide 104 800 people with holidays.[4] As with all other social services, whether or not this provision is desirable must be accepted as open to debate, but the points raised by the class domination theory hardly seem the central issues.

The charge of being laden with middle class values is easily hurled, but it is more difficult to make the indictment stick. Which recreational tastes are shared by the majority of middle class citizens but interest only a working class minority? The most popular forms of recreation including television and holidays transcend class boundaries, while other interests, such as the traditional arts, attract small taste publics rather than entire social classes. Public bodies like the Sports and Arts Councils certainly lie open to the charge that the working class is under-represented among their beneficiaries, but who doubts that if any critics could explain how to attract more working class participants the authorities would be happy to respond? In all formally organised activity, including politics and religion, the working class tends to be under-represented.

The entire spectrum of state-supported recreation cannot be whitewashed so casually. It is impossible to contend that all government enterprise in the leisure field is explicable in one or another of the ways outlined above. Why does the state in Britain support opera, squash, ballet and golf? Answers to these questions would hardly be complete without some reference to the social class compositions of the respective taste publics. Why do we subsidise British competitors in the Olympic Games? The preceding discussion has certainly not exhausted the reasons for state involvement in leisure. What has been illustrated is that there are numerous grounds for this involvement, and accounts that see social control writ large across all these endeavours are refusing to acknowledge the complexity of the picture.

## THE LEISURE MARKET

Listing the diverse explanations for government involvement is not strictly an adequate answer to less vulgar versions of the class domination theory which disclaim conspiratorial overtones and rest content with identifying the covert social structural consequences of leisure provision. These arguments challenge not so much the motives of politicians and bureau-crats as the effects of their actions. A more satisfactory reply, therefore, is to explain that its impact upon the public's uses of leisure cannot be as impressive as the scale of government involvement since, in the leisure industries, the suppliers remain subservient to market forces. Consumer sovereignty remains a reality in the leisure market and one reason is that, to date, neither central government nor the local authorities in Britain have developed anything resembling coherent policies for recreation. Prac-titioners in the public recreation services tramp from conference to confer-ence waiting to be told what their objectives should be. As Smith has noted, '. . . the community has yet to develop its own consensus on the nature of the leisure problem, and the role of politicians in articulating that consensus has to precede administrative reorganisation.'[5] Public bodies deal with a series of youth, educational, arts and sports problems and have encountered little pressure to coordinate their efforts into a coherent leisure policy. Outside observers may note that local authority parks, baths, museums, schools and other services are all in some sense catering for leisure, and likewise at a national level we can observe that the Arts Council, the Sports Council and the Countryside Commission, together with the forestry, broadcasting and water authorities are all active in the leisure field. The fact is, however, that these various agencies have been established at different times with highly specific and sometimes completely non-recreational purposes in view, and the total leisure out-come is an entirely unplanned phenomenon.

Likewise in America it is impossible to identify any clear policy or goals in the public recreation services. In their discussion of public provision in the USA, Godbey and Parker rightly stress the multiplicity of bodies that make up the public sector, their diverse origins, and the absence of any clear objectives.[6] Economists who have examined the work of bodies such as the Arts Council in Britain have deplored the vagueness of its aims and the failure of the Council to evaluate the returns on its investments in a rational manner.[7] Consultants who favour management by clear objectives soon lose patience with the public leisure services.

Given the vagueness surrounding objectives together with the fact that leisure is rarely a matter for party political controversy, it becomes easy to understand how public bodies can become involved in ventures for almost fortuitous reasons. For example, when the head of the Arts Council favoured 'few but roses' the Council's policy was to concentrate its resources upon centres of excellence. The total size of the grants awarded to the Sports and Arts Councils appears highly dependent upon the skills of the recipients in lobbying and discovering sympathetic ears in Westmins-ter and Whitehall, and the views of chief officers and individual councillors can be highly relevant in decisions such as whether and where to build a sports centre, and whether to support the arts. It is impossible to commend this looseness in distributing public largess, and . . . clearer policy guidelines than have operated in the past are now required. At the moment, however, the point at issue is that the unsystematised condition of public provision is hardly consistent with the view of the state either consciously or covertly controlling uses of leisure in order to achieve a desired result.

Equally important, the absence of any coherent leisure policy tends to place the providers at the mercy of the market, subject to rather than manipulators of public taste. No one who works in a public recreation service knows that his job is secure on account of the publicly recognised importance of his work. Personnel operating in different recreation fields have to compete for limited resources, and one way of justifying their claims is to demonstrate public interest and appeal. Meanwhile, members of the public can pick and choose. They do not have to use country parks, Forestry Commission nature trails, arts centres or sports halls. People only use the facilities that they find useful, and if the public sector does not satisfy their tastes, individuals can turn to commercial provision or self-help. Schemes to extend public participation in recreation policy-making and management owe as much to the professionals' interest in discovering the public's tastes as to the public rebelling against alienation in leisure.

In leisure as in other spheres, there is a complex interactive relationship between demand and supply. Demand for a facility such as camping sites may provoke a supply, but it is easy to quote examples of supply-led demand. Until ten-pin bowling was commercially promoted in Britain no one was demanding to play it, and the visible availability of camp sites may increase demand for camping holidays. The relative weight of the influence flowing in each direction between supply and demand depends upon the state of the market. In leisure, as in other markets, a movement towards monopoly increases the power of the suppliers. While pluralism reigns in leisure supply, however, with the existence not only of voluntary and commercial sectors, but an uncoordinated public sector as well, it is the suppliers who are at the mercy of the market forces. It is public taste that has determined how television and radio broadcasting will be used in Britain. Whatever its early aspirations towards educating the public and raising levels of taste, the BBC has found that it can only win a mass audience, thereby justifying its revenue from the government, by catering for existing public interests. Likewise suppliers of sports complexes, arts centres and country parks have to wait and see what uses the public makes of their offerings and respond accordingly. Public provision accounts for only a small part even of organised recreation activity.[8] The providers have no captive audience. It is the public that can pick and choose.

Needless to say, the above comments about consumer sovereignty apply even more forcibly to the commercial sector. It is easy to talk about advertisers foisting their goods and services upon a susceptible public, but things never look so simple from the suppliers' side of the market.

Advertisers may often try to shape public demand, but they are more rarely successful. Nine out of every ten new brands launched are failures. During the last 30 years the British public has largely deserted the cinema, the large dance palais, gents' hairdressers, and the bowling-alleys that were built during a short wave of popularity. Anyone who knows the advertising secret to tempt the missing customers back can make a fortune. The recreation business can be profitable, but leisure is a notoriously risky market. Public taste is fickle. Demand for basic necessities is easier to predict. And to complicate the problems of private enterprise, competition from a subsidised public sector is never far from the foreground. A secure position as a leisure supplier requires either a wealthy patron or a spread of risks across a large number of leisure industries so as to be waiting wherever demand might flow.

## SOCIO-CULTURAL PLURALISM

As far as uses of leisure are concerned, the public remains far from a single, undifferentiated mass. . . .

Life-styles vary in a host of ways that cannot be explained by reference to the interests of a single dominant class. To explain these variations, it is usually more fruitful to refer to the interests and circumstances of the sections of the public directly concerned. Uses of leisure are related to social class. Working class households view more television, while the middle classes predominate at live theatre. There are few forms of recreation where participation is not somehow related to individuals' social class positions, usually assessed in terms of occupation. . . . The point at issue is that while social class is certainly a useful predictor of leisure behaviour, the same applies to numerous other bases of social differentiation. We shall also see that age, sex, marital status and education are among the social determinants of leisure conduct. It is important to keep social class in perspective. Social class is important, but some sociologists of leisure display an unnecessary obsession with the subject. . . .

From exposing the limitations of the mass society and class domination theories we can begin to identify a more valid approach to understanding leisure, and the senses in which its growth constitutes a problem. Both the mass society and class domination theories draw attention to tendencies that certainly operate but which are counterbalanced, in each case, largely by individuals and primary groups developing their own tastes and interests, and using the media and other facilities for their own purposes. The model of society that best enables us to understand contemporary leisure is a pluralist model – the unofficial ideology of Western society. Sociology has always been a debunking subject, but in this case the conventional wisdom is less out of tune with reality than its more vociferous critics. All grand theories necessarily simplify a more complex social reality, but the pluralist theory offers a better fit than its principal rivals, certainly as regards the analysis of leisure. In Britain and other Western societies there exists a variety of taste publics that possess contrasting interests generated by their different circumstances. The uses of leisure of these publics are certainly influenced by commercial and public provision, but the providers are at least as responsive to the public's tastes, and the public has a distinguished history of saying 'No'. In recreation and other spheres the public uses its leisure to nurture life-styles that supply experiences which the individuals concerned seek and value. 'Freedom from' is a condition for leisure. But there is also a positive side of the coin that involves individuals exploiting their 'freedom to' and leads logically to socio-cultural pluralism, meaning societies in which various taste publics are able to fashion life-styles reflecting their different interests and circumstances. This is the reality of modern leisure, and theories that fail to spotlight this aspect of reality prove only their own need of revision.

The pluralist theory incorporates a relatively complex model of society, but its explanations of leisure behaviour are characteristically economical. In contrast, the class domination theory with its more readily assimilated imagery of society consisting of dominant and oppressed strata often has to resort to highly convoluted explanations when faced with the details of leisure conduct. . . .

Students of leisure are well advised to try relating behaviour to the interests of those directly involved before speculating about the significance of the class struggle.

There are numerous patterns of attempted domination and exploitation in leisure, as is the case in most areas of social life. Middle class interests are more diverse than theories which persistently deplore the oppression of the working class suggest. The self-employed complain about expanding government bureaucracies triggering escalating rates and tax burdens, while the salary expectations and career prospects of new middle class armies of executives and professionals including civil servants, teachers, social workers and medical practitioners depend upon the further growth of public expenditure.[9] Within the leisure industries exploitation is not the prerogative of commercial and political élites. Recreation professionals have their own diverse and vested interests. They include holiday camp workers who use campers as easy sources of money, and sometimes sex as well.[10] Then there are the fairground gaff-lads who skilfully and systematically short-change customers.[11] In so far as exploitation is occurring it is not only the state and propertied classes that are the guilty parties.

It is difficult to see how capitalism could ever win the argument with its more determined critics. If workers are employed for 70 hours per week and receive only subsistence wages, the charge of exploitation is sure to follow. Then if hours of work are reduced and wages increased, we are told that this is to enable capitalism to stimulate a demand for its non-essential products. In a capitalist economy it must be possible to make profit from leisure, but the market-place can and does make this conditional upon members of the public receiving goods and services that they value.

One remaining argument in the class domination theory that has so far escaped challenge alleges that even if our leisure behaviour is relatively self-determined, individuals' own choices must be from among alternatives that have been pre-structured by government and commercial interests, which encourage certain uses of leisure while discouraging those associated with values liable to stimulate social dissent. As a result, it is argued, leisure may be a source of some satisfaction, but is less fulfilling than it could be if business and government agencies did not distort the public's appetites. It is easy to make this kind of assertion, but very difficult to supply convincing evidence. Critics who are wholly out of sympathy with modern Western-type societies seem to require no evidence to convince themselves that uses of leisure in these countries are less satisfying than could be the case. Those who find it distasteful to be employed in organisations where individuals sell their labour for the coin of fun are, of course, entitled to their point of view. But what is the alternative? What would leisure be like in a truly humane and liberated society? There are cross-cultural differences, but there are also remarkable similarities in uses of leisure between different countries. The number of hours that people work each week shows little variation between capitalist and communist regimes, while in urban areas throughout the world the amount of time devoted to television shows only modest variation.[12] It is not easy to specify the exact ways in which leisure in modern Britain, America and other Western societies is deformed.

There are romantics to whom formal organisation is anathema whether it is commercially or state sponsored and who insist that, to escape alienation, individuals and communities must organise their own leisure. However, there is already plenty of this communal organisation in our own society. This is the living proof of the pluralist case. There are participant-run dart and domino leagues, golf clubs and photography societies, while kids play street football and arrange their own informal games. We have this and more besides. And is anything lost when schools or recreation departments arrange regular football matches, erect goalposts and provide referees, and when supplies of kit can be purchased? The notion that technology and formal organisation along with their rational values are inherently alienating is surely a misconception. The study of leisure challenges such misconceptions, and the growth of leisure is rendering the broader theories of society from which these notions are derived increasingly suspect.

It is worth noting that despite their deep and often bitter differences, there is little disagreement on basic values between supporters of the class domination and pluralist theories. Both reveal a preference for societies in which members of the public can develop diverse life-styles, supported but not controlled by business and political apparatuses. The disagreement concerns whether this is possible within the present political economy. The pluralist case rests on the claim that while they are certainly at play, class domination tendencies are currently held in check, and that the form of political economy that has developed within Western societies offers a better protection against class domination than any of the known alternatives.

The above paragraphs contain more assertion than systematic proof of the pluralist argument. . . . The preliminary point now being argued is that pluralist thinking allows some credibility to be attached to the propositions in both the mass society and class domination theories without carrying these perspectives to extremes, and can accommodate a great deal of additional evidence besides. Needless to say, the pluralist theory is not only about leisure. Its propositions relate to the composition of the wider social system, as is also the case with the mass society and class domination theories. An examination of leisure, even if absolutely thorough, could cover no more than a tiny fraction of the relevant evidence. But the study of leisure cannot shirk contact with these theories. Leisure is as suitable an arena as any to test their claims. What is more, we can only make sense of the known facts of leisure behaviour by postulating a pluralist social system. Hence the value of this theory in explaining leisure phenomena. In addition, the theory enables us to recognise certain consequences of the growth of leisure, namely the strengthening of pluralist tendencies in society-at-large. The pluralist perspective is preferable to the alternative sociological theories that have been offered. It can incorporate but go beyond their valid contents. And it is superior to specifically recreation theory and research in that it allows us to appreciate how leisure influences and is influenced by the surrounding social context.

## REFERENCES

1. E. Gross, 'A functional approach to leisure analysis', in E. O. Smigel, ed., *Work and Leisure*, College and University Press, New Haven, 1963.
2. P. Gardner, *Nice Guys Finish Last*, Allen Lane, London, 1974.
3. J. A. Patmore, *Land and Leisure*, Penguin, Harmondsworth, 1972.
4. English Tourist Board and Trades Union Congress, *Holidays: The Social Need*, London, 1976.
5. C. Smith, 'The emergence of leisure as a policy issue for central government and the administrative response', in S. Parker and J. Haworth, eds, *Leisure and Public Policy*, Leisure Studies Association, University of Birmingham, 1975.

6. G. Godbey and S. Parker, *Leisure Studies and Services, an Overview*, Saunders, Philadelphia, 1976.
7. M. Blaug and K. King, 'Is the Arts Council cost-effective?' *New Society*, 3 January 1974.
8. S. Mennell, *Cultural Policy in Towns*, Council of Europe, Strasbourg, 1976.
9. See K. Roberts *et al.*, *The Fragmentary Class Structure*, Heinemann, London, 1977.
10. P. Bandyopadhyay, 'The holiday camp', in M. A. Smith *et al.*, eds, *Leisure and Society in Britain*, Allen Lane, London, 1973.
11. D. Dallas, *The Travelling People*, Macmillan, London, 1971.
12. I. Cullen, 'A day in the life of . . .' *New Society*, 11 April 1974.

Reading taken from K. Roberts, *Contemporary Society and the Growth of Leisure*, published by Longman Group UK Ltd, 1978. Reprinted with permission.

# Leisure and inequality | 22

John Clarke and Chas Critcher

Throughout this work on leisure, we have been arguing for a more sophisticated understanding of leisure than any of those currently available in mainstream leisure studies. In this chapter we want to argue that the explanation of leisure activity patterns as the outcome of untrammelled individual choice is deficient. We wish instead to substitute a model of leisure as constituted by a number of subcultures rooted in what particular social groupings have succeeded in claiming for themselves as legitimate and appropriate leisure activity. In particular we wish to extend the point we have initially established that class, race, age and gender are not tangential and incidental but central and fundamental influences on leisure 'choice'.

Earlier, we explained why the nature of leisure 'choice' posited by the consumer model is in large measure illusory. The kinds of leisure goods and services made available and the institutions owning and controlling such provision are in reality highly restricted. The leisure market is neither as comprehensive in scope nor as competitive in ethos as is often assumed. If what can be chosen from is limited, so is who can do the choosing. Consumers are not just the hypothetical figures of market projections. They are also social beings, members of a particular society and of structurally located and culturally defined social groups within it.

This matters for understanding leisure in a way the consumer model cannot begin to encompass. Such a model has to present leisure choice as beyond the influence of group relationships and identities. Potential markets are often targeted through indices of gender and socioeconomic status, but the essential model is one of random individual choice. It is this assumption we are challenging. . . .

Inequality of leisure opportunity has both a material and a cultural

*Sociology of Leisure: A reader.* Edited by C. Critcher, P. Bramham and A. Tomlinson. Published in 1995 by E & FN Spon, London. ISBN 0 419 19420 7.

aspect. The material aspect includes access to key resources, essentially those of time and money. The cultural aspect includes the perception of what is appropriate leisure behaviour for a member of a particular social group. Such perceptions may be variously held by the group itself and by those outside it but in a position to enforce their expectations. It is the ability to negotiate a favourable settlement of such definitions which indicates leisure privilege. Such definitions and expectations abound, distinguishing men from women, middle from working class, white from black, young from old. They may be inconsistent in their application or shift over time but they remain powerful influences on what is culturally sanctioned leisure behaviour.

We see little point in arguing which factor – class, gender or race – is the primary influence on leisure, especially as in practice they intersect. The particular influence of one factor, say age, will depend on the particular combination of other factors present, on the gender and class and race of the person or group involved. . . . A common form of argument is to play these different social divisions off against each other. The undeniable influence of gender, for example, has been used to discredit the factor of class. We therefore begin our discussion of social divisions with what seems an assertion of decreasing credibility; that contemporary leisure can usefully be understood in terms of class. . . .

## IN A CLASS OF ITS OWN

Let us begin by suggesting that there are three classes rather than just two. The upper class, who have or are in the process of acquiring wealth and the power which goes with it, may be numerically small but their influence is large. If we ask whether class affects leisure, perhaps we should start with this group for they, more than almost any other, provide a positive case. It is difficult to think about this group at all without recognising the centrality of leisure to their and others' sense of who they are. The networks and institutions which sustain the upper class may be more economic and political than cultural but leisure is symbolically crucial. From exclusive gentlemen's clubs in the West End to royal garden parties, from patronage of leading national charities to local acts of minor benevolence, from foxhunting to wildlife preservation, from Ascot and Henley to St Moritz, upper-class leisure centres on people, places and pastimes which are prescribed for members of the class. Leisure style and social status become indistinguishable.

The 'middle' classes are altogether more problematic: no one is quite sure who they are. The boundaries of the middle class are not absolute but relative. The boundary between it and the upper class may be marked by the inheritance and accumulation of wealth. At the other end the middle class have in common with the working class the fact that they sell their labour in the employment market but do so under marginally or significantly better conditions. This blurring of boundaries also applies to leisure. Upper middle class interests and life styles may be versions of upper class life writ small; lower middle class people work and live in ways which are less distinguishable than they might like from lower grade clerical or skilled manual workers. This group's leisure activity profile differs in paradoxical ways from other classes. They participate more in the 'private' leisure activities of gardening and house maintenance, yet also appear more frequently at the 'public' venues of theatres and restaurants. Seemingly more individualistic, they are prominent in voluntary and charitable work.

Reflected here are the greater material resources of the middle class compared with the working class. Persistent differences in income and fringe benefits do allow them more open access to the leisure market. . . .

These material differences do show through the leisure statistics, despite the crudity of measurement and categorisation. But there are also cultural inequalities, subtle differences of status, disguised by conventional statistics. Three aspects are worth mentioning: differences in kind between superficially similar forms, differences in the meanings attributed to particular activities, differences in the total leisure context in which individual activities are placed: 'It ain't what you do but the way that you do it'.

First, differences in kind occur where leisure statistics do not and perhaps cannot differentiate within categories of leisure activity. Thus 'going out for a meal' may be a leisure activity common across all social classes but hidden from view are crucial differences in the sorts of food, restaurants and groupings involved.

Secondly, differences in meaning attribution occur when apparently similar activities have an altered significance dependent on the social class involved. For instance, it may be true of the upper and some middle class groups that leisure is caught up in status considerations, often with practical pay-offs. Membership of a private golf club carries a different set of meanings from belonging to a pub football team – though both might be categorised as 'playing sport' or 'club membership'.

Thirdly, and as a result of the first two, there is a sense in which the whole pattern of leisure activities is as important as individual components. Class may less affect the 'choice' of this or that leisure activity than the interrelationship between a set of leisure activities. Community studies of middle and working class neighbourhoods frequently stress the coherence of a leisure culture. . . . These differences are perhaps more subtle than the model which sees middle-class culture as essentially individualistic and working-class culture as collectivist. Rather each contains a different conception of the relationship between individual and collective interests. The point, however, remains that if we are to identify class leisure cultures, it is to the subtleties of kind, meaning and context that we must look, not simply at statistical aggregates of stated participation in individual categories of leisure. . . .

There are, however, some areas where leisure does retain elements of identifiable class conflict. One of these is the continued struggle over definitions of space. There has historically been a disjunction between the ideal of public space advocated by the state and the conceptions of public space embedded in working-class culture. The latter is essentially informal, involving the appropriation for communal purposes of space nominally administered by commerce or government. Thus the idea of the street as a thoroughfare has been continually undermined by an alternative version of its functions as an area of social interaction. Doorstep banter and gossip, children playing and teenagers hanging about, the maintenance of cars and the parading of BMX bikes – all represent thrusts to define the space of the street in a particular direction. These have not generally found favour with public authorities and planners, whose activities have been expressly designed to curtail such activities. The suppositions behind the location and design of tower blocks, housing estates, shopping precincts, sports and leisure centres, have, with notorious consistency, failed to understand the existing and potential meanings of space within a locality.

Thus if the working class has accepted an increasingly 'privatised' notion of space, that may be as a result of the undermining of an alternative definition of public space. The physical and psychological security of the home has come to be contrasted with the insecurity and strangeness of the streets. With one or two exceptions, such as the local 'rec', what is provided as public space is alien – museums, botanical gardens, sports centres. And access to private space is conditional upon the ability to pay. The shopping centre, patrolled by a private police force moving on those who do not show the proper propensity to consume, points up the unequal struggle over leisure space and the potential ugliness of its outcomes.

In this last example, as in all our generalisations and illustrations, it is obvious that not all members of the working class would see their interests in the way we have defined them. The working class is not a homogeneous whole. It is and always has been internally divided by such factors as levels of income and types of housing tenure, conditions of work and patterns of family life, regional economies and cultures, perceptions of 'rough' and 'respectable' elements.

Not the least of these social divisions within the working class is that of race. Differences of culture between the white working class and black immigrants and their descendants have been a marked source of racial antagonism. The religious observances, culinary habits and customs of dress brought halfway round the world have provoked a defensive response by a white working-class culture, eaten away by its own prejudices. We do not know whether leisure surveys have samples large enough, or questions specific enough, to identify ethnic differences in leisure. What we can state with some confidence is that leisure activities superficially similar to those of the white population are contextualised quite differently in Afro-Caribbean and Asian cultures. The roles of family life, religious institutions and musical traditions, the attitudes towards drinking, smoking and sexual relations, are not uniform as between white and black or brown members of society. To talk here of equal access to leisure goods and services, of individual consumer preference, of the democracy of the market-place, is to be blind to the material inequalities and cultural tensions produced by the complex racial mix of contemporary Britain.

## LEISURE THROUGH THE AGES

At first glance, it seems reasonable that age should be found to have a considerable effect on the kinds and rates of leisure activity. The biology and psychology of the ageing process seem likely to involve different physical abilities and personal interests at its various stages. That much is not disputed. More controversial is the attempt to assess how far such stages of life and the leisure activities perceived as appropriate to them are constructed by society. To the extent that they are, the effects of age on leisure are not natural and inevitable but socially imposed and open to change.

We begin with the final stage of the ageing process: old age. Three things need to be noted about this category. First, it is demarcated by retirement. Life may begin at forty but old age definitely begins at sixty or sixty-five. The old are by definition those who have ceased employment or whose partner has. This is not a biological or psychological boundary but an economic one. Secondly, old people are predominantly female and the older the age band considered the more this female predominance occurs. Women who marry are likely to eventually face a period of widowhood, lasting perhaps as long as a quarter of their life span. Thirdly, the conditions under which people enter old age vary considerably, especially by social class. Inequalities of income, housing and physical health are not distributed randomly amongst individuals but systematically between classes.

These are just some of the ways in which old age is socially constructed. We are not here denying as a biological fact the progressive decline of faculties which occurs in old age. These physical factors should not, however, be confused with social ones.

Consistent with status devaluation is the peripheral position of the elderly in relation to the leisure market. Since they no longer have the disposable income necessary to be part of a significant target population, no great effort is made to solicit their custom. When recognised at all, their leisure needs are to be met by councils and voluntary groups providing clubs and outings. For the most part, since ageing is presumed to involve increasing physical and mental passivity, they are quietly left alone.

They are also increasingly left alone and left behind as the consequences of other social processes. Their children may through choice or necessity have moved away. Though the evidence suggests that families do not in fact abandon their elderly members or become indifferent to their fate, the monitoring of their daily lives frequently becomes the exclusive responsibility of whichever relative happens to live nearby. Thus the old are doubly deprived. The limited interest shown by commerce and the state is compounded by decreasing access to the alternative of family-based leisure. The family is increasingly scattered and sooner or later the elderly married couple will become one elderly person living alone. This is 'privatisation' with a vengeance.

It is only when such factors are taken into account that the oft-noted ambiguity of free time for the elderly can be understood. The removal of the structure inherent in the clear demarcation between work and leisure may well be a problem for those who have been habitually in full-time employment, especially men. The domestic work of women does not diminish and in fact becomes more problematic. The budget is tighter, shops less accessible; cooking and washing clothes become more burdensome; the heavy work of cleaning may become impossible. The existence of the home help service demonstrates that it is not the absence of paid work which is a problem for the elderly so much as the continued presence of domestic work.

Thus the leisure problem of old age is not simply one of an excess of time and a deficiency of resources, real enough though those are. It is also one of enforced dependence on a home life progressively more difficult to manage and increasingly isolated from the context of extended family and community. . . .

The economic and social structuring of old age, and the psychological consequences which follow, make it difficult to improve the access of the elderly to a meaningful range of leisure activities. . . .

'Too much time and too little to do' might well be the leisure lament of the elderly. It is a refrain which finds a sympathetic echo at the other end of the age range, amongst those who have not yet reached adult status. Adolescents might justifiably perceive the interest of commerce in their needs as highly restricted and public provision unimaginative and under-resourced. It is not to such similarities but to differences between these age statuses that attention is normally directed. Old age is regarded as a period of physical, psychological and social decline, adolescence as a transitional period of growth. The transition is from childhood to adulthood, marked physically by puberty and its aftermath, psychologically by the exploration of identity, socially by the entry into work roles. These are undeniably experiences common to all adolescents in our society. There must, however, be two severe qualifications to this apparently universal portrait of adolescence. One is that adolescence, no less than old age, is socially structured; it is a social as much as a biological or psychological division. The second is that, again like old age, adolescence has divergent meanings for members of different classes and genders. . . .

## ENGENDERED LEISURE

Gender is the last but by no means the least of the social divisions within leisure. On any statistical measure, gender is a crucial determinant of leisure activity. Figures compiled by the government's Central Statistical Office show this clearly. Men report more leisure activity and of a particular kind. They dominate those activities which involve leaving the home unaccompanied, such as all forms of sport and going out for a meal or a drink. The only things for which women more frequently leave the house are to go to bingo, cinema or theatre. The main household leisure activity of media use shows few gender differences, but men are most involved in gardening and 'do-it-yourself'. Women's other home-based leisure consists of that interest in sewing and knitting 'exclusive' to their sex.

Other data show a few minor activities outside the home where women predominate, in visits to church, leisure classes, opera and ballet. These do little to alter the general picture. Women have less leisure time, participate less in most leisure activities and draw on a narrower range of leisure options than men. They also spend most of their leisure in and around home and family. These differences of form, time and place do not represent a more limited version of male leisure but a qualitatively as well as quantitatively distinct female leisure pattern. The only apparent anomaly is that women in fulltime employment have a leisure profile more similar to men than to other women. . . .

Thus the female forms of leisure are those most easily compatible with the primary domestic role of wife and mother. The contrast between 'compulsory' and 'freely chosen' activity becomes blurred when the times, places and nature of 'leisure' are indistinguishable from those of work. Unlike employment, housework does not have a definite and fixed allocation of time. It contracts and expands according to the needs and demands of the household. This ambiguous pattern means that it is hard to fix the working day with any precision. Children do not fall ill or require attention within the precise and convenient confines of an eight-hour day allocated to 'child-care'.

This timeless nature of domestic work has the apparent advantage of giving women some discretion in pacing their work, though night-time rarely goes according to plan. More fundamental is the experience of being permanently on call: 'a woman's work is never done' (especially by a man). As the time of work dictates the time of leisure, so the place of work dictates the place of leisure. For the woman with children, home may serve as both work and leisure place. . . .

Gender as a social division in leisure does not simply produce the effect that women have less time than men and are less mobile; it redefines time and space for women as compared with men. Women are expected – and come themselves to expect – to participate in those leisure activities defined as appropriate for women, at those times and in those places compatible with established female roles. All these are severe enough limitations on the access to and enjoyment of leisure. But there is more. For the inferior status of women's leisure has as its obverse the superiority of men's interests within leisure.

Throughout our discussion, we have tended to show how leisure reflects social divisions ultimately rooted outside leisure itself. In so far as leisure is dependent on the social organisation of work and family life, this is a valid approach. Leisure, however, does more than simply reflect social divisions. It 'realises' them, becoming one of the powerful means by which social divisions receive expression and validation. This double relationship between leisure and social divisions is particularly evident in the case of gender. The quantitative and qualitative differences between male and female are first an extension of the sexual division of labour within society as a whole. They are also secondly ways in which the dominant definitions of what it means to be male or female are enforced and confirmed. Leisure 'celebrates' gender differences. . . .

## THE SOCIAL DIVISION OF LEISURE

In opening this chapter, we argued that we wanted to reformulate the terms in which the established consensus discussed the topic of social divisions within leisure. We particularly wanted to recast a model of individual choice from a mixed market of leisure orientated around common family needs, into one which revealed the social structuring and economic underpinning of access to a market of imbalanced provision, to which families no less than individuals had far from equal access. This we felt could be understood as the dimension of leisure opportunity.

The argument seems to us (and perhaps to the reader in retrospect) remarkably simple and obvious. If we substitute social patterns for individual choice and systematically interrelated social divisions for independent socio-demographic variables, some straightforward propositions emerge. Leisure has not expelled class from its influence. Superficially similar leisure activities are given differences of form, meaning and context which are class-based. Evident in neighbourhood culture and in conflicts over the definition of public space are class images of family, community and the links between them. The presence of ethnic minorities has complicated the class profile of contemporary Britain but does not obliterate its outline.

Age is another form of social division which affects leisure in more than simply physiological ways. Socially constructed age groups are placed in distinctive relationships to education, family and work, from which follows their economic and social access to leisure. Old and young differ in precisely where they are placed in relation to essentially the same processes. What matters is not how biologically old you are nor how psychologically young you feel but where you are in the systems of economic production and cultural reproduction.

The same basic pattern, although along a different axis, emerges for gender. Women's leisure is quantitatively less than men's and qualitatively dependent on a narrow definition of the female role, especially within the family. Men dominate leisure physically and culturally, of which sport is the most transparent example. Gender relations, in all their complex inequality, are further evident in the sexual rituals without which much public and private leisure cannot be understood.

The supposed capacity of the family to dissolve all forms of social division is not demonstrated in leisure. If anything, the family actively reproduces them in subtle and not so subtle forms: resources of time and income, relations between the generations, interactions between husband and wife. Even the holiday, that wilful attempt to escape the categorical imperatives of everyday life, can never entirely do so.

What we find in leisure, then, is a reflection and expression of the main social divisions of class, age and gender, which the family may modify only within limits. The measures we can take of the distribution of leisure opportunity – time and money, moral prohibition and control, commercial provision and state services – indicate a degree of inequality as profound as, if less immediately visible than, those evident elsewhere in society. . . .

That leisure inequality is less recognised and recognisable than other kinds of inequality does not make it any the less real. . . . Muted and modified though it often is, leisure does ultimately express those social divisions and systematic inequalities inherent in the organisation of contemporary capitalism.

Reading taken from J. Clarke and C. Critcher, *The Devil Makes Work*, published by Macmillan London, 1985. Reprinted with permission.

# Feminism and leisure studies

Rosemary Deem

What I want to explore in this paper is the contribution which feminists have made and continue to make to the study of leisure. It is necessary to make clear that when I say 'feminist contributions' I mean those which have explored the structures and ideological forces shaping women's oppression, taking into account women's life-styles in general and their experiences of leisure in particular. Women's subordination to men in society is seen by feminists as problematic and they seek to find ways in which that oppression and subordination may be overcome. Thus those studies and writers who have analysed women's leisure but do not share this perspective are not the main focus of my argument.

## CONTRIBUTION OF FEMINISM TO LEISURE STUDIES

Much conventional sociology of leisure has taken as its starting-point the boundaries between paid employment and leisure. Almost all the work on the history of leisure has concerned itself with how men have spent their leisure time and what connections there have been between that and their main form of work or employment. A great deal of time has been devoted to studying how the male working class has wrested leisure time away from work time over the course of industrialization, through things like the Ten Hour Act and paid holidays (Thompson, 1967; Burns, 1973). Although a few writers (e.g. Parker, 1983) have pointed out that in some circumstances paid work and leisure are so blended together that they are

*Sociology of Leisure: A reader.* Edited by C. Critcher, P. Bramham and A. Tomlinson. Published in 1995 by E & FN Spon, London. ISBN 0 419 19420 7.

difficult to disentangle (vicars or residential social workers, for instance), this has been regarded as the exception rather than the norm. . . . House-work has also had its status raised to that of work proper (Malos, 1980; Maynard, 1985), although the reluctance of most male leisure researchers to follow through the implications of this reorientation for men and house-holds in general is quite remarkable.

Looking at forms of work outside the formal economy has consequences well beyond that of providing new areas for research. Feminist analyses of housework, home working and other forms of unpaid work, like care of children and adult dependants, have shown that the notion of time being set aside only for leisure is very difficult to achieve for those outside full-time paid employment. The problems are enhanced for those with dom-estic responsibilities because such work is not highly structured, is often contingent on the actions of others and cannot simply be stopped or forgotten about at the end of the day (Deem, 1986; Graham, 1984). Leis-ure, for many women, is of a quite different order from that experienced by most men. It is feminist writings which have so sharply exposed this contrast and its theoretical, social and political consequences.

In tracing some of the contributions which feminists and feminism have made to the study of leisure, I want to make clear that feminists have not worked in a vacuum. Just as feminism has had some, though regrettably so far small, impact on mainstream leisure studies, so more general devel-opments in social science have where appropriate been taken on board by feminism, as in the need to consider class and age alongside gender. Hence not all the territory marked out here should or can be seen as the exclusive terrain of feminists. It is clear, for example, that the field of cultural studies has been one which has contributed quite significantly to the development of approaches to sport and leisure which take gender seriously (Hall and Jefferson, 1975; CCCS 1977; Clarke, Critcher and Johnson, 1979). Similarly, for instance not only feminists have found it worthwhile to study the life-cycle and life-course (Rapoport and Rapoport, 1975).

But at the same time, feminist approaches to sport and leisure have not just confined themselves to studying women's leisure or even incorporating gender into their analyses of leisure experiences. What is distinctive about the feminist contribution is the endeavour to set the study of leisure firmly in the context of women's oppression and gender relations and the concern to bring about a positive change in the social position of women. So feminism has not just looked at what women's lives are like but has also examined the connections between those life-styles and femininity. There is almost no counterpart to this in the study of male lives and leisure. Thus, despite the massive attention paid by leisure studies to male leisure and sport, little of that research looks at how masculinity and the role of men in gender power relations has shaped and influenced that form of leisure. There is, for instance, only one study of football hooliganism which claims to do this (Dunning and Murphy, 1982).

## THE DEVELOPMENT OF FEMINIST STUDIES OF LEISURE

During the 1970s most mainstream leisure studies texts considered women either not at all or only in so far as they took into account institutions like the family (Dumazedier, 1974; Cheek and Burch, 1976; Roberts, 1978; Kaplan, 1975). For example, one textbook (Smith, Parker and Smith, 1973) made significant mention of women in only two of its twenty-two chapters, one on the family and one on adult education. It constantly refers to 'man', 'he' and 'his' in connection with leisure, and the only mention of women in the Introduction is the intriguing sentence that 'the housewife can escape from the triviality of being a domestic servant by taking an Open University degree' (p. 5). Knowing the problems that married women OU students often have in leaving their domestic responsibilities and persuading their husbands to allow them to attend tutorials and summer schools, I wonder what the authors actually meant by that statement!

Feminists have questioned conventional notions of leisure which are constructed around a separation of paid work from leisure (Green, Hebron and Woodward, 1985; 1987a; McIntosh *et al.*, 1981). The impact of others, especially men and children, on women's leisure has been closely studied (Wimbush, 1986; Deem, 1986; Green, Hebron and Woodward, 1987a), and there has been some exploration of the impact of sexuality on sport and leisure participation by women (Scraton, 1986, 1987). Feminists have begun to analyse how male social control over women has constrained the where, when and how of women's leisure (see Green, Hebron and Woodward, 1987b). In the process of doing all this feminists have also shown how important it is that women should be involved in sport and leisure because of the potentially liberating effects such involvement can bring (Scraton, 1987; Graydon, 1983; Talbot, 1981, 1984).

At the behest of the SSRC/Sports Council Joint Panel on Sport and Leisure research, in 1979 Margaret Talbot produced a report setting out the 'state of the art' in the study of women's leisure. This review uncovered a considerable amount of relevant studies and findings, linked them together in a logical way and posed a number of important questions for future research. So the necessity to look carefully at women's leisure and to take seriously the analysis of gender relations was beginning to appear on the leisure studies agenda by the beginning of the 1980s.

In 1980 itself, another important contribution was made at a joint British Sociological Association and Leisure Studies Association seminar on Leisure and Social Control by a group of researchers from the Birmingham-

based Centre for Contemporary Cultural Studies. They developed a critique of male-centred leisure studies and pointed to important researches
of their own about girls, young women, and housewives (McIntosh *et al.*,
1981). Another major input was made by Liz Stanley (1980) who stressed
the necessity to explore the meaning of leisure, the fact that women were
not just deviant men and that women are a heterogeneous group with
many different interests. Rachael Dixey and Margaret Talbot's (1982)
researches on bingo revealed the game to be a leisure activity dominated
by women and valued by them not just for its own sake but because it
provided somewhere out of the home where unaccompanied women could
go without being harassed or policed by men.

In 1982 the SSRC/Sports Council Joint Panel finally launched a research
initiative on women and leisure, although the panel which interviewed
the shortlisted applicants was all-male! The funding was awarded to two
Sheffield Polytechnic researchers, Eileen Green and Diana Woodward,
who subsequently were joined by Sandra Hebron. Their project ran from
1983 to 1986 and uncovered a wealth of data about women and leisure in
Sheffield, material which also has a much wider applicability (Green,
Hebron and Woodward, 1985, 1987a). Two other projects funded by the
Joint Panel have also looked at women's leisure – the Leisure in the Home
study headed by Sue Glyptis at Loughborough University (Glyptis, McInnes and Patmore, 1987) and the study of shift work at Liverpool University
(see Chambers, 1986) – although neither project has taken a feminist
approach as its main standpoint. Contributions have also been made by
non ESRC funded research. For example, in Edinburgh Erica Wimbush
has done important work linking the study of health and well-being to
considerations about women and leisure in a study of young mothers
(Wimbush, 1986).

The 1980s have also seen important developments in the field of women
and sport (see Green *et al.*, 1985; Graydon, 1983; Talbot, 1984; Ferris, 1981;
Brackenridge, 1987). Amongst the issues which they have explored have
been the growing success of women in competitive sport, the continuing
barriers to wider female sports participation, the problems faced by women
in sports leadership, the ways in which men have tried to exclude
women from certain sports as well as the benefits of sport to women. . . .

## NON-FEMINIST CONTRIBUTIONS TO GENDER AND LEISURE

It is of course perfectly possible to study women and leisure without doing
so from a feminist perspective. Indeed, mainstream leisure studies have
not so much neglected women altogether, as treated them within limited
contexts. For example, women are considered as part of family leisure or
as housewives who have little in common with paid and by implication

male workers; women are viewed as of only slight significance to the analysis of leisure as an aspect of male experience. Another mainstream approach, noted by Liz Stanley (1980), has been to view women as the problem, rather than seeing women's experiences of leisure as something of importance because it directs our attentions to new aspects and dimensions of leisure in ways which the study of men does not.

With the development of feminist analyses of leisure, there are signs that the male-stream of leisure studies has at least noticed that it might be necessary to mention gender occasionally, even if it has not entirely shifted the preoccupation with class, capitalism and paid employment as determinants of leisure. Thus more recent books like Stan Parker (1983) and Ken Roberts (1981, 1982) have tried harder than before to use non-sexist language. At the same time, their inclusion of gender has produced a series of even more pluralistic analyses which treat class, age, race and gender as though they were similar and cumulative factors. This view is particularly problematic because it implies that gender itself, and more importantly gender relations of power between men and women, are not of major importance in determining leisure choices and experiences. Feminists, on the other hand, have argued strongly for the crucial import- ance of gender and gender relations to leisure, irrespective of other important factors like class or age. To say otherwise is to argue, for example, that men's leisure is as much affected by fears of sexual harass- ment, assault and violence as is women's leisure, a standpoint which is patently not supported by the evidence.

Not all the analyses which have taken gender on board the lower decks are necessarily pluralist though. Chris Rojek's theoretical treatise on leis- ure published in 1985 does not exclude women's leisure and even has index categories for sexism, although it does not fully incorporate gender into its analysis. The improvement is not across the board however. Tony Veal (1987) manages to use both sexist language and minimize references to women in his latest book.

But there are gender-aware-analyses of leisure beginning to appear from non-feminists. This is particularly true of John Clarke's and Chas Critcher's work (Critcher, 1986; Clarke, Critcher and Johnson, 1979; Clarke and Critcher, 1985) and the study of sex differentiation in physical education by Oliver Leaman (1984). John Clarke and Chas Critcher (1985) make a serious and sustained attempt to incorporate a gender analysis in their recent study of leisure in capitalist Britain. In reviewing radical theories of sport, Chas Critcher (1986) suggests that recovering gender relations is one of three crucial directions in which the sociology of sport has to move. Why I do not refer to such analyses as feminist is because none of these writers fully accept that women are oppressed primarily by gender relations and patriarchy rather than by class relations and a capitalist mode of production. Moreover, none are fully committed to a theoretical and political analysis which will point to ways of overcoming the subordinating effects of gender relations and patriarchy.

## NEW DIRECTIONS FOR THE SOCIOLOGY OF LEISURE

### Exploring the boundaries of work and leisure

I have already drawn attention to the ways in which feminism has both widened the concept of leisure beyond the point at which it is only applicable to those in full-time employment and brought in an analysis which looks at the effects of unpaid work on leisure. These are important developments which have also begun to be taken on board by more mainstream analyses (Deem and Salaman, 1985).

Paradoxically, however, some feminist analyses have also shown that for those women who are in employment, the kind of compartmentalization practised by many men for their leisure is more likely to be possible (Deem, 1986). This is despite women's dual role in the home and in employment. Indeed, studies of women who have been made redundant or otherwise become unemployed say they find it difficult to reorganize their lives so that either unpaid work or leisure are again possible (Coyle, 1984; Martin and Wallace, 1984).

Ironically, the idea of paid work being crucial to life and leisure is one that some leisure theorists have begun to reject in discussing the possibilities of leisured society (Jenkins and Sherman, 1981). To argue that women may be more able to claim leisure time and rights when they are in paid employment is neither to say that women are not often exploited in employment nor that they need to become like men if they are to have equal access to leisure. In a differently organized society there might be other kinds of boundaries drawn around paid and unpaid work and leisure and the sexual division of labour might be such that women who work at home are not disadvantaged in leisure terms by that situation. But at present we live in a society where the sexual division of labour, although shifting (Gershuny and Jones, 1987), is not disappearing, and where paid work, despite unemployment, is still seen as very important. It gives access to money, friendships, status and legitimate claims to leisure to an extent that unpaid work does not. Furthermore, the number of women spending the majority of their adult lives in paid employment is continuing to rise (Martin and Roberts, 1984).

Our knowledge of what happens to women in paid work is much greater than our knowledge about women in unpaid work, because unpaid work is less visible and harder to research, as well as being an area which is less likely to attract research funds. Hence, despite a considerable amount of research into unpaid work already, there is still much more scope for expanding further how unpaid work affects and relates to leisure. For example, the extent to which those who do only unpaid work think themselves less worthy of leisure than those in paid employment, where unpaid work includes not just domestic work and childcare (Wimbush, 1986) but also the care of sick, elderly and disabled dependants and a wide range of community and voluntary work. There is also much to be done exploring why and how women and men attach different priorities to paid work, unpaid work and leisure. So for example, Debbie Chambers shows that because of their domestic commitments, women find shift work more attractive than men do (Chambers, 1986). They are less concerned about shift work's effects on their leisure because they are already used to unpaid commitments disrupting their leisure.

### Leisure and time

Stan Parker has drawn my attention to my understating of the importance of time (Deem, 1986). Other feminist researchers have begun to consider the importance of time to leisure, as indeed have some non-feminist time-budget researchers as well as John Clarke and Chas Critcher (1985). The ways in which time is important to leisure have of course already been pointed out to us on numerous occasions by social historians (e.g. Thompson, 1967). But such analyses have focused almost exclusively on how the switch from agricultural work to industrial employment affected the male working class. Women's conceptions of time and the ways in which time organizes their days are still very much underresearched. But Graham notes that the peaks of women's personal timetables are usually very different from those of the men they live with, and that the main time periods devoted to leisure by men and children are often those least available to women for leisure (Graham, 1984). In my own research I found this particularly true of holidays, which for women, especially if they are on so-called self-catering holidays, can involve more time committed to work than if they were at home. When the male working class fought for holiday time, they did not have in mind their wives' rights to leisure as well as their own.

Many definitions of leisure talk about leisure taking place at times when other activities do not – in other words, when there are periods of choice and actual spaces. But much of the research on women suggests that the quality of women's time is such that several things are done at once (Sharpe 1984; Wyatt, 1985) and leisure is combined with other activities. . . .

### Life-styles and leisure

Leisure studies have for a long time operated in an empirical (and sometimes also theoretical) vacuum separated from research on other aspects of social life. What feminist contributions to the sociology of leisure have done is to stress the importance of analysing leisure in the context of individuals' lives as a whole. It is not possible to understand why, for instance, women have far more leisure at home than men unless the rest of their lives are explored too. For women the home is a workplace, even if they also have a job outside it, and their responsibilities for others, their relationship with their children and male partners, the community they live in and their friends as well as their living standards are all crucial to an understanding of why they do what they do in their leisure. Hence Rachael Dixey and Margaret Talbot, in their study of bingo, also undertook a community study of a working-class area of Leeds so that they could better understand the significance of bingo in the lives of women (Dixey and Talbot, 1982). Erica Wimbush (1986) has explored the connections between well-being and leisure for mothers; in terms of women's life-styles as mothers, she shows the significance of leisure for developing and maintaining women's support systems (Wimbush 1986). Studies of women with children in paid and unpaid jobs suggest that tiredness is a constant problem which may prevent leisure even when time is available (Yeandle, 1984; Sharpe, 1984; Wimbush, 1986). . . .

The lesson here is that we must look at life-styles as a whole and try to utilize methods of research which will allow us to place leisure within the context of community and region as well as class, race and gender.

## Context and meaning

Context itself is an important aspect of whether women gain enjoyment and relaxation from activities – going for a drink in a pub with two women friends is very different from going to a wine bar with a husband to meet his work colleagues. It is crucial that such nuances are detected. That women may sometimes enjoy cooking or sewing or looking after children is often adduced as evidence that women 'enjoy' housework, whereas more careful analysis shows that it is only certain aspects of cooking or sewing or children which are enjoyable – for example, baking cakes when no one is at home, or playing with children in the park when you don't have to hurry back to get a meal and do the washing. Activities are not in themselves necessarily pleasurable or relaxing. My own Milton Keynes research found that women enjoyed cooking meals for friends, but did not enjoy entertaining their husbands' work colleagues or fellow football players (Deem, 1986).

Meaning and context are very closely linked. Although mainstream leisure studies have paid some attention to the meaning of leisure, this has often been a theoretical debate detached from the groups and individuals who construct those meanings. It has been feminist analyses which have drawn particular attention to the ways in which leisure and sport can provide women with a sense of liberation if they are doing something they choose to do and over which they have some control.

## Gender relations and power

As I said earlier, more recent mainstream analyses of leisure have begun to take on board the importance of analysing gender as a dimension of leisure. But it is not always evident that the full import of this is understood. Taking gender seriously means much more than noticing the existence of women. Gender relations involve studying relations of power, ideologies and other mechanisms whereby one gender wields power over the other, just as accusations of sexism involve relations of power and not simply mentioning one sex to the exclusion of the other. Women are constrained by patriarchal relations of male dominance to a much greater extent than many male researchers realize. Liz Stanley has pointed out the ways in which men 'police' many public places such as pubs and clubs where women on their own or with other women are not welcome (Stanley, 1980). More recently, Eileen Green, Sandra Hebron and Diana Woodward have drawn attention in their Sheffield research to the reluctance of most women to go on their own to city centre leisure venues ranging from cinemas to pubs (Green, Hebron and Woodward, 1985). Even travelling on public transport can be problematic for women, whether at night or by day. In my Milton Keynes research I found many women who were frightened of using the city's cycle and footpath network because of previous sexual attacks on women during daylight hours (Deem, 1986). It is scarcely surprising that so much women's leisure takes place in the home, although, even there, little guarantee of peace exists, because violence is as likely to be experienced by women in their own homes as outside them (Hanmer and Maynard, 1987).

Inside the household gender power-relations continue to exert their influence. Although it is often claimed that the sexual division of labour in the household is becoming less rigid (Gershuny and Jones, 1987), there is little evidence to suggest it is disappearing altogether and much to suggest that it remains the responsibility of women to do housework and provide childcare (Maynard, 1985; Malos, 1980; Yeandle, 1984). It is not in men's interests to disturb these arrangements, because it would decrease the support for their own leisure. Even where men are unemployed they are not always willing to take on more domestic work and may inhibit women's social spaces for leisure by hanging around the house (McKee and Bell, 1984). The research on women's leisure in Sheffield and Edinburgh (Green, Hebron and Woodward, 1985; Wimbush, 1986) found that women had to spend a good deal of time negotiating with male partners over leisure entitlement and going out, although no equivalent negotiations usually take place over male leisure time away from home. Men are often heard to complain about having to babysit – for their own children! The Sheffield researchers also found that men were reluctant to allow women to go where alcohol was to be found. Yet if a similar control were enforced by women over their husbands, pubs would long ago have ceased trading! Women are in general the facilitators of others' leisure – husbands, children, male relatives – rather than the recipients of leisure. In my research I found that few women thought of themselves as having a right to leisure (Deem, 1986); many men do see themselves as having such a right.

But how many mainstream studies of leisure or sport have looked at the power struggles over leisure which take place in households every day? How many have thought beyond the 'they are individuals and they choose not to do . . .' aspects of women's failure to participate in many male-dominated sports? Having seen the way male members of my cycling club provide their wives and girlfriends with the heaviest and most difficult-to-ride bikes they can find and then complain about how slow the women are on touring rides, it is difficult not to believe in male conspiracy theories. But it is easy to see much scope for further research in the sociology of sport well removed from the sphere of football hooligans and schemes for the young unemployed.

There is, however, a more general point here, concerned with the necessity of directing feminists' attention not only to the existence of power relations but also to how and why those power relations are sustained by ideological and material factors. There is much discussion about the importance, for example, of gender ideologies but little attempt to explore how these actually work in the field of leisure.

## CONCLUSIONS

### A good many gaps to fill?

What I have tried to do in this paper is to show how feminist analyses of leisure and sport have begun to rectify some of the deficiencies in conventional approaches to leisure studies. This, however, is not to say that there are no other non-feminist attempts to do the same (e.g. Clarke and Critcher, 1985). The major difference, however, is that these parallel endeavours do not take gender relations as central to their enterprise. There are many other issues which could have been included here, some of which are taken up by other contributors. For example, feminist researchers are on the whole much more sensitive to other social divisions like age and race than are non-feminist researchers.

While not pioneering the life-cycle approach (see Rapoport and Rapoport, 1975) feminists have been more ready to utilize life-cycle approaches to leisure and sport. It is of course also true that feminist approaches to leisure studies have not always learnt from more conventional approaches – for example, in the treatment of class. But the significance of taking gender relations seriously is inescapable, and it is high time that male leisure researchers began to examine carefully the connections between male leisure, male power and socially constructed notions of masculine gender identity as well as considering some of the other new directions which I have sketched out here. As Debbie Chambers says in her study of shift workers, 'Men appear better able to preserve normal life-styles irrespective of their work schedules; women are a central part of men's resources to overcome [these] . . . women do not have equivalent resources' (Chambers, 1986: 321). It is up to all leisure researchers, not just feminist ones, to find ways in which women can enjoy such resources and support too.

## REFERENCES

Brackenridge, Celia (1987) 'Gender inequalities in sports leadership', paper given to the 'Future of Adult Life' conference, Leeunwenhorst, Netherlands, April.

Burns, Tom (1973) 'Leisure in industrial society', in Mike Smith, Stan Parker and Cyril Smith (eds) *Leisure and Society in Britain*, London, Allen Lane, Penguin.

Centre for Contemporary Cultural Studies (1977) *On Ideology*, London, Hutchinson. (1981) 'Women and leisure', in Alan Tomlinson (ed.) *Leisure and Social Control*, Eastbourne, Brighton Polytechnic, Chelsea School of Human Movement.

Chambers, Debbie (1986) 'The constraints of work and domestic schedules on women's leisure', *Leisure Studies* 5(3): 309–25.

Cheek, N. and Burch, W. R. (1976) *The Social Organisation of Leisure in Human Society*, New York, Harper & Row.

Clarke, John and Critcher, Chas (1985) *The Devil Makes Work*, London, Macmillan.

Clarke, John, Critcher, Chas and Johnson, Richard (1979) *Working Class Culture*, London, Hutchinson.

Coyle, Angela (1984) *Redundant Workers*, London, Women's Press.

Critcher, Chas (1986) 'Radical theories of sport: the state of play', *Sociology of Sport Journal* 3: 337–43.

Deem, Rosemary (1986) *All Work and No Play: The Sociology of Women and Leisure*, Milton Keynes, Open University Press.

Deem, Rosemary and Salaman, Graeme (eds) (1985) *Work, Culture and Society*, Milton Keynes, Open University Press.

Dixey, Rachael and Talbot, Margaret (1982) *Women, Leisure and Bingo*, Leeds, Trinity and All Saints' College.

Dumazedier, John (1974) *The Sociology of Leisure*, Amsterdam, Elsevier.

Dunning, Eric and Murphy, Philip (1982) 'Working class social bonding and the socio-genesis of football hooliganism', University of Leicester, Department of Sociology.

Ferris, Liz (1981) 'Attitudes to women in sport; prolegomena towards a sociological theory', *Equal Opportunities International* 1(2): 32–9.

Gershuny, Jay and Jones, Sally (1987) 'The changing work/leisure balance in Britain: 1961–1984', in John Horne, David Jary and Alan Tomlinson (eds) *Sport, Leisure and Social Relations*, Sociological Review Monograph 33, London and Keele, Routledge & Kegan Paul.

Glyptis, Sue, McInnes, Hamish and Patmore, Alan (1987) *Leisure and the Home*, Sports Council/ESRC, London.

Graham, Hilary (1984) *Women, Health and the Family*, Brighton, Harvester Press.

Graydon, Jan (1983) 'But it's more than a game. It's an institution. Feminist perspectives on sport', *Feminist Review* 2.

Green, Eileen, Hebron, Sandra and Woodward, Diana (1985) 'A woman's work . . . is never done', *Sport and Leisure*, July/August, pp. 36–8.

Green, Eileen, Hebron, Sandra and Woodward, Diana (1987a) *Leisure and Gender*, final report to Sports Council/ESRC, London, Sports Council.

Green, Eileen, Hebron, Sandra and Woodward Diana (1987b) 'Women, leisure and social control' in Jalna Hanmer and Mary Maynard (eds) *Women, Violence and Social Control*, London, Macmillan.

Hall, Stuart and Jefferson, Tony (eds) (1975) *Resistance through Ritual*, London, Hutchinson.

Hanmer, Jalna and Maynard, Mary (1987) (eds) *Women, Violence and Social Control*, London, Macmillan.

Jenkins, Clive and Sherman, Barrie (1981) *The Leisure Shock*, London, Eyre Methuen.

Kaplan, Max (1975) *Leisure Theory and Policy*, New York, John Wiley.

Leaman, Oliver (1984) *Sit on the Sidelines and Watch the Boys Play: Sex Differentiation in Physical Education*, London, Longmans for the Schools Council.

McIntosh, Sue, Griffin, Chris, McCabe, Trish and Hobson, Dorothy (1981) 'Women and Leisure', in Alam Tomlinson (ed.) *Leisure and Social Control*, Eastbourne, Brighton Polytechnic, Chelsea School of Human Movement.

McKee, Lorna and Bell, Colin (1984) 'His unemployment; her problem', paper given to British Sociological Association Conference, April.

Malos, Ellen (1980) *The Politics of Housework*, London, Allison & Busby.

Martin, Jean and Roberts, Ceridwen (1984) *Women and Employment: A Lifetime Perspective*, London, HMSO.

Martin, Robert and Wallace, Jean (1984) *Working Women in the Recession*, Oxford, Oxford University Press.

Maynard, Mary (1985) 'Houseworkers and their work', in Rosemary Deem and Graeme Salaman, (eds) *Work, Culture and Society*, Milton Keynes, Open University Press.

Parker, Stan (1983) *Work and Leisure*, London, Allen & Unwin.

Rapoport, Rhona and Rapoport, Robert (1975) *Leisure and the Family Life Cycle*, London, Routledge & Kegan Paul.

Roberts, Ken (1978) *Contemporary Society and the Growth of Leisure*, London, Longmans.

Roberts, Ken (1981) *Leisure*, London, Longmans.

Roberts, Ken (1982) *Youth and Leisure*, London, Allen & Unwin.

Rojek, Chris (1985) *Capitalism and Leisure Theory*, London, Tavistock.

Scraton, Sheila (1986) 'Images of femininity and the teaching of girls' physical education', in John Evans (ed.) *Physical Education, Sport and Schooling*, Barcombe, Lewes, Falmer Press.

Scraton, Sheila (1987) 'Boys muscle in where angels fear to tread: the relationship between physical education and young women's subcultures', in David Jary, John Horne and Alan Tomlinson (eds) *Sport, Leisure and Social Relations*, Sociological Review Monograph 33, London and Keele, Routledge & Kegan Paul.

Sharpe, Sue (1984) *Double Identity*, Harmondsworth, Penguin.

Smith, Mike, Parker, Stan and Smith, Cyril (1973) *Leisure and Society in Britain*, London, Allen Lane.

Stanley, Liz (1980) 'The problem of women and leisure: an ideological construct and a radical feminist alternative', paper given to the 'Leisure in the 80s' Forum, Capital Radio, 26–8 September.

Talbot, Margaret (1979) *Women and Leisure: A State of the Art Review*, London, SSRC/Sports Council.

Talbot, Margaret (1981) 'Women and sport: biosocial aspects', *Journal of Biosocial Science*, Supplement 7: 33–47.

Talbot, Margaret (1984) 'Women and sport; a gender contradiction in terms?' paper presented to International Conference of Leisure Studies Association, Brighton, Sussex, July.

Thompson, Edward P. (1967) 'Time, work-discipline and industrial capitalism', *Past and Present* 38.

Veal, Tony (1987) *Leisure and the Future*, London, Allen & Unwin.

Wimbush, Erica (1986) *Women, Leisure and Well-being*, Edinburgh, Centre for Leisure Research.

Wyatt, Sally (1985) 'Science Policy Research Unit time-budget studies', paper given to 'Women, Leisure and Well-being' Workshop, Dunfermline College of Physical Education, Edinburgh, April.

Yeandle, Susan (1984) *Women's Working Lives*, London, Tavistock.

## FURTHER READING

Deem, Rosemary (1987) 'The politics of women's leisure', in David Jary, Jim Horne and Alan Tomlinson (eds) *Sport, Leisure and Social Relations*, Sociological Review Monograph 33, London and Keele, Routledge & Kegan Paul.

Gregory, Sarah (1982) 'Women among others: another view', *Leisure Studies* 1(1): 47a–52.

Reading taken from E. Wimbush and M. Talbot (eds), *Relative Freedoms*, published by Open University Press, 1988. Reprinted with permission.

# Vb Leisure and the Future

# 24 | The leisure forecasting tradition

Anthony J. Veal

## MEASURING LEISURE

A key aspect of any forecasting exercise is the decision about how the phenomenon under consideration is to be measured. Some five different measures of the scale of the leisure phenomenon can be identified, as set out below:

1. *The Participation Rate* – the proportion or percentage of the population which engages in specified leisure activities, for example: '6 per cent of the adult population swim at least once a week'.
2. *Number of Participants* – the number of people from a given community or geographical area who engage in specified leisure activities, for example: '20 000 *people* in Blankshire swim at least once a week'.
3. *The Volume of Activity* – the number of visits made or games played in particular activities in a particular area over a given time period, for example: 'There are 1.2 million *visits* to swimming pools in Blankshire in a year'.
4. *Time* – the amount of leisure time available to the individual or collection of individuals, in a specified time period, for example: 'The average working male has three hours leisure time per day'.
5. *Expenditure* – the amount spent in pounds or dollars on leisure by individuals, families or communities in a given time period, for example: 'Consumer expenditure on leisure in Britain in 1983 was almost £50 billion.' (Veal, 1980a, p. 3)

*Sociology of Leisure: A reader.* Edited by C. Critcher, P. Bramham and A. Tomlinson. Published in 1995 by E & FN Spon, London. ISBN 0 419 19420 7.

There are certain relationships between a number of these measures, particularly the first three. The Number of Participants is equal to the Participation Rate multiplied by the population of the area under study. The Volume of Activity is equal to the Number of Participants multiplied by the frequency of participation. Expenditure on a particular leisure activity is equal to the Volume of Activity multiplied by the expenditure per visit.

Of particular importance to all these measures is the *time period* to which they relate. This is obvious in the case of the last three measures which relate to volumes of activity, time, or money which must be related to a time period to make any sense. But it is also true of the first two which relate to levels of participation. Information on levels of participation in leisure is largely obtained from social surveys. Many of the early leisure social surveys asked people what leisure activities they had participated in over the previous *year*. This had the advantage of covering all seasons, which is particularly important for many outdoor leisure activities, but had the disadvantage of straining respondents' memories about events up to a year ago and thereby possibly introducing errors into the results. Generally the trend in surveys has been to reduce the period of recall in the interests of accuracy. In Britain, for instance, the General Household Survey asks respondents what activities they have done in the *four weeks* prior to interview. This has the effect of excluding many, although not all, of the less frequent participants, so producing apparently lower levels of participation than surveys based on a one-year period. The level of participation recorded is therefore dependent on the period of time referred to and is dependent on people's own accuracy of recall.

All the measures outlined above have their uses and users. The commercial sector is more interested in the volume of activity and expenditure, whereas the public sector provider is very often more interested in increasing the participation rate and the number of participants. Broadcasting organizations are particularly interested in the time measure of leisure activity. All these measures are used in forecasting.

## FORECASTING TECHNIQUES

The range of forecasting techniques available to the social scientist has been much discussed (Encel *et al.*, 1975) and most have been utilized in some form by leisure forecasters (Burton and Veal, 1971). Here we review techniques under nine main headings: speculation, trend extrapolation, respondent assessment, the Delphi technique, scenario writing, the comparative method, spatial models, cross-sectional analysis and composite methods.

## Speculation

The term speculation is used here to cover all those predictions which appear to be based on writers' own experience, knowledge, thoughts and informal observations rather than on some explicit, formal technique. Such speculation can be a source of ideas both for policy-making and research. Much of the work of the 'visionaries and philosophers' would come under this heading. Contemporary examples include Burton's essay 'The Shape of Things to Come' (1970), Bailey's *Futuresport* (1982), Jennings's (1979) paper 'Future Fun' and Asimov's (1976) paper of the same name. Some of the speculation in such papers is based on observation of current trends – such as Burton's prediction that team sports would decline in popularity relative to individuals sports or Jennings's prediction of the growth of non-competitive games. Others rely on some creative thinking about the possible implications of science, technology and space exploration for leisure.

## Trend extrapolation

Trend extrapolation or 'time series analysis' simply involves examination of the pattern of increase or decrease in a particular phenomenon in the recent past and extending, or 'extrapolating' this into the future to obtain a forecast. Examples are given in Figure 24.1 relating to visits to US National Parks and attendances at cinemas in Britain.

In its simplest form this is clearly a very unsophisticated approach. It is based on little more than a hunch that what has gone on in the past will continue to go on in the future. It can produce some unlikely results if not used with care. For instance a straight line extrapolation in Figure 24.1(B) would suggest that cinema attendances in 1990 would fall to zero, whereas in practice they are more likely to 'bottom out' before then, even if at a very low level. At the other extreme there are times when certain activities experience booms in participation – for instance, squash in Britain in the 1970s – when, if current trends were continued far enough into the future, the whole population would be doing little else! In common with most others, this technique is not able to predict sudden changes in trends: for example, at the time of writing, British cinema attendances have recovered from their long-term decline, at least for one year, and have shown a 35 per cent increase over 1984. The technique, in its simplest form, is therefore only suitable for short- to medium-term forecasting – say, over a period of three or four years in most leisure forecasting exercises, and even then must be treated with caution and be constantly updated.

An unsophisticated technique needs to be handled with some sophistication if it is not to make fools of the forecasters. Trend extrapolation can

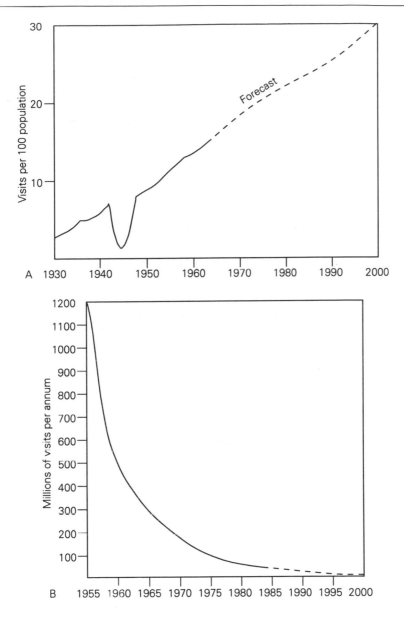

**Figure 24.1** (A) Visits to US national parks. (Source: ORRRC, 1962.) (B) Visits to the cinema in Britain. (Source: Central Statistical Office, *Annual Abstract of Statistics*, HMSO, London.)

be made more sophisticated by looking not just at trends in the activity or other phenomenon of interest but also at trends in some additional, more basic, or predictable, but related series of data. Thus, for example, trends in cinema attendances might be related to the sales of television sets and video-recorders and trips to the countryside might be related to the growth in the level of car-ownership. Television set and video-recorder sales and the level of car-ownership might be more predictable than the leisure activities themselves. If more than one underlying variable is included, the techniques evolve into what Stynes (1983) calls a 'structural model'. The problem for the forecaster is to identify suitable variables for which reliable forecasts exist and whose relationship with the leisure activity in question can be expected to continue into the future (Burton and Veal, 1971, p. 88).

A final practical problem in the use of trend extrapolation lies in the absence of adequate data. The method depends on the existence of a series of data collected in the past over a number of years. Such data series are few and far between, although the situation is slowly improving.

## Respondent assessment

In a number of leisure surveys respondents have been asked what leisure activities they would like to take up in future, as a guide to the likely future popularity of activities. The problems associated with the use of such questions are numerous. Is the respondent indicating a wistful hope, or a firm intention? To what extent does the fulfilment of the wish or intention depend on the provision of additional facilities, the respondent's own personal circumstances or other factors? If all the external conditions were to become suitable – for example, the provision of a new, reasonably priced, conveniently located facility – would the individual actually partici- pate? At the individual level all sorts of problems can be foreseen, but if enough respondents in a survey express a desire to participate in a particu- lar activity this would give a strong pointer to the providers of facilities, commodities or services at least to investigate the matter further. The results of such exercises can be of value to policy-makers in a sort of democratic or public relations sense – they can be seen to have consulted the public – but in practice they would need to be treated with extreme caution. . . .

Another approach of this general type is to ask people about their past patterns of leisure activity. What activities have they dropped and why? What activities have they taken up and why? Some of the answers would be related to changing personal circumstances and the life-cycle but it might be possible to detect changes and trends in tastes as well (Hedges, 1983). . . .

As with so many of the forecasting exercises reported on here, the practicalities of actually testing the validity of these methods mean that very few have ever been evaluated. It would be necessary to repeat the surveys of the 1960s using the same wording for this sort of test to be done. The declining interest of funding agencies in forecasting means that the substantial funds necessary to carry out such repeat surveys are rarely available.

## The Delphi technique

The Delphi technique can be used for both quantitative and qualitative forecasting but is particularly suited to the latter. It was developed in the early 1960s for the RAND Corporation of America, and is a means of producing a consensus of expert opinion about future events.

The technique involves three or more stages. First, a panel of experts in the particular field of interest is each presented with a series of questions concerning the likelihood of a range of events happening in a given time period, or alternatively they are themselves asked to suggest developments which they see taking place in the field of interest over the given time period. In the second stage the answers from the experts are collated; average probabilities are assigned to each of the developments, based on the experts' answers, or a list of possible developments and their possible timings, as put forward by the panel, is drawn up. Members of the panel are then sent this collated list and asked to revise their own opinions, if they wish, in the light of the information presented on their colleagues' views. These replies are then collated and the process repeated until a stable situation is reached. The technique is therefore a process of distillation of expert views on the future. Of course its success depends to a large extent on the choice of a suitable panel of experts . . .

The technique appears simple but can be very time consuming to set up and administer (Moeller and Shafer, 1983). While it has the advantage of throwing up possibilities which other methods could not, it is still ultimately dependent on the quality of the experts chosen; the experts may or may not be gifted with 'Delphic' vision.

## Scenario writing

Discussion of the Delphi technique and its derivatives leads naturally to a consideration of 'scenario writing' as a means of looking at potential futures. Scenario writing involves the drawing up of alternative hypothetical futures as characterized by key variables and the relationships between them. For example, one scenario might involve a future of high economic growth and low unemployment and all that flows from that, while a second, alternative scenario would involve low economic growth and high unemployment. The implications for leisure would then be explored within these 'scenarios'. The aim is not to produce hard predictions but to present policy-makers with alternatives so that they are prepared for all conceivable eventualities. . . .

Scenario writing can be seen as complementary to other, more quantified forecasting. In the past some forecasters have simply assumed that the political, social and economic environment would not change radically over the forecasting period and that such phenomena as economic growth would continue. In the 1980s such assumptions have become less tenable. Economic growth seems less assured and political values have become polarized in the West. Forecasting must, therefore, of necessity, involve alternative scenarios.

## The comparative method

Joffre Dumazedier, in his book *The Sociology of Leisure* (1974) ... suggests that society A can consider its future by reference to society B, a more advanced society. Thus he suggests that Western societies in general should look particularly to the United States as a means of studying their own futures. He refers to America as the first society to pass into a post-industrial state.

Dumazedier recognizes that differences in cultural, political, historical and environmental contexts will make comparison difficult. He attempts to outline a method by which the essence of leisure and the causal relationships between leisure and other aspects of life can be isolated. ...

Dumazedier's attempt to develop the comparative method as a scientific method of forecasting would seem to be doomed to failure. Far too many variables are involved and, even if the necessary data were available, disentangling the effects of different variables on leisure behaviour would be virtually impossible. ...

## Spatial models

The pattern of a great deal of leisure behaviour outside the home is affected by the availability and spatial distribution of facilities for leisure. In fact even leisure in the home is directly affected by facilities available outside the home – if attractive facilities are not available outside the home then people are likely to spend more of their leisure time in the home, watching television or engaging in other home-based activities. The significance of this rather obvious statement for the future of leisure is that certain activities cannot grow substantially in popularity unless facilities are available in which they can be practised.

Activities which depend on specific facilities in this way might be termed *confined* activities, and those less dependent upon specific facilities *unconfined* activities. Confined activities are those like squash, ice-skating (in temperate climates), swimming (indoors) and watching professional theatre, where participation is virtually totally dependent upon the availability of specific, usually purpose-built, facilities and where facilities have a fairly clearly defined capacity. Once any spare capacity in existing facilities has been taken up, any increase in levels of participation depends on the provision of additional facilities or an increase in the capacity of existing facilities. Unconfined activities on the other hand, are those which, like trips to the countryside or jogging, while they may make some use of facilities, are nevertheless not dependent in any clear way on specific facilities and so increases in participation are not dependent on the provision of additional facilities. The notions of 'confined' and 'unconfined' lie at opposite ends of a continuum: in between are activities displaying both confined and unconfined characteristics, such as fishing or visiting museums.

It is, therefore, possible to think of leisure futures not simply in terms of gross 'levels of participation' in different activities, but in terms of patterns of demand arising from specific residential neighbourhoods and workplaces and being catered for by specific facilities. Forecasting then becomes a matter not of predicting total demand for a whole country or region but of predicting the spatial patterns of that demand, the origins and destinations of leisure trips, the relative impact of facilities with differing attractions, and the effect on the 'system' of the introduction of additional facilities, new transport routes, new residential neighbourhoods or new workplaces. This is what transport planners do when they consider the generation and distribution of journeys to work or shopping journeys, with the difference that in those cases workplaces and shopping centres, rather than leisure facilities, are the destinations of the trips.

Such a perspective lends itself to modelling – the mathematical representation of the leisure trip 'system'. A number of attempts have been made in the academic literature to develop such models but there have been few practical applications for recreation planning purposes.

How do such models work? Models of human behaviour can be constructed when people behave in some predictable manner. Many might object to the idea that people are assumed to behave 'predictably'; such a statement seems to deny people their individuality and freedom. But the statement is not based just on assumption but on observation. People, *en masse*, do often behave predictably. This is not to say that everybody behaves in the same way – in certain situations there is only a limited choice of courses of action which the individual can take and models are based on the observations of the proportion of the population who choose each course. Models are quite limited in what they set out to do. . . .

The fundamental observation upon which spatial recreation planning models rely is that travel distance, travel time and travel costs affect people's use of leisure facilities. Concentrating on distance for the moment, this means that, other things being equal, the further a person has to travel to visit a leisure facility the less likely that person is to visit it. Figure 24.2

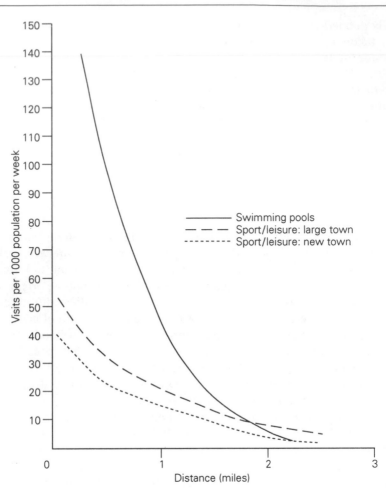

**Figure 24.2** Effect of distance on participation.

illustrates the general truth of this observation for a number of different
types of leisure facility. Since the number of visits from an area will to
some extent be a reflection of the number of people living in that area,
the diagram shows visit *rates* at different distances from the facilities, that
is, the number of visits *per 1000 population*, in a given time period.
There is generally a marked fall-off in visit rates as distance from the
facilities increases. The pattern varies from facility to facility – more attractive facilities will attract larger numbers of people from greater distances
than the less attractive facilities. The pattern is also affected by the type
of clientele which uses the facility – for example, a swimming pool which
has a large proportion of children among its users or a library which has

a large proportion of elderly people among its users, will have a smaller 'catchment area' than a theatre which attracts mainly the more mobile sections of the middle class.

The relationships between residential areas, recreation sites and the trips between them can also be viewed from the perspective of the 'gravity model'. Newton's law of gravity states that the force between two bodies is proportional to the product of their masses and inversely proportional to the square of the distance between them. This provides an analogy for recreational-trip-making: the recreation facility is seen as one of the 'bodies' and its size and attraction as its 'mass'; the second 'body' is the residential area from which trips are made, the 'mass' of this body being its level of population. The 'force' between the two bodies is then the number of recreational trips. The 'gravity model' then accords with observed trip-making behaviour:

1. the greater the population of the residential area the greater the number of trips generated;
2. the larger and more attractive the recreation facility the greater the number of trips attracted to it;
3. the greater the distance between the residential area and the recreation facility the less will be the number of trips between them. . . .

Using the gravity model and derivations of it, models of a system of recreation sites can be developed. Such models can include not only a system of sites and the residential (and possibly business) areas from which trips are generated but also the transport routes between them.

## Cross-sectional analysis

Cross-sectional analysis is probably the most widely used technique in quantitative leisure forecasting. As its name implies, the basis of the method is the examination of leisure participation levels among a *cross-section* of the population. Levels of participation in many leisure activities are usually found to vary between different social groups such as different age groups, different income groups or those with and without access to private transport. These patterns are illustrated in Figure 24.3 for a range of activities and social characteristics. The basis of the forecasting part of the exercise is the proposition that the changing social composition of the population in the future will lead to corresponding, predictable changes in the levels of participation in leisure activities. For instance, it can be seen in Figure 24.3 that outdoor physical recreation is engaged in by more middle class groups (professional, managerial and other non-manual workers) and car-owners than by working class and non-car-owning groups. Therefore, the cross-sectional method assumes that, if the proportion of middle class people in the population increases and if car-ownership

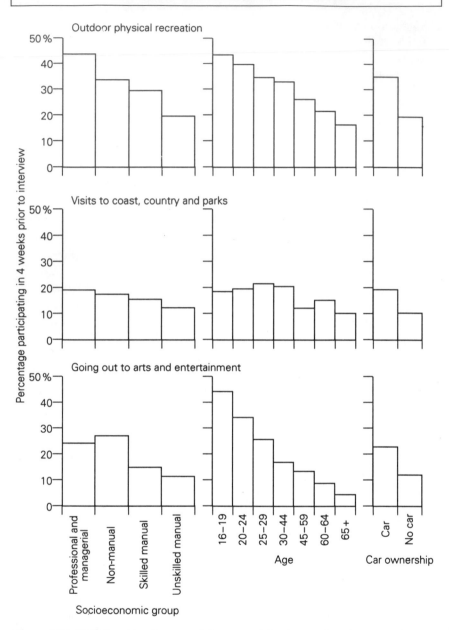

**Figure 24.3** Relationships between leisure participation and socioeconomic characteristics. (Source: General Household Survey, 1980: England and Wales.)

increases, then so will participation in outdoor physical recreation. Furthermore, this can be quantified because we know the levels of participation among these groups.

The method uses the statistical technique of multiple regression (and sometimes discriminant analysis) to quantify the relationships between participation in a leisure activity and the various relevant social characteristics. As with the spatial models discussed above, the model must first of all be set up ('calibrated') using observations of existing patterns of behaviour, such as those illustrated in Figure 24.3. These data are generally drawn from substantial social surveys. The analysis can be based either on groups defined according to the average characteristics of the group (e.g. male car-owners in professional jobs ages 30–45) or on individuals and their individual characteristics (Veal, 1980a).

The approach has a number of limitations. The first, which is apparent from the description given above, is that the method does not forecast changes in levels of participation *per se* but merely the effects on participation of certain structural socioeconomic factors. Thus, for example, if young male car-owners have a higher than average participation rate in a certain activity and the number of such young male car-owners in the population is expected to increase in the future, then the number of participants in that activity will be predicted to increase. But if the existing young male car-owners themselves participate more in the activity in future, this will not be reflected in the model forecasts. Thus the model is based on changes in the *structure* of the population rather than on the changing tastes of the population. We have already noted how, in the 1960s, when many of these methods were first devised, the changing size and structure of the population were indeed very important causes of changes in demand. Currently it is more likely that other factors such as changes in taste will be important.

A second limitation is that, generally, the method does not take account of changes in the supply of facilities. For some activities facilities are necessary, as discussed above; for these 'confined' activities the omission of supply considerations from the model is a serious limitation. For 'unconfined' activities this is not a problem. Another aspect of supply is technological change. Thus the appearance of cheap glass-fibre boats had a significant effect on levels of participation in boating in the 1960s and the invention of the video-recorder has affected home-based leisure. Neither of these phenomena could be foreseen by the cross-sectional model.

A third limitation is the extensive data requirements of the method. If the method is based upon the characteristics of groups rather than individuals then a worthwhile statistical exercise would need to be based upon perhaps some forty or fifty social groups. This places a strain on any sample survey in that some of these groups may contain very few subjects, calling into question their statistical reliability. Further, the more social variables included, the more difficult it is to obtain forecasts of those variables upon which to base the forecasts of leisure activity. If individuals rather than groups are used in the analysis, all sorts of problems arise because of the non-quantifiable nature of many of the variables used and the necessity to use 'dummy' variables, and also because many leisure activities are of a minority nature so that any sample divides unevenly into a small number of participants and a large number of non-participants. . . .

The most comprehensive piece of work was carried out by Young and Willmott (1973). The study was comprehensive in terms of the range of activities covered and, although the data base was from the London and south-east region it was adjusted to reflect the national population structure, so it was the first attempt at national forecasts. The social variables included in the study were age, income, occupation, age of finishing full-time education and car-ownership. Table 24.1 reproduces the key forecasts and demonstrates the range of activities covered, including not just sport and outdoor activities but arts and entertainment and home-based leisure activities as well. The measure of participation used is unique to this study, so it is difficult to monitor progress as we move towards the year 2000, nevertheless a number of trends in participation, as revealed by the General Household Survey (Veal, 1984), are moving in the opposite direction from that predicted by Young and Willmott. For instance, attendances at most spectator sports is in decline, cinema attendances have been in decline, and athletics and skating are increasing rather than being static.

**Table 24.1** Young and Willmott's 1973 leisure forecasts

| Activity | % Participating* | | % Change† |
| --- | --- | --- | --- |
| | 1970 | 2001 | |
| Swimming | 29 | 37 | 28 |
| Sailing | 3 | 4.5 | 50 |
| Golf | 7 | 10 | 43 |
| Fishing | 9 | 10 | 11 |
| Soccer | 6 | 7 | 17 |
| Cricket | 4.5 | 5 | 11 |
| Tennis | 8 | 10 | 25 |
| Table tennis | 11 | 13 | 18 |
| Bowls | 2 | 2 | 0 |
| Ten-pin bowling | 9 | 10 | 11 |
| Athletics | 2 | 2 | 0 |
| Badminton and squash | 3 | 4.5 | 50 |
| Rugby | – | 1 | 250 |
| Boating | 1.5 | 1.5 | 0 |
| Skating | 1.5 | 1.5 | 0 |
| Horse riding | 1 | 1.5 | 50 |
| All sports | 44 | 52 | 18 |
| Watching swimming | 6 | 6.5 | 8 |
| Watching golf | 2.5 | 3 | 20 |
| Waching soccer | 20 | 22 | 10 |
| Watching rugby | 3.5 | 4.5 | 29 |
| Watching cricket | 10 | 13 | 30 |
| Watching tennis | 5.5 | 7.5 | 36 |

**Table 24.1** Continued

| Activity | % Participating* | | % Change† |
|---|---|---|---|
| | 1970 | 2001 | |
| Watching athletics | 3 | 3.5 | 17 |
| Watching motor sports | 7 | 8 | 14 |
| Watching boxing | 3 | 3 | 0 |
| Watching wrestling | 4 | 4 | 0 |
| Watching horse racing | 5.5 | 7 | 27 |
| Watching winter sports | – | 1 | 250 |
| Watching showjumping | 2 | 2.5 | 25 |
| All watching sport | 40 | 45 | 13 |
| | | | |
| Listening to music (on radio, records) | 68 | 70 | 3 |
| Playing an instrument | 9 | 11.5 | 28 |
| Home decoration/repairs | 60 | 66 | 10 |
| Car maintenance | 20.5 | 27 | 32 |
| Car cleaning | 33 | 50 | 51 |
| Knitting/sewing | 46 | 44 | −4 |
| Reading | 67 | 74 | 10 |
| Gardening | 63 | 67 | 6 |
| Model-building | 5.5 | 6.5 | 18 |
| Collecting (stamps, etc.) | 12 | 13.5 | 13 |
| Handicrafts | 5 | 5.5 | 10 |
| Technical hobbies | 5 | 6 | 20 |
| Playing cards/chess | 8.5 | 11.5 | 35 |
| Crosswords | 3 | 4 | 33 |
| Cooking | 2.5 | 3.5 | 40 |
| Painting/sculpture | 3 | 4.5 | 50 |
| Working at home | 4.5 | 7.5 | 67 |
| | | | |
| Going to cinema | 53 | 58 | 9 |
| Going to theatre | 37 | 45 | 22 |
| Going to museum | 25 | 32 | 28 |
| Going to art gallery | 17 | 25 | 47 |
| Going out for a meal | 62 | 70 | 13 |
| Going to pub | 62 | 69 | 11 |
| Attending church | 37 | 41 | 11 |
| Voluntary work | 15 | 19 | 27 |
| Billiards/snooker | 12 | 12.5 | 4 |
| Darts | 21 | 22 | 5 |
| Dancing | 31 | 35 | 13 |
| Going for a walk of 1 mile+ | 65 | 68 | 5 |
| Going for a drive | 68 | 78 | 15 |
| Camping | 7 | 8 | 14 |
| Caravanning | 10 | 11 | 10 |
| Bingo | 3.5 | 3 | −14 |
| Adult education | 3.5 | 6.5 | 9 |

* Percentages of adults aged 18 and over doing the activity at least once a year.
† Young and Willmott produce a range of increases, reflecting the uncertainties in the data and method. The % changes given here are my own calculations from the data given.
– less than 0.5%.

*Source*: Young and Willmott (1973, pp. 369–72).

The growth mentality and environment of the 1960s and 1970s is reflected in Young and Willmott's conclusion to their exercise:

> The outstanding feature of the forecasts is that almost everything is likely to increase. This is a reflection of the main finding of the survey – that richer, higher-status, more educated, car-owning people did most of almost everything. Since we assume that people will be richer, more educated, doing higher-status jobs and owning more cars, it follows that almost every activity should have more participants in 2001. (Young and Willmott, 1973, p. 372)

My own study using the 1973 General Household Survey data for Britain was the first national exercise using national data (Veal, 1979). The projections for 1991, which are produced in Table 24.2, were based on predicted demographic, income and car-ownership changes. If the General Household Surveys are continued it will eventually be possible to test these predictions. But, for all the reasons we have discussed, they are unlikely to prove at all accurate. For example, swimming in indoor pools is predicted to rise by 21 per cent between 1973 and 1991. In fact, largely because of a 70 per cent increase in the number of swimming pools in the country between 1973 and the end of the decade, indoor swimming increased by a similar 70 per cent in that period (Sports Council, 1982; Veal, 1984). Unless there is an unexpected decline, participation is likely to have at least doubled between 1973 and 1991. So it would appear that British forecasts based on the cross-sectional model are proving the same point as already demonstrated by the American work: that without a supply component they are grossly inaccurate.

**Composite methods**

Two agencies in Britain are well known for their continuous monitoring and forecasting of the leisure scene: they are Leisure Consultants, otherwise known as Martin and Mason, and the Henley Centre for Forecasting. They produce annual and quarterly monitors largely, but not entirely, devoted to trends in leisure expenditure. To produce such forecasts requires a combination of virtually all the techniques reviewed so far, plus a fair measure of common sense, experience and instinct. . . . Such detailed work depends on extensive knowledge of market trends for individual products and services and a grasp of the total picture of consumer behaviour and expenditure patterns. For example, while future purchases of video-recorders might be predicted by means of simple extrapolation of trends in recent years, this must be set against, and if necessary modified by, knowledge of the 'product life-cycle' of such new consumer durables, 'cross-sectional' information about which groups in society are buying the machines, and the overall trends in disposable income and the share of

**Table 24.2** 1991 leisure forecasts (Britain)

| Activity | % increase in number of participants 1973–1991 |
|---|---|
| Camping | 33 |
| Golf | 33 |
| Soccer | 7 |
| Cricket | 21 |
| Tennis | 37 |
| Bowls | 17 |
| Fishing | 19 |
| Swimming outdoors | 25 |
| All outdoor sport | 23 |
| | |
| Badminton/squash | 59 |
| Swimming indoors | 21 |
| Table tennis | 29 |
| Billiards/snooker | 23 |
| Darts | –5 |
| All indoor sports/games | 23 |
| | |
| Watching horse racing | 10 |
| Watching motor racing | 33 |
| Watching soccer | 15 |
| Watching cricket | 19 |
| All watching sport | 19 |
| | |
| Visiting parks | 6 |
| Visiting seaside | 17 |
| Visiting countryside | 21 |
| Visiting historic buildings | 25 |
| Visiting museums | 25 |
| Visiting zoos | 18 |
| Going to cinema | 18 |
| Going to theatre | 20 |
| Amateur music/drama | 25 |
| Going out for a meal | 21 |
| Going out for a drink | 15 |
| Dancing | 17 |
| Bingo | –4 |

*Source*: Veal (1979, p. 62).

that income available for leisure products. Monitoring of events in other countries, particularly America – the comparative method – is also part of the battery of techniques used in what might be termed the 'composite' method. As with national economic forecasts, these are not once-for-all exercises, but must be modified in the light of changing economic circumstances and government policies. . . .

Clearly all the individual forecasting methods reviewed here have their weaknesses. It is therefore no coincidence that those who earn their living from forecasting leisure tend to use what we have called the 'composite' method, which draws on a variety of techniques, compensating for the weakness of one with the strengths of another. For all the weaknesses of the methods employed there remains a demand for forecasts from those who must make investment decisions for the future. We could do worse than leave the last word on leisure forecasting to the Outdoor Recreation Resources Review Commission which said, in 1962:

> Many individuals and indeed whole groups of individuals in public and private agencies remain averse to the idea of forecasting and adamantly refuse to become involved in any project which attempts to envision the future. Certainly their position is a comfortable one, and history will never prove them wrong. (ORRRC, 1962, Study Report 26, p. 1)

## BIBLIOGRAPHY

Asimov, I. (1976), 'Future Fun', in *Today and Tomorrow and . . .* (London: Scientific Book Club), pp. 199–209.

Bailey, A. (1982), *Futuresport* (London: Pan)

Burton, T. L. (1970), 'The shape of things to come' in T. L. Burton (ed.), *Recreation Research and Planning* (London: Allen & Unwin), pp. 242–68.

Burton, T. L. and Veal, A. J. (1971), *Experiments in Recreation Research* (London: Allen & Unwin).

Dumazedier, J. (1974), *The Sociology of Leisure* (The Hague: Elsevier).

Encel, S., Marstrand, P. K. and Page, W. (eds) (1975), *The Act of Anticipation: Values and Methods in Forecasting* (London: Martin Robertson).

Hedges, B. (1983), 'Personal leisure histories' in M. F. Collins (ed.), *Leisure Research: Current Findings and Future Challenge* (London: Leisure Studies Association/Sports Council/SSRC).

Jennings, L. (1979), 'Future fun: tomorrow's sports and games', *The Futurist*, vol. 13, pt 6, Dec., pp. 417–31.

Moeller, G. H. and Shafer, E. L. (1983), 'The use and misuse of Delphi forecsting', in Lieber and Fesenmaier (eds), *op cit.*, pp. 96–104.

Outdoor Recreation Resources Review Commission (1962), *Outdoor Recreation for America* (Washington, DC: ORRRC).

Sports Council (1982), *Sport in the Community: The Next Ten Years* (London: Sports Council).

Stynes, D. J. (1983), 'Time series and structural models for forecasting recreation participation', in Lieber and Fesenmaier (eds), *op. cit.*, pp. 105–19.

Veal, A. J. (1979), *The Future of Leisure*, Report to the Social Science Research Council, Centre for Urban and Regional Studies, University of Birmingham.

Veal, A. J. (1980a), *Trends in Leisure Participation and Problems of Forecasting: The State of the Art* (London: Sports Council/SSRC).

Veal, A. J. (1984) 'Leisure in England and Wales', *Leisure Studies*, vol. 3, no. 2, pp. 221–30.
Young, M. and Willmott, P. (1973), *The Symmetrical Family: A Study of Work and Leisure in the London Region* (London: Routledge & Kegan Paul).

## FURTHER READING

Bell, D. (1974), *The Coming of the Post-Industrial Society* (London: Heinemann.)
Lieber, S. R. and Fesenmaier, D. R. (eds) (1983), *Recreation Planning and Management* (London: Spon).
Veal, A. J. (1980), 'The future of leisure', *International Journal of Tourism Management*, vol. 1, no. 1, March, pp. 42–55.
Veal, A. J. (1987), *Using Sports Centres* (London: Sports Council).

Reading taken from A. J. Veal, *Leisure and the Future*, published by Allen & Unwin, 1987. Reprinted with permission.

# Activities

## INTERPRETATIVE EXERCISES

1. Make a list of your own five favourite leisure activities and/or those of your group. Assess the extent to which each of them is affected by class background or gender. What might be done to make such activities open to everyone?
2. Select any one major planning document in the private or public sector (e.g. the Sports Council's 'The Next Ten Years'). Which of the forecasting models identified by Veal are present and how aware are the authors of the pitfalls he identifies?
3. Check the demographic trends outlined in a recent copy of *Social Trends* or the PSI survey *Britain 2010*. What implications do they carry for future leisure policies and practices?
4. What are the likely impacts of new technologies (e.g. 'virtual reality' simulation) on more traditional forms of mass leisure?
5. List some examples which would suggest that there is a growing 'globalization' of leisure practices and tastes.

## ESSAYS

1. Compare and contrast any two of the pluralist, Marxist and feminist theories of leisure, explaining which you find the most convincing and why.
2. What are the major problems in predicting the future of leisure?
3. Critically evaluate the view that traditional theories, unlike 'green' perspectives, fail to think abut the impact of leisure practices on the environment.
4. 'During the 1960s experts were predicting the 'coming of a leisure

revolution'. That prospect seems even more unlikely as UK society approaches the millenium.' Discuss.

5. 'In the future, work will no longer be an individual's central life interest and, more importantly, neither will leisure.' Discuss.

# Index